VEILS, HALOS & SHACKLES

International Poetry on the Oppression & Empowerment of Women

Charles Adès Fishman, Editor

Smita Sahay, Associate Editor

Kasva Press / Alfei Menashe

The December 2012 rape and murder of Jyoti Singh Pandey in Delhi moved thousands of people to pour into the streets in protest. *Veils, Halos & Shackles* was conceived in response to that vicious gang-rape and to the unprecedented public activism for women's safety that followed it.

Front-cover art "The Core," acrylic on canvas, 30 x 24 in., © 2006 by Lucy Liew, and used by permission of the artist.

Back-cover photo copyrighted by and reprinted with permission of Sheri Vandermolen.

Book design & layout: Yael Shahar

First edition published 2016
Printed on paper certified by the Forest Stewardship Council.

Kasva Press LLC
www.kasvapress.com
Alfei Menashe, Israel / St. Paul, Minnesota
info@kasvapress.com

www.veils-halos-shackles.com

Veils, Halos & Shackles:
International Poetry on the Oppression & Empowerment of Women

ISBN
Trade Paperback: 978-0-9910584-5-7
M 0 9 8 7 6 5 4 3 2

Dedication

To the Memory of Jyoti Singh Pandey, Nadia Anjuman, and the uncountable number of other women and girls who have been victims of gender violence

and to Malala Yousafzai, whose leadership and courage have inspired millions

and for all of our daughters.

Jyoti has become a symbol. In death, she has lit such a torch that not only this country, but the whole world, got lit up. But at the same time, she posed a question. What is the meaning of "a woman"? How is she looked upon by society today? And I wish that whatever darkness there is in this world should be dispelled by this light.

— Badri Singh Pandey

I am not free while any woman is unfree, even when her shackles are very different from my own.

— Audre Lorde

We realize the importance of our voices only when we are silenced.

I raise up my voice — not so I can shout but so that those without a voice can be heard . . . we cannot succeed when half of us are held back.

— Malala Yousafzai

Contents

Veils, Halos

& Shackles

INTRODUCTION

In the wake of the rape and murder of a woman in Delhi in December 2012, Charles Fishman and Smita Sahay began building this anthology, which brings together nearly two-hundred voices to break the silence about gender violence, to raise awareness, and to offer alternative narratives. The poems in *Veils, Halos & Shackles* witness oppression, rape, female infanticide, acid attacks, victim-blaming, marginalization, female genital mutilation, incest, and more. But they also document the movements and organizations that seek to offer help, such as women's shelters and movements like One Billion Rising, Women's Day, The Vagina Monologues, and V-Day.

While reading these poems and the accompanying testimony of the poets, I was reminded of the time when scholar and activist Jackson Katz spoke at a university a few blocks from my home in Lincoln, Nebraska, during Sexual Assault Awareness Month. As an undergraduate at Iowa State University, I had taken a class in Masculinity Studies where we read *Our Guys: The Glen Ridge Rape and the Secret Life of the Perfect Suburb,* a book that recounts and tries to make sense of the gang-rape of a mentally-handicapped girl by her high-school classmates, who were athletes. That semester, we also watched Katz's video *Tough Guise.* Both texts helped us to explore men's violence against women within the larger framework of a culture of violence. I was horrified by the book, even as the texts we studied sought to explore a violent masculinity and the ways some groups were organizing to train athlete leaders in bystander approaches that would enable them to interrupt gender violence before it occurred. When I learned Katz would speak, I left early from work, biked the few miles to the lecture hall, locked up my bike, and found a seat in the auditorium. The day was bright, balmy, and filled with promise — spring in the Midwest.

One of the things I admired about Katz's talk was the way he foregrounded the power of language. For instance, he pointed out that the word "male" is often dropped from the phrase "male violence against women." He also discussed issues of privilege and power and how those who have power are often missing from the discussion, so that violence against women becomes a "women's issue" rather than a cultural one, and helping women in crisis becomes "women's work" rather than essential action that is the responsibility of us all. To end men's violence against women, Katz said, we need more men involved. Only then would the paradigm begin to shift.

Over a decade after taking my first Women's Studies classes at ISU, I am now teaching classes in Women's and Gender Studies that explore violence against women. Though the world has changed in innumerable ways since I was an undergrad, women and girls are still molested, abused, raped, and oppressed by the men and boys who are sometimes strangers, but — more often than not — people they know.

This semester I taught "Introduction to Women's and Gender Studies" and showed *Dreamworlds 3,* a video that documents men's violence against women in music videos and ends with footage from the attack on women that occurred during a festival in Central Park in 2000 — real-life images that eerily echo the ways women are treated in music videos. Even though I'd been in college during the actual Central Park incident and had previously taught the *Dreamworlds 3* video, that day while I watched the film with my students I felt my body chill, my throat close, and my breath grow heavy with horror and shame.

This video is part of a sequence of texts that prepares my students for the assignment that asks them to write about one music video that was recently produced. I look forward to this part of the class — the presentations, the papers, the critical thinking of young people engaging with issues that concern them. As someone who enjoys pop culture, I'm always eager to see how musicians are challenging gender roles, calling attention to gender violence, and presenting new ways of being female in this culture. I'm always hopeful for serious change and look forward to seeing videos where women are strong, powerful, and unharmed, in which words and images that signal misogyny have faded. Watching my students' video clips this time, and reading their papers, I was both delightfully surprised by some artists and undeniably disturbed by others, especially those who perpetuated the "dreamworlds" we'd studied. I say "we" because, though I am the teacher in the classroom now, I am forever the student. I learn as my students learn, and they have much to teach me.

I would be lying if I said some of the videos didn't make me cry, much as I would be lying if I said *Veils, Halos & Shackles* didn't move me to tears. Sometimes the culture of gender violence feels hopeless, as if there's no way to delete the horrors and create something better. This was brought home to me when I had the opportunity to work with the artist Sally Deskins, who mentioned that when she was a girl, her mother taught her that when it feels like there's nothing that can be done, it's time "to make a book."

The poetry in *Veils, Halos & Shackles* is important. Such poetry is subversive and dangerous because it critiques violence myths presented in the media that perpetuate stereotypes which, in turn, promote ignorance, logical fallacies, and fear. Such poetics do more than speak to power. They resist the abuses of power by imaging a better world. They enable poets to claim power over experiences and stories that are frequently missing from the culture at large. Fishman and Sahay have put together a book of hope.

Veils, Halos & Shackles is a brilliant anthology with powerful and moving poetry from a wide range of voices. It's distinguished by both a deep cross-cultural awareness and a close attention to the intersectionality that fosters power and privilege as it operates transnationally, locally, and in the home. The biographies of the poets offer a sense of who these writers are, from where they're writing, and what they're doing both individually and among communities that seek change for women.

The poetry is accompanied by testimonies from the poets that contextualize their poems within the culture and document the place from which the poems emerged. Sometimes it's a place of media representation and the news; other times, it's the community in which the poet grew up, or it's the location in which the poet now resides. They offer news accounts and personal stories, historical and literary research, and pop-culture presentations. As in texts like Carolyn Forché's *Against Forgetting,* this contextualization enables readers to enter into a larger conversation about gender violence, one that might go beyond their experiences, or is missing from current dialogs, or is representative of the insidious ways violence against women manifests everywhere. They allow the reader the opportunity to explore poetry of witness and poetry of resistance within the historical and cultural climates from which these poets tell their stories.

Make a book when you're bored. Make a book when you despair. Make a book as an act of resistance. Open such a book when you need change.

The words from poets in this anthology are powerful, informative, and necessary. Inside the college classroom, around the conference table at a library where a book club meets, in the seminar room of a writing workshop, or in the safe space of a women's group at a crisis center, this anthology has the possibility to extend the discussion and enable a multi-layered approach as readers consider the art of the poems and the poets as the makers of the art — individuals who are, just as they are, active participants in a world where men's violence against women continues. These are poems and statements written to imagine a better, more peaceable world. For example, Stephen J. Cipot, one of the more than two dozen men whose poems appear in the anthology, explains that his inspiration for writing "Prayer for Malala Yousafzai" was a girl who "spoke out so eloquently for the kinds of things that we take for granted as basic human and women's rights in this country," things like "education, freedom of belief and religion, the right to self-development and self-expression, without overbearing masculine impingement," a sentiment this anthology speaks to again and again.

Women deserve the right to live free from violence because it's a basic human right. We all deserve it. We are all worth so much. As Fishman writes, "human beings crave dignity and freedom and, insofar as they are able to, resist efforts to chain them or beat them down." *Veils, Halos & Shackles* is an act of resistance. It is a collective act of poets who ask us to act, to imagine, and to work to bring about change. We can. Janine Harrison writes, "I want a better world for the generations to come." The resistance work that anthologies like *Veils, Halos & Shackles* do will help take us there.

Laura Madeline Wiseman
Lincoln, Nebraska
May/June 2015

PREFACE

The December 2012 rape and murder of Jyoti Singh Pandey in Delhi moved thousands of people to pour into the streets in protest. *Veils, Halos, & Shackles* was conceived in response to that vicious gang-rape and to the unprecedented public activism for women's safety that followed it. The anthology includes more than 250 poems by over 180 poets, who represent dozens of countries, from Brazil to Bangladesh and from New Zealand to Nigeria. Many of our contributors are among the most accomplished living poets.

These diverse, impeccably crafted poems tell us that Afghanistan, Australia, Canada, Ireland, India, Israel, Mexico, Norway, Sweden, the USA, the UK, and dozens of other countries, are not so dissimilar where the oppression of women is concerned. Many of the contributors to this anthology are survivors of rape and other crimes that affect women and girls every day or are the kin of victims and survivors. Other contributors have written about this subject out of empathy and concern, having been moved deeply by the fate of human beings who just happen to be women.

In addition to the poems, we have included statements by the poets, in which they explain why they have chosen to address this subject in their work. We believe that this feature of the anthology will not only add to its value as an adopted text for classroom teaching but that it will also widen the circle of potential readers.

We also believe that our anthology will be an essential and timely contribution to the cause that so deeply concerns us: telling the truth about the violence and oppression women are subjected to, and moving individuals, and even governments, to protect and support women, through intelligent laws and the transformation of cultures. It's clear to us that *Veils, Halos, & Shackles* will speak to a global audience and that, tragically, its subject will remain current in the foreseeable future.

Charles Adès Fishman – Bellport, Long Island
Smita Sahay – Mumbai, India
October, 2015

JIM PASCUAL AGUSTIN

Jim Pascual Agustin writes and translates in Filipino and English. He grew up in the Philippines during the Marcos dictatorship and moved to South Africa in 1994. His work has appeared in *Rhino Poetry, GUD Magazine, Rusted Radishes,* and *Modern Poetry in Translation*. Agustin's recent poetry books were published by the University of Santo Tomas Publishing House in Manila: *Baha-bahagdang Karupukan* (2011), *Alien to Any Skin* (2011), *Kalmot ng Pusa sa Tagiliran* (2013), and *Sound Before Water* (2013).

PERHAPS TO SENEGAL TO LISTEN TO ISMAËL LÔ?

"You're my sedative, your cheeks
a tangerine in my fist." His words
make her think of bruising again.
She pretends her skin grows leathery,
supple and able to take knuckles
out of nowhere.

He talks funny just as he surrenders
to slumber, she tells herself. She smiles
when he makes that last involuntary kick
followed by drool. Tomorrow he'll have
no memory of this, like most nights. Pillow talk
if you lay your head on shattered bricks.

There's a spade in the garage
that she's never touched.
She imagines seeking the center
of its weight before she swings,
as if it were a bat. But where
would she run? Her back traced
with blue. The door, a flap
of skin.

AGUSTIN: I moved to South Africa in October 1994 and only after a few years of living here did I begin to learn of the disturbing history of violence against women and children in this country. The statistics are frightening and the daily news reports can often numb one into accepting the deplorable situation, even after 20 years of democracy. My poem is an attempt to capture the state of mind of a woman in search of a way out of a situation, but first she has to find the courage to face her real and imagined fears.

KAREN ALKALAY-GUT

Karen Alkalay-Gut has been writing on walls, clothes, and artwork for many years. She writes lyrics for rock groups like "Panic Ensemble" and "Una Selva"and has performed her own work with "Thin Lips," as well as with Jazz pianist Liz Magnes, with whom she recorded "The Paranormal in our Daily Life." Alkalay-Gut has also published over twenty-five books of poetry, hundreds of academic articles and books (including *Belly Dancing in Tel Aviv,* in English and Italian versions from Audible books and Kolibris), and she has worked with Israeli designers such as "Comme il Faut"and "Shihar" to combine poetry and dress. She is retired from Tel Aviv University where she taught English Literature.

THE VEIL

Before My Hidden Face
the veil that fixes my gaze
within the frame of womanhood.
Beneath the gauze between you and me
may be nakedness

GUY BREAKS UP WITH A GIRL

Guy breaks up with a girl
she tries to kill herself
girl breaks up with a guy
he tries to kill her

either way it's her fault

PANTIES

After I got home that night,
I raced past my parents to my room
(Now they were merely naive in my eyes
— no longer the worst threat in my life).
Pulled down my panties to see
if they were stained, if he had really
made it inside me with all that struggle,
all the blows and writhings, all the pains.

And there was the blood — bright and shining —
even though the red was already dried,

the little game of the rapist
played out to the end.

ALKALAY-GUT: In the decade of my Middle-Eastern dancing, I discovered a great deal about the body and its relationship with costume. The veil became an extension of the self, accentuating movements, manipulating others, modest and flirty at the same time. The veil seems to hide a secret, or perhaps the absence of secrets. The veil is a declaration of womanhood, and a woman is free behind her veil to express whatever she wishes. At the same time, it is an acceptance of slavery, an acknowledgement that self-expression in the world outside is forbidden. "The Veil" has not previously appeared in print, but it was printed on one of the veils I practiced with. I danced for myself: I never did perform in public.

"Guy Breaks Up With A Girl": With these three lines, I was summarizing all I know of opera, literature and life. The plot of romance seems to have been constant since the nineteenth century, and it's pretty clear that women usually blame themselves when something goes wrong, while men tend to blame others. I wrote this for a musical that used a series of my poems about love. The music was written by Roy Yarkoni and most of the poems were sung by Yael Kraus. This poem, which I wrote to conclude the section about the breakdown of a relationship, was recited by me. We performed this musical drama at the Jerusalem Festival in 2010 and recorded it in an album entitled *Night Hawks*. It was never published.

The original idea for "Panties" was to print it directly on panties. I had the notion that sometimes underwear is a lot of wasted space that could be used for poetry. Sometimes you'd be the only one who knows that the poem is there, or that you have on the sexiest panties in the world, and that would give you a special secret which, like your sexuality, you don't need others to enjoy. In a sense, the poem, like the panties, would be something that was unique for each individual.

JOEL ALLEGRETTI

Joel Allegretti is the author of five collections of poetry, most recently *The Body in Equipoise* (Full Court Press, 2015), a chapbook on the theme of architecture and design. His other books include *Father Silicon* (The Poet's Press), which was selected by the *Kansas City Star* as one of 100 Noteworthy Books of 2006. Allegretti is the editor of *Rabbit Ears: TV Poems* (NYQ Books, 2015), the first anthology of poetry about the mass medium, and wrote the texts for three song cycles by Frank Ezra Levy, whose work is released on Naxos American Classics. He is a member of the Academy of American Poets and ASCAP.

THE MARITAL HYGIENE POEM

The bruise on the left cheekbone was the last straw,
Purple-black and stark, as if Denny had surgically implanted a plum.
Your arm is healing, but the high shelves are still part of your future.
You agreed: The rip in the dress shirt was your fault, Kathleen.
So was the miscarriage, because it's called spontaneous abortion.

The suburban professional's wife is supposed to know other kinds of days.
The nostalgic aroma of baking chicken and chopped apples flees the oven
And finds you at the top of the stairs. Your mother's Wednesday tradition.

6:15 p.m.
The November sky is the color of 8 p.m.
The BMW purrs up the driveway into the garage, a mechanism of stealth.
Leukemia is also quiet as it advances, Kathleen.

You hear Denny enter through the recreation room singing "Eleanor Rigby."
You know he rearranges the decorative Japanese tea cups on the coffee table.
He calls your name. The tone is candy coated. Stay where you are, Kathleen.
The second call is not so sweet. The third is inflammable.

He eyes you from the bottom of the staircase, motions for you to come.
You've seen the smile often enough. It's *that* smile, Kathleen.
He's on the first step now. Don't submit.

He's on the fourth step.
Draw the air deep into your lungs, Kathleen.
The dinner is overcooked. Don't you dare go down.
Fifth step.
Five to go before he reaches you.
Resolve, Kathleen.
Sixth step.
Denny's clenched teeth.
Resolve.
Seventh step.
Denny's extended hand.
Eighth step.
Goddamn it, Kathleen,
Pull the trigger!

ALLEGRETTI: "The Marital Hygiene Poem" is about an abusive marriage. The cliché of the physically violent husband is that he is uneducated, downwardly mobile, or holds a blue-collar job, if he holds a job at all. When we picture this type of individual, how often does a well-compensated business executive come to mind? The physically abusive impulse doesn't understand the meaning of "net worth."

SUZANNE ALLEN

Suzanne Allen is an interior designer turned teacher from Los Angeles, California. Her poems have been published in many anthologies and journals, including *Not a Muse, Strangers in Paris, The Heart of All That Is, Villanelles, Tears in the Fence, Spillway, Nerve Cowboy, Upstairs at Duroc, Spot Lit Mag, Pearl, California Quarterly*, and *Cider Press Review*. Online, selected poems are archived at *Carnival, Hobo Camp Review*, and *Crack the Spine*. Allen holds an MFA in Poetry and is a Pushcart Prize nominee and a co-editor of *The Bastille: The Literary Magazine of Spoken Word Paris*. Her first press-published chapbook, *Verisimilitude*, is available at CorruptPress.net.

AN HOUR WITH MADAME SABATIER[*]

> *True art, when it happens to us,*
> *challenges the 'I' that we are.*
> — Jeanette Winterson, "Art Objects"

Mistress to many, including her sculptor,
and muse   to Baudelaire,
she lies
stretched across a bed of flowers carved
as intricately as her sinewy locks, her
parted lips — in French, she whispers
décadence, punition.

Objectification circa eighteen forty-seven —
torso twisted, head thrown
back in that way that intensifies
climax, marketability, by simply elongating
the neck.   Cliché that I
am drawn to her.   Temptation —
serpent bangled 'round one wrist,
her gown   falling softly away —
marble complexion   cold,   waist

---

[*] "Femme piquée par un serpent," Auguste Clésinger, Musée d'Orsay

kinked in a fine crease — flawless — breasts full;
otherwise   sexless.
A husband listens   to his audio guide.
        Obscene
critiques his wife as he lingers.

A mother explains to a four-year-old girl:
She didn't want to live —
Why?   The girl asks why.
She was so sad   having been separated
from her lover.   How death can look like
pleasure   on a woman —
but she doesn't get into that.

ALLEN: I have been witness and victim in too many abusive scenarios to list here, but, truth is, the poem says it better than I can. I do think the poem explains itself, but I obviously owe a huge debt of gratitude to Jeanette Winterson, who suggests in *Art Objects* that we learn to sit and really look at Art…for an hour, at least, and so I did.

IVY ALVAREZ

Ivy Alvarez is the author of *Mortal* (Red Morning Press, 2006), *Disturbance* (Seren, 2013), and three chapbooks. Her poems have appeared in many journals and anthologies, with several translated into Russian, Spanish, Japanese and Korean, and she has been a recipient of writing residencies from MacDowell Colony, Hawthornden Castle (UK), and Fundación Valparaiso (Spain). A visiting lecturer at the University of Chester in 2010, she has served on the editorial boards of *Cordite Poetry Review, qarrtsiluni,* and *Cha*. Born in the Philippines and raised in Australia, Alvarez became a British citizen in 2010, after living in Cardiff, Wales for 10 years.

REPLACE BROKEN MIRROR

Excerpt from "Jane's To-Do List"

I was raised on polite silences
my daily bread
my long hair shed and combed and bound again
my gaze lowered
my hands quiet
the pulse at my wrists a lie
this seemed the pattern of my life
learn to lie down
let myself be poured into
this strange shape
called wife

SIGNATURES

I was sure
I was dying a slow death
who knows if this would hasten it
my decision
to take the paper
and sign, sign, sign
in triplicate to make it real
to make him feel it where it hurts
change the locks and tell it true
all those bruises
his ruse — I wasn't clumsy
just tongue-tied
well, I'm undoing the knot
that held my breath for fifteen years
my daughter might come back
my son might smile again
and all I have to do
is seal this envelope
slip it in the slot
let drop
from my suddenly nerveless hand

ALVAREZ: I wrote "Signatures" to show, at this point of the story, how the speaker finally nerves herself to leave the pain and abuse she endured during her marriage — to "make it real." Similarly, "Replace Broken Mirror" reflects on how the lessons of decorousness and restraint one learns early on as a girl child might perpetrate a social oppression that extends into marriage. Both poems appear in my second poetry collection, *Disturbance,* a verse narrative about a man who kills his wife, his son, and then himself, leaving the daughter as a sole survivor of this sadly all-too-common crime.

NADIA ANJUMAN

Nadia Anjuman was born in Herat. She graduated from high school, despite the two-year interruption caused by Taliban rule in Afghanistan. During that time, she had begun to write poetry that described the oppression of Afghani women, which made her a disgrace to her family. Her first collection of poetry, *Gol-e Dudi* (*Smokey Flower*), was published when she was 25, the last year of her life.

THE SILENCED

Nadia Anjuman's "The Silenced" could not be included in this anthology because permission to use her poem, in both existing and new translations, was denied by official representatives of Wisehouse Publishing, AB.

For further information about Anjuman's short life, her death, and the impact of her work, please visit these sites:

www.nytimes.com/2005/11/08/world/asia/afghan-poet-dies-after-beating-by-husband.html

en.wikipedia.org/wiki/Nadia_Anjuman

universeofpoetry.org/afghanistan.shtml

www.thehypertexts.com/Nadia_Anjuman_Poet_Poetry_Picture_Bio.htm

AMEERAH ARJANEE

Ameerah Arjanee is a university student in the humanities. Her poems have appeared in such magazines as *Magma* and *The Cadaverine* and have received the Foyle Young Poets Award and the Dorothy Sargent Rosenberg Prize. Her first collection, *to the universe*, was published by l'Atelier d'Escriture in 2011; her second, *Morning with My Twin Sister*, was released in 2014 by La Librairie Mauricienne Numérique. Arjanee lives on Mauritius, a small island in the Indian Ocean east of Madagascar.

MARRIAGE IS A MOSQUE

"Marriage is a mosque — don't tear it down."
Green churidars, gold bangles, the gossip of empty cupboards.
"Marriage is — " Green churidars, gold bangles — "You are from
a good family, he is from a good family." "He is a doctor, a well-
educated man, how can he do this?" A broken set of porcelain
tableware; the imam gives good advice, he is kind and ignorant.
"Marriage is a mosque — pray in it, have patience in it, sabr,
women must have sabr, women can —" "Think of your family,
your parents have such a good reputation; the woman waits
and then everything is alright. He is a good man, he has a degree,
his family has no scandal, he wears polished black, black, black shoes."
Somebody in a fit of anger broke the dining room table. Good oak.
"He is a good man, he just can't control himself. A mosque is a marriage —
don't tear it down and don't walk with your shoes into it." Your youngest
child is going to the psychologist, he smashed your face into the bathroom
mirror because — He is a good man, but he just can't control himself
       sometimes.
The gossip of empty cupboards. "Women must have patience, sabr. He will
change. And if he doesn't, so what? Women must — . He is a good man,
from a good family, he doesn't mean it."

ARJANEE: Because of the taboo on divorce and the importance of the "reputation" of families, some women in Muslim communities who find themselves in abusive marriages are told by elders and religious leaders that their husbands will stop being violent if they have patience (*sabr*) and perform a certain prayer enough. Sometimes the "counselors" are well-intentioned but ignorant, giving out folk wisdom unthinkingly and fearing to transgress norms. Some are so pro-family that they are ready to ignore the suffering of an individual, in order to maintain the family unit *just* for the sake of maintaining it. They believe that preventing a divorce is the best thing in *any* circumstance. I witnessed such a case in a relative's life when I was in elementary school, and later, in my late teens, remembered the case and felt very angry. The relative's husband was an engineer (a "good job"), who had anger problems and was violent. The woman was convinced by her relatives that it was her role, as a woman, to keep working on the marriage and that destroying the marriage would be bad because, in their words, "Marriage is a mosque"; any marriage is holy, abusive or not.

LINDA K. ARNOLD

Linda K. Arnold's poetry has appeared in *Mindprints, The Oleander Review, Tipton Poetry Journal, HeartLodge,* and *The Master's Hand: Reflections on Rane.* She has also been published in such professional journals as the *NEA Journal, English Journal,* and the *Journal of the Colorado Language Arts Society.* Arnold is the author of numerous education grants and award applications, including two United States Department of Education Blue Ribbon awards and the 2011 Colorado Schools-to-Watch, National Reform for Excellence in Middle Level Education Award.

THE BACKBONE OF OUR SOULS*

after Ayaan Hirsi Ali's memoir, Infidel

Malala, we applaud you who fractured Allah's wisdom —
ancient scripture of patronage and prosperity.

But like women of promise before you — Benazir Bhutto,
Mukhtaren Bibi — our lives remain miserably the same.

At 2:37,
our Muslim sister stole onto a foreign city bus.
Her patriarchs mocked her blasphemy
of divorce, in forked-tongued syllables.
She left behind her trousseau of silk dirhas
and frankincense.

In Holland,
she pulled her headscarf over her eyes
in a safe haven...on her own. Through petals,
she learned to wonder, through sepals to ponder.
Why were infidels living Allah's promises
while believers were shackled to conflict and suffering?

---

* This poem, told in third-person plural, portrays Muslim women speaking to Malala.

We beg, Malala:
study Voltaire with this *Holland Infidel*. Though
the Qur'an proclaims men and women equal before God,
we cower as faithful wives and daughters dwindle
to customary honor killings and acid throwings.

A difficult irony
prevails for those of us who disclose wedded abuses:
cast from societal graces, we taint our families' honor.
It is our learned Dark Age dignity that batters us,
grooms our children to ignorance.

Bid your Somali sister to press her cheek to your fissure:
activism only incites bearded shadows so traditions endure.
Let education be our staff; reform, the backbone of our souls.

ARNOLD: In the United States, I was a member of the first generation of women who were encouraged to work outside of the home. I enjoyed a 36-year career in education and, with my husband's help, raised three successful children. Unlike most of the women mentioned in *Veils, Halos & Shackles*, I was lucky. When the Taliban attacked Malala Yousafzai, a thirteen-year-old girl, on her school bus, I really struggled with that abuse against a child. As luck would have it, I had just checked out Ayaan Hirsi Ali's memoir, *Infidel*. After much thought, I wrote two versions of the same poem. I wanted this little girl to know that other Muslim women were living her beliefs.

YOLANDA ARROYO-PIZARRO

Yolanda Arroyo-Pizarro has been published in Argentina, Bolivia, Chile, Colombia, Denmark, France, Guatemala, Hungary, Mexico, Panama, Spain, and Venezuela. Her works have been assigned at the Stockholm Cervantes Institute, the Black Cultural Center at Purdue University, the Centro de Estudios Avanzados de Puerto Rico y el Caribe, the University of California (San Francisco), and in other graduate-studies institutions in North and South America. Arroyo-Pizarro has participated in the cultural summits of Bogotá39 at the Hay Festival, the Guadalajara International Book Fair, the Vivamérica Festival in Madrid, the LIBER Barcelona, and other major cultural events. She is also founder and editor in chief of *Revista Boreales*.

RAZA POEM

When I was eight years old
I was already astute
a smart worm
a perceptive cactus
who knew at that point
that during school recess
in order to prevent
my classmates' jokes about my hair
my skin color
mis bembas grandes
big lips
big hips
I must get into the bathroom
to hide
or to picnic there
to write novels
to talk to my imaginary friends
there were many
legion
to laugh
to recite poems

to practice what I was taught in class
to review the math test
to fancy the teacher
and imagine she was my girlfriend
to conclude my science project
to inhale the albuterol medicine
for my asthma attacks
to cough
to perform an invisible kiss
waiting for it to happen
I learned to see my world
stuck in that bathroom
of Colegio San Vicente Ferrer
spent many years making that place my den
my cave
my hideaway
I also knew
that once I sat in class
if Mrs. Guzmán mentioned the word "Africa"
while teaching Social Studies
I was supposed to wear a stoic mask
pretend it did not happen
assume an I-do-not-care attitude
thereby obviating the long-awaited reaction
of José Manuel or Eliseo
or anyone else who joined in the harassment
there was always the cry proclaiming funny
Yolanda, you are African!
you are so black
so ugly black
so bembetrueno
big lips thunder
big hip hurricane
while the teacher tried to scold the commotion
(silent children

show respect for others
remember that God punishes without rod and no whip)
while she tried to implement bullying policies
that had not yet been invented
by 1978

ARROYO-PIZZARO: I am an Afro Puerto Rican woman. I was a much-bullied kid in my childhood, due to my skin color. That was in the 1970s. Unfortunately, today, in 2015, racism continues to be an active part of our daily life.

LANA HECHTMAN AYERS

Lana Hechtman Ayers is a consulting editor for *Crab Creek Review*, manages three poetry presses, and works as a manuscript organizer and writing workshop facilitator. She lives across the Puget Sound from Seattle, where, on clear days, she can see Mt. Rainier from her desk. She has published five collections of poems to date and is at work on her first novel.

BLUE SKY

The room tilts after
you flip the coffee table
and fly at my neck —

never mistake love for violence —

passion cracks bones,
blasts china to smithereens

You could break your own teeth
clamping them down

when I repeat that other woman's name —

here I won't give
her the black and white
but in our living room

her name explodes

like a sparrow
against the windowpane —
feathers everywhere —

one pump of your fist
and I'm horizontal

blood pulsing out the back of my skull
staring
at a ceiling that's not

sky blue

THIS ROSE-SHAPED SCAR

serves as permanent reminder
of when my brother pushed me
facedown on Far Rockaway sand
and from beneath spongy bracken
a jagged busted beer bottle
gnawed at my knee
while he held me there
bumping against me
until he was done,
leaving the impression
I'd been bitten by a rose.

AYERS: As a child, I was physically abused by family members. As a young adult, I entered into relationships with men who were violent. I feel very strongly that writing openly and honestly about these experiences is healing for myself as a writer and for readers who have experienced similar strife. These poems let women know they are not alone and are a badge of survival and transcendence.

HIRA AZMAT

Hira Azmat is a writer, editor, and feminist based in Lahore, Pakistan. Her first published poem, "The Trials and Tribulations of a Well-Endowed Woman," originally appeared in *The Missing Slate* and was included in *Hallelujah for 50ft Women: Poems About Women's Relationship to Their Bodies* (Bloodaxe Books, 2015).

THE TRIALS AND TRIBULATIONS OF A WELL-ENDOWED WOMAN

my breasts offend my father
even more than my opinions;
it's the size that's insolent — bursting
out of t-shirts, spilling
out of kameezes that hang
demurely on any other girl.

the most mundane actions inspire a filial
mistrust that extends well beyond your
garden-variety middle-class moral suspicion:
going out for coffee with a friend, being on the phone;
in our lounge, leaning back
dupatta-less on the couch becomes
an act of sexual rebellion.
my sisters get hugs;
I, at best, get awkward back-pats.

felt up by a darzi at 10, groped by a driver at 11,
and too many times to count since; intrusive
hands years of poor posture couldn't deflect.
I envy other women their ability to wear
their sexuality like a mask, to take
off and put on as they please
and, not least, I envy them
their delicates that actually

look delicate; mine, all hefty
cotton and industrial-strength
underwire, look just like armor.

fortunately, though, the man I love
loves warriors.

AZMAT: This poem comes from a place of lifelong, chronic discomfort with my body, reinforced by people's reactions to it as something repulsive, something shameful and, somehow, almost inherently evil. For all that, it's a poem that refuses to take itself seriously. I wrote it impulsively, laughingly, and the fact that it resonated with so many women around the world has me completely floored and strangely comforted.

MAX BABI

Max Babi, born Mushtaque Ali Khan Babi, was an advanced trainer in plasma technology and wrote prolifically in four languages, though the bulk of his writing was in English. Due to the poor quality of translations into English from various Indian regional languages, he adopted the concept of "transcreations," whereby he assimilated a poem and then wrote a fresh poem in English that was never a word-for-word translation, in order to preserve the aroma and essence of the original. Babi conducted workshops on serendipity, creative intuition, and tacit knowledge, and also led discussions on biomimicry or bio-inspiration. He was married, with one daughter, Maujiza, and lived in Pune, India. He died in March 2015.

A PIERCED SOUL

Males rarely ruminate with profundity on
penetrative rape, that females tend to cringe from
when a discussion rears its ugly head
like a spirit emerging
foggily from a womb
searingly from a wound.

I am a normal male with no history of rapes
and half a century of treading my twisting paths
on this tongueless planet,
but I suffered agonies once
when an over-enthusiast herbalist
shoved a stainless steel cone up my rectum
till my screams rattled the windows and juddered
his Man Friday holding a platter.

I am slightly abnormal because the word rape
runs its electric course through my veins my blood
my electric impulses through the neurons,
I think I abhor no other four-letter words more
than R A P E.

This is one of those rare
double conspiracies:
males shrug it off, just one of those things,
females sweep it under a carpet of
mild umbrage —
rape thus remains obscure as an orphan
ubiquitous as oxygen and yet
corrosive as acid.

Ladies often arrange their words
as if they were part of an Ikebana
flower show
— and who wants to touch a rotting fish,
who wants to fondle a dismembered member
or shrunken meatballs in shriveling skin?

Those men should be castrated, hisses a lady,
and I do visualize the predator now
carrying a plastic piss bag tied to his belt,
all starch gone from his de-membered self,
gone forever his gung-ho pelf.

But reality wouldn't jell into such a scenario.

Reality is ugly enough to kill you or me
lest we invent a myth or two —
and start to believe in it.

BABI: I have been a feminist all my life, and a huge majority of people who influenced me deeply have always been female. While I jump at the slightest opportunity to highlight the wrongs done by males to females in human societies anywhere, it hurts me to see that most women today are not really serious about doing something desperately effective to reduce these rampant cases of trafficking, child abuse, maltreatment and rape, including sub-human cruelty to women (often with other women conniving with the perpetrators — a "madam" who runs a brothel is always a lady, never a man). I hope and trust that better efforts, which can be sustained worldwide, have finally been started and supported. A most depressing scenario.

NED BALBO

Ned Balbo's *The Trials of Edgar Poe and Other Poems* (Story Line Press) was awarded the 2012 Poets' Prize and the 2010 Donald Justice Prize. *Lives of the Sleepers* (University of Notre Dame Press, 2005) received the Ernest Sandeen Poetry Prize and a *ForeWord* Book of the Year Gold Medal. *Galileo's Banquet* (Washington Writers' Publishing House, 1998) shared the Towson University Prize for literature. Balbo has received three Maryland Arts Council grants, the Robert Frost Foundation Poetry Award, and the John Guyon Literary Nonfiction Prize. He was also co-winner of the 2013 Willis Barnstone Translation Prize. Balbo's fourth book, *Upcycling Paumanok*, will be released by Measure Press in 2016.

HOME FOR GIRLS, LONG ISLAND

for my adoptive mother Elizabeth, c. 1929

They've got someone's attention, finally:
photographer unknown, this mob of girls
in dresses bleached to near-transparency
squeezes before the lens, set free to smile —-
all faded, water-stained over the years.
Who brought them here, to this Victorian house
built on bare land, dune-drifts, clumps of weed,
or just bad soil? Is this their residence?

And you, too: starched and scoured with the rest —
cleansed, almost — still astonished when you think
of all that changed the day you choked back tears,
struggling to tell who hit you, held you down,
who tore your dress. When blows began to fall
before you'd finished speaking, how surprised —
and yet, beyond surprise — you found yourself,
past all thought she would pull you close again...

— And yet, each time she visits, you forgive
your mother, and wait to be taken home.

BALBO: When I was growing up, my mother, Elizabeth — "Betty" to friends and family — would refer to her time in "the home," a period that she shrouded in secrecy yet mentioned often enough to ensure I always knew she *had* a secret. Later, in my teen years, she began displaying the faded photo that inspired "Home for Girls, Long Island." In my teen years, she suffered from crippling arthritis and clinical depression yet confided more about her past, acutely aware that our time together was growing short. In fact, she died of cancer in the fall of my first year of college.

One story Betty told me is the one depicted in the poem: as a thirteen-year-old, she was raped, blamed — as if she, and not her rapist, were the person who'd transgressed — and sent to live in the "home" I now saw in a faded glimpse. Another story I have yet to write about. Always at odds with her own mother — the Polish immigrant who'd treated a daughter's rape with scorn — always seeking approval, but finding only rejection, Betty once confided that if "Nanny" ever told me about the time that she, Betty, had been arrested with a group of prostitutes, I should know it was all a mistake: she'd been locked out of the house after yet another argument with her mother, and a working girl had kindly offered her shelter for the night. In later years, I realized the likelier truth was that Betty herself was a prostitute at some point during her Depression-era youth and that she'd invented a cover story before her mother could betray her.

RICHARD BALLON

Richard Ballon has been writing poetry and plays for thirty years. His full-length plays *One Good Look* and *In the Name of God,* and his short plays and monologues, among them *Benefit, The Accident, Cassandra's Choice, Forsythia,* and *How We Began,* have been performed in major US and Canadian cities. Ballon's six-part mini-series *Zephyr* was seen on ACTV-Amherst, and his short films "Dear Edward," "Benefit," and "The Pure Dark" won placements in several film festivals. A selection of Ballon's monologues, poems, and short plays appeared in *Enough of a Little to Know the All* (Levellers Press, 2007). He has an MFA in Playwriting/Screenwriting from Lesley University and is a member of the Dramatists Guild.

THE COMMANDMENT

You do as you're told, young man,
and my whimper so small,
like a wounded bird, like a bedspring
and him, my Grandpapa
parroting No? No?
His meat, his poker, sausage, no-no
You do as you are told.

If Moses knew what those words would do
to all his children.
If Moses knew that Honor Thy Father
would brand the hearts
of the innocent
he would have smashed those tablets down
and forsaken the Law.

BALLON: I have written this poem because I am a survivor of sexual child abuse. In my recovery from the experience, I have met a lot of women who have been through similar circumstances. I am a playwright and poet and my creativity has allowed me to unlock some of these feelings and share the experience with others in an original, thoughtful manner.

RITA BANERJI

Rita Banerji is an author, photographer, and gender activist from India. Her book *Sex and Power: Defining History, Shaping Societies* (Penguin Books, India), is an historical study of the relationship between sex, sexuality, and gender in India. She is also the founder of the 50 Million Missing Campaign, an online, global initiative that raises awareness about India's ongoing female genocide and lobbies for official action to stop it.

THE CALL OF REVOLUTION

I. *Maya ad Infinitum*

Deeper than gravity
she anchors
earth to the womb,

she is the journey
fifty million women
could not make
through life.

More will be trashed;
flesh ridden life-less.
Fragmented
after birth,
garbage,
street dog food.

But she lives!

Baby hands strong
grab destiny.
The world opens.
Black skin
robe beautiful,
sweeps past the blind land,

stomps on traditions,
buries them in history.
Mud in a grave,

inconsequential
to mourning.

Life swings her high
into new air,
she pauses,
smiles,
to recompose the song
unwinding,
in the protection
of soul.
A breath births
the unbroken chain,
the lotus of infinite openings,
still gestating,
life!
Maya!

II. *Undressing*

I ripped them off
one at a time,
painfully,

layer after layer
of identities,
woven into the fabric
of my being,
since birth.

And each time I thought
I had stripped to the core,
there was always one more.

When will I be done?
I ache to dance
naked in the sun.

III. *Colors of Kranti*

Here where the sun does not exhale,
a year is twelve unbroken months
of rolling steam.
Here where feet are stilled
by languid quagmires,
the trees announce
the shifting of time.

Mulberries bomb the roads
with pools of purple.
Virulent green mosses
scale the walls.
Flames of the forest
crown and crackle
and scatter red cinder on roof-tops.

Laburnums hung in yellow
take up arms
of brown swords.
White jasmines
silently ambush the night.

If you stand under the dancing
pink skirt of the bougainvillea,
and listen with your eyes open,
you will hear the call
to revolution.

BANERJI: This is a poem in three parts. "Maya ad Infinitum" was inspired by the daughter a Swedish friend adopted from India and named Maya. Ninety percent of children in Indian orphanages are "unwanted" daughters. Maya's adoption was long and painful; Indian families did not want to adopt her because she was a girl and also because of her dark skin. "Maya" as a concept is attachment, affection — that natural tie that bonds parents to their children, but also that which ties each of us as human beings to the larger and more compassionate process of living. "Undressing" is about freedom, especially the need Indian women have to affirm individual identities and resist the social imperative that imprisons women in confined roles in the context of family, society and culture. "Colors of Kranti" is about a feminist revolution in the offing, in India. Often Indian women, even outside India, are viewed in a cultural context that's seen as colorful and exotic, and the Kranti (revolution) is about looking beyond that.

DONNA BARKMAN

Donna Barkman is a writer/actor who has had her feminist solo plays, *Hand-Me-Downs: Scenes from a Life* and *Sticks and Stones and Women's Bones*, produced in New York City and elsewhere. Her poetry has appeared in *Adrienne Rich: a Tribute Anthology, Common Ground, Chautauqua, Boston Literary Review, String Poet, Per Contra,* and other journals and anthologies. She has enjoyed writer's residencies at Brush Creek and Jentel, both in Wyoming. In the late 1960s, Barkman was converted to feminism by the persuasive writings of the radical women of that time, including Robin Morgan, Germaine Greer, and Audre Lorde, and she continues to be a fierce and active feminist, both in the United States and abroad.

LUCK OF THE DRAW

She was chosen, Tessie Hutchinson,
                    by lottery
We read of her in 10th grade English,
urged by Miss Porterfield
to find meaning in the stoning
                    of a woman,
her name plucked in a raffle.

We thought Shirley Jackson a sadist —
who else but a fiend could imagine
                    such carnage?

We rejected the possibility
of a murder like that,
performed by neighbors and friends
                    for what? —
to preserve the community?
Our guess at a meaning,

Years later, our scruples effaced,
we have become casual consumers
                    of atrocity
gazers at screens,
            shruggers of shoulders

Wretchedly unfortunate
in the cultures of their birth:
Fatima Bani, Mini Kolvat,
Sakinah Mohammedi-Ashtiani
Saba Abdali, Zhila Izadi
                    the youngest at 13
each buried to her waist
slowly executed by stones hurled
by fathers, brothers, uncles, friends
who find meaning, Miss Porterfield,
in preserving
                    family honor.

We accept the possibility,
        click the switch.

A WOMAN IS TALKING TO JUSTICE (selection)

after Judy Grahn's "A Woman Is Talking to Death"

Hey judge
Hey judgment
Come and get me
Put me in the witness box
I've seen it all
or most of it
I'm dying to testify

Well, no, in truth
(if that's what you care about)
others are dying
Mutilated little girls in Egypt
    genitals cut with jagged glass
Fistula women in Kenya
    stinking of rot
    banished to their stinking huts
Swaziland where
    multiple wives are shrinking to sticks
    as AIDs-infected husbands extort sex
Soldier-gang-raped girls in Iraq
Congo, Thailand, Mexico, Burma, Laos
Sri Lanka, Nepal, Japan and
(fly that flag)
Columbus, Georgia, USA.

Y chromosomes
crow their power

Everywhere

BARKMAN: The long struggle for women's rights is central to my life, as a writer, a woman, a feminist, an activist, and a citizen of the world. Women hold up way more than half the sky, with little recognition of their work, talent, and responsibilities and with little compensation in most countries. Until the underclass status of women is acknowledged and corrected, we will not have the peace and justice we deserve. Because of the harsh truth of women's circumstances, I write and perform works that address our oppression, hoping that words (written and spoken) can foster change in those who read and hear them and, thus, ultimately, change in women's lives, just as I believe that this anthology can better the lives of women.

HELEN BAR-LEV

Helen Bar-Lev was born in New York in 1942. She has lived in Israel for 42 years and has had over 90 exhibitions of her landscape paintings, including 33 one-person shows. Her poetry collections include *Cyclamens and Swords and Other Poems About the Land of Israel* and *The Muse in the Suitcase,* both with Johnmichael Simon, illustrated by Bar-Lev, and *In Moonlight the Sky Will Slide,* with Katherine L. Gordon. *Everything Today,* her most recent collection, is a book of poetry about colors, with her illustrations. Bar-Lev is assistant to the president of the Voices Israel group of poets in English, and senior editor of Cyclamens and Swords Publishing.

WHY SHOULD THE SUN SHINE?

He needs no excuses
to be abusive
it's as natural
as the hair he wears
as the skin he's in

Aggression brings out
the best in him,
shows the world
he's masculine

Why praise
when he can complain?
why should the sun shine
when it can rain?
why smile
when shouting is superior?

Why explain
when it's easier to blame?

THE MASTER OF THE HOUSE

He doesn't want affection
just snap to attention
the moment he demands it
or by George you've had it
he'll be madder than an adder
and you'll have to run for cover

He needs a slave
not a lover

BAR-LEV: These poems were written after observing some friends interacting with each other. I am an artist who paints from nature, so I observe every nuance of light and shade, every nuance of human interaction.

TINA BARRY

Tina Barry's short stories and poetry appear online and in print publications, including *Drunken Boat*, *The Camrock Press Review*, *Lost in Thought*, *The Orange Room Review*, and *Exposure*, an anthology of microfiction from Cinnamon Press (2010). She is the author of *Mall Flower*, her first book of poems and short fiction (Big Table Publishing, 2015). Barry lives in High Falls, New York.

PINE

Air freshener dangling
from a cabby's window.
A freshly mopped floor.
The surprise of Christmas trees
in a November farmer's market
where a woman waved a branch,
proud of its healthy aroma,
as I fled.

I thought of going back
if only because she'd said, *Miss?*
with such concern.

Because she was kind,
I didn't return to explain,
Your trees smell like a man
who locked me in his car,
or burden her with details:

The warped cross of black
moles on his cheek.

Burnt evergreen of
stale cologne.

His weight, the crush
of an overturned tree.

Chilly fingers in my coat pockets,
I began:

Heart
Mouth
Hands
Breath
Heart

Until the smells became street smells.
The noise street noises.

Until my tongue tasted like nothing
but my tongue.

BARRY: I've written "Pine" because violence happens to women every day, every minute, everywhere.

Roberta Beary

Roberta Beary is the haibun editor of *Modern Haiku*. Her book of short poems, *The Unworn Necklace* (Snapshot Press, 2007, 1st HB ed. 2011), was named a Poetry Society of America award finalist and a Haiku Society of America Merit Book Award prizewinner. She is on the editorial staff of the annual *Red Moon Anthology* and is a longtime member of Towpath, a Washington, DC poetry group. Her poetry has been featured on National Public Radio and in the *New York Times*.

Irish Twins

We share an attic room. In the corner is an old double bed
that smells and sags on one side. My side. Late at night I hear my
heart beat. Loud. So loud he will hear it. He will think my heart
is calling him and come up the attic stairs. His footsteps are heavy.
He smells of old spice and cherry tobacco. My eyes shut tight. I
know he is there. I feel his weight. Never on my side. Always on
the side where she sleeps. When the bedsprings sing their sad song
I fly away. Up to the ceiling. My sister is already there. Together
we hold hands. Looking down we see our bodies. We are not moving.
We are as still as the dead.

BEARY: My hope is that at least one incest survivor reads my poem and finds in it the strength to confront the fact of the abuse and/or the abuser.

B. ELIZABETH BECK

B. Elizabeth Beck is a writer, teacher and artist. She is the author of two books of poetry: *insignificant white girl* (Evening Street Press, 2013) and *Interiors* (Finishing Line Press, 2013). In 2011, she founded the Teen Howl Poetry Series, the only under-twenty-one poetry series in Central Kentucky. The series was specifically designed to give teenagers the mic — for teens/about teens.

GRANDMA'S MINK & ARMY JACKETS

I. *Edelweiss & My Mother's Apron*

My mother's family speaks Hungarian, German, English all in one
sentence. We kiss on both cheeks, exclaiming *Szervusz!,*
hug & interrupt; yell to be heard; reek of garlic, onions;
crowd around a large table to eat goulash & paprikash,
cucumbers, plums, apple strudel & dobos torte
served on flamboyantly hand-painted pottery.
Omi plants blackberries to wind around a chain-link fence;
Wolfie, Chris & I pick to eat until our stomachs ache. We reach
for glass bottles of 7-Up corked with rubber & metal stoppers
we open then chug; each taking our turn.

Emi Tante picks up her guitar; Filli Baci turns to his piano;
their strains of Mozart, Haydn, Bach fill the room.
Ferns, palms, jades dance in the solarium Aunt Martha
carefully plants with exotic blooms. Music floats over the end
of the evening, Reverend Uncle Emil only a shadow in my memory.

I erase him from these snapshots to forget other weekends
at Emi Tante's & Uncle Emil's home, when he would hold me hostage
on his lap in the living room and jack himself off inside his pants
by grinding against my bottom while Emi Tante made crepes
with clotted crème, blackberries, and dark chocolate, in the kitchen.

II. *Silver Spoons & Daddy's Little Girl*

I have a photograph of myself at age eleven,
thin, brown-eyed girl in a cotton nightgown,
sun bleached, long blonde hair cascading
over Grandma Helen's mink jacket
she let me try on for just one moment
after Grandpa Harry finished nine holes
at the country club, where we ate roast beef,
shrimp cocktail, petit fours from buffets decorated
with carved ice sculptures — after too many Manhattans —
back when white-jacketed waiters used little sterling silver brushes
to sweep away crumbs & ashes because everyone smoked
in those days.

Hypocrisy is the worst form of cowardice
like my father's ivy league education — his legacy as only son
of a doctor and a debutant. Raised in a world where manners floated
between the ice cubes in cut crystal glasses of Johnny Walker Red
and tea in bone china was served at weekly bridge games
on linen tablecloths in the living room, where white & ivory keys
polished by the maid could not wipe clean the shame, degradation,
and dark secrets that echoed through the hallways of his life, my father
carefully removed his seersucker suit, Brooks Brothers tie & penny loafers
before climbing under my Laura Ashley nightgown.

BECK: I wrote the poem as an introduction to my book *insignificant white girl,* which details the story of an American suburban girl in the 1970s who survived childhood sexual abuse, rape, and domestic violence. The purpose of the book is to raise awareness and to empower other incest survivors. It is a continuation of my lifelong devotion to social justice — first as a social worker, then as an inner-city school teacher, and now as a writer.

I teach high school students *Catcher in the Rye.* It is my own red hunting hat, my cry for the sanctity of innocence. *Protect the children, Holden! Rail against authority & scream at the top of your lungs,* "Sleep tight, you morons!" The prep-school boy who raped me in the ninth grade deserved more than that rant from me. Instead, I went on the pill.

LYTTON BELL

Lytton Bell has published five books: *A Path Before Winter* (He & She Publishing, 1998), *The Book of Chaps* (24th Street Irregular Press, 2002), *Nectar* (Amazon Digital Services LLC, 2011), *Poetica Erotica, Volume One* (The Poetry Box, 2012), and *Body Image* (CreateSpace Independent Publishing, 2013). She has also won six poetry contests and has been the featured reader at many California literary venues. Her work has appeared in over three dozen publications. As a teenager, Bell won a scholarship to the Pennsylvania Governor's School for the Arts, where she studied with Deb Burnham and the late Len Roberts. She graduated Magna Cum Laude from Bryn Mawr College.

CALL ME SCHEHERAZADE

The man wanted to rape me
There is no other way to say it than that
How he had gotten me into his trailer
and then blocked the door
is a story for another day
Why I was 2,000 miles from home,
alone and gullible at 20 years old, is another

Still, he had me trapped
What could I do?
I told him jokes and stories
kept him distracted, laughing
Encouraged him to drink
Until finally, he passed out
and began to snore

Maneuvering him, a man twice my weight
away from the narrow, squeaky door
without waking him, was my next ordeal
It took me twenty minutes
moving an arm here, a leg there
always gently and softly
without breath or sound

Freed then (though I was in the middle of the Arizona desert
miles from where I had parked my car)
I began to run, literally leaping for joy
I whispered a grateful prayer to every goddess I could think of:
Artemis, Baba Yaga, Bast, Erzouli, Freya
Let me be worthy of this deliverance
And I know I wasn't imagining it when I saw that
the stars now burned brighter than they ever had before

BELL: I am concerned for women because, so often in our society, it is assumed that we bring violence upon ourselves by not being "safe." "Safe" means to conclude in advance that all men are potential monsters waiting only for an opportunity. So it becomes the woman's imperative never to let that opportunity occur, rather than the man's imperative not to commit a crime. In this scenario, men are only following their true natures, which women must hide from with careful diligence, or else they are complicit and "wanted it." Someday, the world won't be like this. Women will be free to follow their natural curiosity about their surroundings, without a big target being draped over them at all times.

JANE BHANDARI

Jane Bandhari was born in Edinburgh in 1944 but has lived in India for 47 years. Her writing includes reviews, articles, poems, and short stories for anthologies, publications, and websites; two collections of poems, *Single Bed* and *Aquarius;* and two books for children, *The Long Thin Jungle* and *The Round Square Chapatti.* Bhandari coordinates Loquations, a Mumbai poetry-reading group. Her poems have appeared in a variety of magazines and anthologies, including *60 Indian Poets* (Penguin), *To Catch a Poem, We Speak in Changing Voices* (Sahitya Akademi), *Rattapallax, Fulcrum,* and *The Little Magazine.* After being widowed for 16 years, she remarried and is editing her husband's biography of his father, the actor Madan Puri.

THE WIDOWS

We widows sit together, dry-eyed.
The other women
Overflow like rivers.
We dry wells will not yield.
Our eyes feel no water,
Know no tears.

One day she will wonder
How it was she felt no pain
After the first dreadful hurt,
The day her heart stopped with his,
And then
Went on beating without him.

On this day we widows, the dry wells,
Sit with your mother in the dismal hall
And drily, tearlessly,
Make her one of us.

FERTILITY CLINIC

Sometimes they come
With a husband, often
With another woman.
The mother-in-law
Sits stiffly apart, unsmiling:
The girl has not conceived,
Or has borne only girls.
The girl's mother sits closer,
Smiles and chats, but anxiety
Underlines her lips.
The girl says nothing.
What is there to say?

The lone husband
Is a man out of context.
The women stare at him,
Accusing: We do this for you.
We try to please you, and you
Are not pleased.
What must a woman do
To please a man and his mother?

Then the doctor comes. Her power
Flows out into the waiting women.
They glow and pulse, their eyes shine,
And this power is only for them.
The men sit abashed by this effulgence.
After the doctor leaves, the room fades,
But power remains with the women,
And for a while
They wear their men like handbags.

SATI: REQUIEM FOR CHARAN SHAH

Hear the whispers:
Head shaved,
Bangles smashed;
You might as well
Step into the pyre
And become legend.
Otherwise what is left?
Reviled for his death,
To sleep on the floor,
Eat others' scraps,
Be less than a servant.

The whispers, urging:
Walk towards the pyre.
Step into the fire
And become Goddess,
Revered, not reviled.
One breath of the fire
Is all it takes, to be
United with the beloved.
There is not much room
For widows, even now.

Drugged by the ecstasy
Of grief and despair,
An unwanted widow
Leapt into the flames.
You who were there,
Did you hear the whispers?
Or were you the whisperers?

BHANDARI: "The Widows": I attended the funeral of a close friend's husband. As I embraced the new widow, I thought, *Here I am, a widow myself, bringing you into the closed group of women who have lost their husbands.* The poem is intentionally bleak. "Fertility Clinic" was prompted by my daughter's quest for pregnancy. I went with her on one occasion and was struck by the different attitudes of the mothers and the mothers-in-law. I think the poem speaks for itself. On the same day that Princess Diana died in a car crash, Charan Shah committed *sati*. "Sati: Requiem for Charan Shah" was my take on why she might have done so.

LAURE-ANNE BOSSELAAR

Laure-Anne Bosselaar is the author of *The Hour Between Dog and Wolf* and *Small Gods of Grief,* which was awarded the Isabella Gardner Prize for poetry in 2001. Her third poetry collection, *A New Hunger,* was selected as an American Library Association Notable Book in 2008. She is the recipient of a Pushcart Prize and is the editor of four anthologies, including *Outsiders: Poems About Rebels, Exiles and Renegades* and *Never Before: Poems About First Experiences.* Bosselaar taught at Emerson College and at Sarah Lawrence, and she currently teaches at the University of California, Santa Barbara. Bosselaar is also a member of the founding faculty at the low-residency MFA program at Pine Manor College.

THE CELLAR

I want my father to stop sending me down there
to fetch his daily gin, and potatoes for supper.
But there's no saying no to him, and no more places to hide:
he's found them all. Outside, the cellar's rusted door
stains my hands as I yank it open, scraping a branch
that whips back, grabbing at me — like he does.

Six steps stop by a second door, with a hasp
and a slit between two thick planks. I press my face to it,
whisper to the bottles and potatoes: Go away, I'm coming!
But how can they? We're all dammed in this big
brick house in Antwerp, and I'm the *Kapo,*
I have no choice: it's them or me.

I kneel in the cellar, pray: Don't let me separate
families, don't let me kill a child . . . then inch
toward the shelves — and reach. Sometimes
I think I hear a moan, a sob; sometimes it's a child's wail
so exactly like mine I think it comes out of me — so I quickly
put the thing back: I'm sorry, I'm sorry.

The worst are the potatoes. I know exactly
how they lived before, rooted deep in wild, salted polders,
where lapwings titter between cattails and winds,
where rows of loam run past the horizon —
and here they are now, uprooted and cluttered in crates,
limbs groping for a wedge of light from a cellar door.

But then, from up there, comes father's call, weary, irked,
with that pitch and threat in the last vowel of my name.
I grab the gin, the potatoes, hold them as far as I can from my body,
run up, throw them on the table, and escape to my room
where I stand pounding my ears with my fists so as not to hear
yet another cry for mercy.

FROM MY WINDOW, I SEE MOUNTAINS

The morgue man pulls my father out of wall C,
the drawer so heavy he must brace his foot
against another one to pull it open. It jams
half-way — this is how far it will go: one half
available for viewing, the other no.

A voice cries out in the anteroom, then turns
into a wail so unbearable the morgue man leaves.
I'm alone with my father again. This time, I
lift the sheet further than allowed, and look.
This time, it is he who is frozen. And I see his

rage, down there, dark — like a fist
crammed between his legs. I touch his hands, the huge
Dutch hands that almost killed me, almost killed
my daughter, but once — on a shore in The Hague —
built me a sandcastle, the morning after

his mother's funeral. It took him all day,
the deepest terror I remember, watching him
build that castle with the odd tenderness of brutes,
stroking the sand with weightless hands while I
sat at a distance, not knowing what to think,

what to do, Dutch rain sprinkling the sands
like a blessing. When the castle was done, he raised
moats around it, and mountains circling them,
while dusk wrapped us in its cerements, then night.
Not a word was uttered, even when we climbed the dunes

back to his mother's house, where I watched him
rock her wooden shoes in his lap, a hand in each
battered thing, the kitchen stove sighing.
After I buried him next to her, I flew back to this new
country, to this house surrounded by mountains,

with mountains around them. Some days, they seem
so quiet, so unchangeable, I think: shock, fissure, fault;
I want: chasm, quake, wave. But pray: plant me here
a while longer, plant this in me deep: nothing's perpetual,
eternity is only a word — kind as consolation, but as brief.

BOSSELAAR: "The Cellar" — I fear I don't have much to add about this poem: it narrates what I wanted to express: how children often personify objects, how their imaginative space is filled (or haunted) by imagery and stories or things they witness. I was raised in Antwerp in the years just following the end of WWII. Antisemitism was still rampant (Antwerp was full of ex-collaborators), and all around, one heard stories from the war… and my father was not only very abusive but also an antisemite. "From My Window, I See Mountains" was written in Snowmass, Colorado, more than 15 years after my father's death. After a three-day blizzard, the view from my window was an immaculate white and gave me a sense of stability, of immutability, and I thought of the landscape of my youth: the wind- and rain-swept flatlands of Belgium and Holland. The blanket of whiteness also reminded me of the sheet covering my father at the morgue. I started writing this poem out of those images.

MARY BRANCACCIO

Mary Brancaccio has an MFA in poetry from Drew University. Her poetry has appeared in *Minerva Rising, Edison Literary Review, Adanna, Naugatuck River Review,* and *Lake Affect.* She was included in *Farewell to Nuclear, Welcome to Renewable Energy: A Collection of Poems by 218 Poets,* which was published in Japan and America as a bilingual edition. A former broadcast journalist and public school teacher, she is currently an Assistant Professor in the Caspersen School of Graduate Studies at Drew University.

TRANSFIGURATION

At eight, we were best friends, hanging from bars
by our knees in a park by the creek. Did we argue

about our futures? Or did I dream that later?
That month of Our Lady, livid with lilies,

we walked to the altar in white, as our mothers
shushed a baby. The Host, a blind eye in a brass sun.

Let's call it another May, when grass bends
beneath the weight of your body prostrate in grass,

under a pimpled boy pummeled by anger, that red,
carnivorous flower that devours throat and tongue.

He scours the meadow. *You ugly girl,*
open your mouth and swallow. You lost belief

in your own transcendence, some sidewinder missile
of spirit-gift that shoots its path across an alien sky,

some god of buttons and pins and strings that twist. Now,
you turn to a man with a gun, open yourself to his bullet.

Can you die only once? Silence is caught in the mouth
of the temple bell between clapper and bronze.

Your dead eyes like walls: *I did what I did to survive.*

TO NORA, WHO CAME TO CLASS WITH A BRUISED FACE

She holds her head up, not out of pride
but to cup tears in the levees of her eyes.
She pastes one hand against her cheek, as if
for shelter. Not the first time.
I calculate the physics of that punch —
loci of potential energy: fist.
Pendulum that pivots backward: arm.
It gains momentum. The same swing threshes
grass with a hand-held scythe or sweeps dirt
off a wooden porch. All brainfire and heart
logic: when hand strikes flesh, shock
waves blast through skin, tendon and cartilage.
Fist sears its silhouette onto bruised flesh.
It lingers for days.

BRANCACCIO: My poetry often focuses on the struggles women face to gain equity and standing in a world dominated by institutions that marginalize, oppress, and silence those who identify as female. "Transfiguration" addresses the oral sodomy of a close friend. She and I were raised Catholic. In adolescence, we began to realize gaps between our faith's ideals and its silence on sexual assault. Once a priest advised us to always resist an attacker to preserve our virginity. The implication was that if you were raped, you had accepted what was happening to you and were therefore culpable. My poem is an attempt to reclaim sacred space for women who've been raped. "To Nora Who Came to Class with a Bruised Face" was a response to an all-too-common event that I encountered as a high school teacher: violence committed against young women (and sometimes young men) by their boyfriends. Despite how far women have risen in American society, many young women still accept violence as part of the compact of a relationship.

SHEVAUN BRANNIGAN

Shevaun Brannigan is a graduate of the Bennington Writing Seminars, as well as the Jiménez-Porter Writers' House at the University of Maryland. Her poems have appeared, or are forthcoming in, such journals as *Best New Poets 2012, Rhino, Washington Square Review*, and *Crab Orchard Review*. She is the first-place recipient of the 2015 Jan-Ai Scholarship, through the Winter Poetry and Prose Getaway. Her favorite poetry gig is the workshop she leads at her local domestic violence shelter.

WHY MY MOTHER IS AFRAID OF HEIGHTS

When he held her by her ankles
        upside down off the roof   like she was

a bird he was plucking,   feathers
        flying in clumps through the streets of India,   like the dandelion fluff

from home   that you blew to make a wish like
        I wish he doesn't drop me   I wish this hadn't

happened,   this being   the molesting, the threats, then   — to come —
the disbelief,   when a girl came forward and said   *he made me*

touch him,   and she, my mother, said *me too,*   they told her she was
a naughty girl who just wanted attention,   like that was always

        such a crime, to want your parents   to look at what they had made,
what the body was doing, what   was being done to the body,   it was

too much to ask, and she   always was asking   for someone to
        love her, just   a little bit, and   they believed the first girl, who must not

have been held   over the roof, if she was telling,   she was older, heavier,
perhaps he couldn't   hoist her up and display her   like the Indian flag,

and when he held my mother by her ankles   while below her, the open
     dumpster's   mouth yawned,   spun around,

waited to receive her body,   to swallow her up,   she knew
     the bags of trash would not   cushion her fall, she was learning

at that very moment   the mass of her body   was immense,
     she was learning   to have a body

was a gift, to have a body   was to have a weapon,   was to
     be desired and that you could control   nothing, not even

which way was up.

BRANNIGAN: My family and I were at an amusement park, and my mother always
refused to ride the roller coasters. I asked my father why many times, and one day he
finally answered me, though likely still at far too young an age. "Why My Mother
is Afraid of Heights" is a poetic interpretation of that answer. It is based on a true,
horrifying story of my mother's early-childhood experience. The poem came out very
organically, as a story I needed to tell. The caesuras, or blank spaces, in the poem capture
a haltingness that I felt must be conveyed when telling a narrative of so unsettling a
nature. My mother does not mind my having written the poem, but it pains her to
reread it.

CINDY BROWN

Cindy Brown lives in Taos, New Mexico, where she writes about women finding strength and healing in nature. Her poetry has recently appeared in "Women Writing Nature," a special edition of the literary journal *Sugar Mule*, and she writes a monthly column for the *Taos News* on hiking. Her website, *The Girl's Guide to Swagger* (www.girlsguidetoswagger.com) encourages women to find their voice and speak their truth. Her latest book, *Taos Hiking Guide*, was released in 2015 by Nighthawk Press.

MY PRETTY JAILER

on the airplane
my pretty jailer

he leans against the window
long black hair falling from the turquoise and silver rosette hair tie
brawling bad boy, his twisted lips parted below the sensuous aquiline nose
I've seen his face carved in Mayan stone

my pretty jailer
he sleeps now

so I can breathe and live a moment
hear my own voice — a whisper

when he wakes
eyes fly open
he twists in the seat toward me
finds something wrong —
that I sleep or don't, that I read a book or don't
that I'm screwing someone else
that I don't love him enough,
            can never love him enough

in the middle seat, my prison without bars,
I withdraw, hide my soft body like a sea creature inside a secret, shiny
        pink shell

I stay small, quiet, pleasing
and false

nighttime on the plane —
in the row in front of us
a woman lies across the seats
her head in her husband's lap, and both gently sleeping
their seats tilted back toward us

I see love there,
he sees inconvenience and empty seats
shoves the seats forward, roughly
she wakes
sits up
looks back

suddenly my body comes alive
I stand up
can stay silent no more
shoot from my shell
break from my jail
"enough, no more," I say
knowing it is over
I free myself
dare to hear my voice
one more time
speak out loud: goodbye

BROWN: After being sure that I could never be caught in an abusive situation, I fell into a passionate relationship that became unhealthy and controlling. I write poems about the experience to help me release the pain and to begin to live my own life again. In sharing my story, I hope to give permission to other women to do the same.

LAUREN CAMP

Lauren Camp is the author of three collections; the most recent is *One Hundred Hungers* (Tupelo Press, 2016). Her poems have appeared in *Slice Magazine, The Seattle Review, World Literature Today, Hobart,* and elsewhere. Her literary honors include the Dorset Prize, the National Federation of Press Women poetry prize, the Margaret Randall Poetry Prize, an Anna Davidson Rosenberg Award, and a Black Earth Institute fellowship. She produces and hosts *Audio Saucepan* — a global music program interwoven with contemporary poetry — on Santa Fe Public Radio.

INFILTRATION

In school, she arranged words and pencils to suit her.
She savored the slurry of students, an hour-to-hour cascade
of skittering footsteps. Bells rang in her ears at intervals,
the brief album of engagement. Fifty-minute slots abbreviated days,
and she settled to the sequence of study and space, a canopy
of teachers clotted with questions and chalk. For lunch,
she swallowed a jam-butter sandwich, then raced to the art room
for rich moments of blue and droplets of green. Almost alone,
she owned the marvelous room. Over desks, she studied
each gesture someone had folded or painted.
Seeing was a miracle, and she walked onto its page.

But one day her art teacher bent up the last note
of her childhood and tasted the thing he was taking.
He drew on her lights with his darks and his traces: equal parts
phrasing and brushstroke done with his tongue
in her mouth. He fell on her like a playground for a moment,
sliding until the weight of what he needed dislodged into ropes
and wheels of mud colors. From then on, the place he had broken,
she fenced in and called her worst self. Art unsweetened
with each cup she added to the kiln. Each word she spoke
was a cartoon cloud, rapidly drawn, so she entered the library
and hid between creases and pages with shelves of herself.

TACTICS

After one pure moment,
she refuses. Still he multiplies
into her buttery skin

and downturned mouth,
sucks the glow from her
calligraphed belly with his spit

and liquor. He sucks
her whole as her mind dabbles
in a room where chaos

has climbed into bed
and never stops loosing
available flesh. Night bends

low to blue. She knows
to obey when the man moves
again, slurping at her salt

and waste, his hard spittle
staining her neck hollow
to down her fringe

and deep mat of her wilderness.
The night tips back, flavorless,
as she continues saying *no* —

no name, no face,
no home to crawl to,
and her *no* bleeds out

between his grunts, and *no*
becomes her home,
no — the place she's leaving.

WOMAN KEPT CAPTIVE FOR 24 YEARS

Whatever they tell me on the news this time,
I will see three children raisined in the dark
between the basement and the old man. I will hear
the mother's eyes lock down with each unwanted entry,
each night passing through a boundary
of shame, each night swallowing the same wrong
as her father splays the petals between her legs
with his body. Her eyes will shut hard,
closing over the black ruin of her flesh,
and her smile will leak hope. At 42, she is buried
beneath eight locks, hidden
from the sun, folding missing time like an answer
into years. The story repeated six times
this morning, and whatever attention I give it
feels as if I've rotted inside, as if the wild
pollen of my own love will pour out of my body,
dark and bitter, naked and ashamed. A basement!
such a silent haunted place to plant a family.
Home is never false, never clean. Her children
will perfect their childhood, bending
promises like broken birds into the landscape
of their small selves, washing
in the only invisible strip of untouched light.
The mother keeps unwrapping edges and listens
to herself get older. She is news
and I am innocent, stepping off the curb
into my life, and wavering.

CAMP: I host and produce a music/poetry show on Santa Fe Public Radio. I wrote "Woman Kept Captive for 24 Years" to understand and process a news headline I heard five times during one of my broadcasts. This was the headline that was repeated each hour that morning: "Austrian police have arrested a 73-year-old man believed to have imprisoned his daughter in a windowless basement for 24 years. The woman told police she gave birth seven children after being repeatedly raped by her father during her captivity" (Associated Press, April 28, 2008).* The other two poems address the more typical abuse and improprieties that most, if not all, women (and girls!) face at some point in their lives. It is unfathomable to me that my society, and no doubt many others, values silence when such things happen — an unspoken law that we must keep such transgressions hidden, private, unspoken. In this way, societies seem to value lies over truth, danger over safety.

---

* March 2009 — Josef Fritzl was sentenced to life in a psychiatric ward for enslaving his daughter, Elisabeth, raping her more than 3,000 times over 24 years, fathering her seven children, and letting a newborn son die in captivity.

NEIL CARPATHIOS

Neil Carpathios teaches and is Coordinator of Creative Writing at Shawnee State University in Portsmouth, Ohio. He is the author of three full-length poetry collections: *Playground of Flesh* (Main Street Rag Press), *At the Axis of Imponderables* (winner of the Quercus Review Book Award), and *Beyond the Bones* (FutureCycle Press), and is the editor of *Every River on Earth: Writing from Appalachian Ohio* (Ohio University Press, 2015). Carpathios won the 28th annual Slipstream Press poetry contest for his collection *The Function of Sadness*, which was published in the fall of 2015.

BACK PAGE, FRONT PAGE

On the back page of the newspaper
is the story of a girl
who can't feel pain,
who might at first glance
be a superhero,
her face emotionless
as she steps on a nail
or the hornet's barbed stinger
pierces her skin.
What the government wouldn't do
for an army of men like her,
perishable yes,
but marching straight into danger,
with no fear.
She has not been trained
like some elite warrior
who practices exposure to torture —

she is ten, with a disorder
that affects the central nervous system,
the way pain signals travel
to the brain,
one of only 100 humans worldwide

with anhidrosis,
a genetic disorder.
She never cried when she had
diaper rash,
her parents state.
Everyone thought *what a good baby*
but she almost died
from appendicitis
because there were no warnings.

It is not right to think it,
but the notion rises:
what if she had switched places
with the girl on the front page,
twelve years old,
finally found after being missing
for two years
chained in the basement
of a deranged neighbor,
kept as his sex slave,
who told police
the man shoved things
way up inside her —
bottles, sticks, a live rat —
and carved into the skin on her belly
his name with a straightened hanger,
glowing hot,
and claimed he actually loved her
in his own way
and told her many times —
the girl is quoted in the article as stating —
"I am making you into a Wonder Woman
who can take anything."

This coincidence — or is it,
how can one fathom? —
these two stories, front and back, appearing
like two sides of the same coin
on the same day
meant for us to neatly file away
somewhere in the orderly catalogue
of memory.
And the way the articles end
as if the two girls
for some sick joke
had consulted,
the one on the back page
stating she regularly attends
a camp called Painless But Hopeful,
the one on the front page
who can't remember
or refuses to say
her own name
as if that person is dead now,
closing with her answer
when asked what is the secret
of survival:
"You have to learn not to feel."

CARPATHIOS: "Back Page, Front Page" deals with a true experience I had one day, as I was reading the newspaper. The poem makes this incident clear, so I will let it speak for itself. Primarily, though, the subject is the suffering of two young women.

SHANE CARREON

Shane Carreon has received the Carlos Palanca Memorial Award for Literature for her poetry, and the Nick Joaquin Literary Award for her short fiction. Her works primarily articulate the experiences of women loving women in her largely conservative country. She lives in Cebu and teaches at the University of the Philippines. Her first collection of poems, *travelbook*, was published by UP Press.

ELLIPSES

Sometimes when you forget
or when you're braver
without you knowing, you
tell me stories about your father —
how, on a good day,

you and he took the new
red motorbike for a break-in
around the countryside,
how, when it rained,

he asked you to hold
him close and closer
and you felt his wet skin
soaked against yours.

We always pretend the story
ends endlessly where the rain
falls, your blue kite soars
your father holding the thread

hero stories that go on and on
as whenever we visit him
lying there in his own peace.

CARREON: Because my writing is informed by lesbian experiences in the Philippines and the nuances of silence, surviving incest is a subject that naturally has a place in my work. For even though incest survivors, of their own volition, keep the horror in their own locked memories, and the very few whom they tell are also sworn to secrecy, society *must* know of this violence in order to stop it. Among many other factors, the primacy of family and family ties makes the many, many cases of incest largely unreported and undocumented in my country. Many Filipino women and young girls keep silent while living with this horror in their own homes because of trauma, shame, and the instilled need to protect their family's social reputation. These instances of violence are even more complicated and horrific in the households of lesbian children, where fathers, uncles, and other male relatives believe a lesbian can be "cured" by forced heterosexual intercourse.

Susana H. Case

Susana H. Case is a professor at the New York Institute of Technology. Her many chapbooks include *The Scottish Café* (Slapering Hol Press), which was re-released in a full-length Polish-English annotated version, *Kawiarnia Szkocka,* by Opole University Press in Poland. Her other books of poetry are *Salem in Séance* (WordTech Editions), *Elvis Presley's Hips & Mick Jagger's Lips* (Anaphora Literary Press), and *4 Rms w Vu* (Mayapple Press, 2014).

The Acid Thrower's Wife

> *Fakhra Younas, disfigured and partly blinded by acid when she left her abusive husband, died after she jumped from a sixth-floor apartment, her fourth suicide attempt in the 12 years following the attack.*

Burned: melted breasts,
ear, hair no longer there.
Breath not moving in, not moving out,
braking in front of the corroded necrosis.
Lips fused,
her face, effaced by the *sharp water* —

nitric,
or hydrochloric — cheap.
The life that's worse than dying —
her good name ruined,
he tells her, satisfied
her desecration incises her disgrace

in others' eyes.
One eye can't see. Her son can't
see behind her corrugation of scars.
Returned by the authorities
to the husband who threw her life away
like tossing wastewater

out the back door,
he hides his monster wife-wraith
in the kitchen, sobbing
as she scours pans.
There is little escape
from 39 surgeries, the scrape and graft.

There is little escape from pain.
Self-cancellation, its brief flight into space
in which there is no flight.
The little escape to being the dancing girl
she was, now known always as
the acid thrower's wife.

DISAPPEARANCES

After the close of the Lyovikha, Siberia,
copper mine in the swampy woods
down the road from rusted houses
a hungry dog finds fifteen
decomposing girls,
abducted for prostitution.
Broken-boned and strangled in their fervor
to break free,
they sleep under a thin blanket of sticks and brush.
For a long time,
only the animals notice.

Every year in Nazhny Tagil,
a thousand missing-person reports.
Girls.
History counts its skeletons in round numbers,
Szymborska wrote. No flowers
grow on tundra.

A fisherman discovers fetuses
bundled in industrial barrels,
mummified,
curled up,
tags with surnames.
The police count 248.
(Mathematicians will tell you 248 is round.)
Were they to be trafficked for vaccines?
Adrenals for Parkinson's?
Stem cells for rich women's face lifts?

The sign says, *Glory to Miners!*
No peace of mind — painted signs are cheap.
The mine closes and its hole
fills with brown water.
The town fills with brown water,
the entrenched scrofulous stench.
What's left for the residents is getting
high — a birrus of jug wine and cough syrup.
Death and vanishing every day.

THE ONLY ONE SHE FOUND

In the end, there's room for only one
in the small blue house,
a petty treason, husband killing.
There's the good wife and the aberrant wife
— her devious life, dressed
in the wrong clothes,
don't care if you hurt me some more.

She does care, does not mean to belong to him
like a pair of his boots.
Too easy to confuse abuse with love
and the other small blue house

where a gang of men
rape her when she's eleven,
but that's a different story —
don't care if you abuse me again.

She does care. When she runs
away from all she's got, he finds her,
tries to drown her, to wash off the stench
of disobedience.

She does not know
there will be better friends
in prison than she's ever had.

She stabs him in his sleep —
the bread knife
goes in quiet and quick.
Sometimes she sees double
from the times he hit her in the head,
sees two victims, two knives, two deaths,
two wives.

CASE: In addition to being a poet, I'm an academic sociologist, and so my interest in gender and gender roles is longstanding and occurs on several levels. Part of the way gender plays out, of course, is through violence, and all three of my poems in this anthology were inspired by women who were victimized in some way, though only in the second of these, "Disappearances," were women murdered. This is the only one of my three poems to make reference to international trafficking. The first poem, "The Acid Thrower's Wife," was inspired by a suicide that occurred in Rome, that of Fakhra Younas, after a horrific history of violence and the medical trauma of the resultant damage. In "The Only One She Found," a woman who has had a long life of abuse ends up killing her husband after running away fails. Whereas the first two poems were inspired by specific actual incidents, the third, "The Only One She Found," derives from a composite of many case studies of violence against women with which I am familiar. It was inspired also in part by a classic rock song, "You're All I've Got Tonight," by the Cars, released in 1978, and it contains some references to the song.

PRIYA SARUKKAI CHABRIA

Priya Sarukkai Chabria is a poet, novelist, essayist, and translator, with five books published. She has been recognized by the Indian government with an Outstanding Contribution to Literature citation, and her works have been translated into six languages. Chabria's poems have been published, or are forthcoming, in *Adelphiana, Soundings, South Asian Review, Caravan, Post Road, The British Journal of Literary Translation, Drunken Boat, Pratilipi, Language for a New Century, The Literary Review, IQ,* and *Another English: Anglophone Poems from Around the World*, among others. Her book of translations of Andal, a Tamil mystic poet, was released by Zubaan, and a short story collection was published by Niyogi Books. She edits *Poetry at Sangam*.

DIALOGUE 1

She says to her lover:

I'll tell you this in advance —
You who will be enclosed in my flesh, your rhythms
mine, our hands like a thousand comets descending
towards pleasure, your sweat becoming my skin,
listen: All this I want, and more.

Yet in your passion, do not scar me.
Do not split my lip, nor stifle speech.
Do not force my cervix out of shape
nor ram my individuality.

I am parched. Riven
by longing, caked by the long dust of denial.
And yet I'll come to you like the first rain,
fragrant and trusting.

SEE:

Till the horizon
the body of the earth curves like a leaping cod's
shimmering
with scales of grain.
See its harvesting. Cut pound winnow:
seeds small as a cod's eyes fall fall fall fall.

See:
This body is still curved as the earth.
See through the swimming gloaming: see
its hills and valleys and furrows. Harvest it.
Cut veins pound hair winnow breath.
See what falls —

and if it renews itself.

CHABRIA: "Dialogue 1" was written years after reading Tamil *akam* poetry that was composed between the 2nd century BCE and the 2nd century CE. Unlike contemporaneous *puram* poetry, which spoke about war, was largely panegyric, named the heroes, and was situated in the public domain, *akam* addressed the inner landscapes of love, and most of those poems were "assigned" to women, though written by men who adopted the personas of women and men in love, foster mothers, and best friends. Unlike the better-known tradition of Sanskrit and Hindi poetry, which linked the emotions of love with the six seasons, *akam* locates love in specific geographies — fertile mountainsides, wastelands, etc. Both the subaltern anonymity of the personas adopted and the commingling of space — inner and outer — pulled me to this form. The earlier writers of *akam* were men; I wish to pay tribute to this form by giving it a passionate and contemporary female voice.

SAMPURNA CHATTARJI

Sampurna Chattarji is a poet, novelist, and translator. Her thirteen books include four poetry collections: *Space Gulliver: Chronicles of an Alien* (HarperCollins India, 2015), *Absent Muses* (Poetrywala, 2010), *The Fried Frog* (Scholastic, 2009), and *Sight May Strike You Blind* (Sahitya Akademi, 2007); two novels: *Rupture* (2009) and *Land of the Well* (2012), both from HarperCollins; and *Dirty Love* (Penguin, 2013), a short story collection about Bombay. Her anthology appearances include *60 Indian Poets* (Penguin), *The Bloodaxe Book of Contemporary Indian Poets, The HarperCollins Book of English Poetry,* and *The Literary Review* "Indian Poetry" issue. She is the editor of *Sweeping the Front Yard,* an anthology of women's writing.

ALL THE GODDESSES

All the goddesses
are gathered at my door.
It is an old rejection they come to reverse,
not benign, perverse.
I do not let them in.
They are not like me.

Not Kali, the loudest,
clamoring for attention,
the slow dance of skulls around her neck
bone music to my fears.
She is aggressive, that one,
and rude.
Look at the way she sticks out her tongue
at all who dare to look at her.
A red tongue, thirsty
for another demon to quench.
She drank his blood,
each self-perpetuating drop.
A furious suckling that saved the world.
Blood mother,

she would have killed us all.
It took a husband
(Lord Shiva trembling
half-trampled beneath her feet)
to make her stop,
and bite her tongue in shame.

Not Lakshmi, the meekest,
sprung perfectly beautiful
out of a tumultuous ocean of milk,
a lotus at her breast,
she, a lotus at the breast
of Vishnu, Lord Protector,
inseparable bride,
gentle breathing light,
riding her white owl
into the homes of the propitiatory,
casting dark glances and blight on all
who dare to slight her.
Mother of the world,
a whimsical tyrant,
feminine and full of wiles.

And not Durga, the fiercest.
A cosmic blaze of energy
in her eyes,
a pinwheel of mace and trident and sword.
Terrifying, but derived.
Free of husband, lord or lover,
but formed fully of all their powers.
A sum total of gods then,
an essence of,
Shakti, distilled, concentrated,
burning the throat as it goes down.
Mother to none,
a lion between her thighs.

But
(and now I sense them listening, hushing,
pushing flat against the door)
I have taken Kali's anger and made it mine.
My black moods are hers,
my irreverence.
I whoop, I rant, I rage,
a belt of severed hands at my waist.

I have swallowed Lakshmi whole.
She runs through me now,
a river of desire.
I drown myself, and again
I rise, a dreaming weed,
clinging to love, unworldly-wise.

And Durga?
Durga has given me freedom,
and I have paid for it,
gladly.
She made a fighter of me.
She taught me when to raise my weapons,
screaming,
and when to lay my head in my mother's lap,
a daughter come home again.

As a Son, My Daughter

When you grow up,
you will be a healer
loved for your smile
and your sorceress skill.
You will be a composer
of concrete dreams,
songs of towering glass.

You will be the one
to split the gene
and shed light
on every last particle of doubt.

You will know numbers so well
that you will reject them all
save two,
for they will be enough
to keep you engaged endlessly
in running the world,
efficient and remorseless,
a network of binary combinations.

When you grow up,
you will be all that I am not.
Wise, patient, with shiny long hair
and good teeth,
radiant skin to go
with your razor intellect,
as brilliant as you are beautiful.

You will be a wife
and a mother,
your children will be
brilliant and beautiful,
exactly as I see them,
perfect miniatures
of all
that I am not.

I brought you up as a son,
my daughter,
fierce and strong and free.
But now, now
that you are, have become,
all that I am not,

you are too fierce, too strong, too free.
Your hair is too short.
Your absences too long.
You fear nothing.
You frighten me.

MARKINGS

I.
Trouble is an amulet
singed into your arm.
You need protection
from yourself.

In the softness of your elbow
the faded blue of old ink
stitches your skin
into impossible calligraphies.

Veined tapestry to pain.

Some things are best unseen.
I am looking at the mark
on your cheek
where a fist has been.

II.
Pierced through ears nose and
tongue you draw my gaze like gauze across your face
your skin is paper the unchanging
blue calligraphy of your veins pains me
on the inside of your arm needles have punctured
the words that will save you from harm
you are a marked woman: your look
pierces me through the heart.

CHATTARJI: In these poems, I look at the violences that permeate a woman's everyday experience in an insidious, sometimes invisible, but always simmering and hurtful way: the violences done to her by men, by other women, by her own perceptions, traps and expectations of herself; the ways in which patterns of oppression are replicated, from generation to generation, through mythology, religion, stereotypes, in the domestic, marital, and sexual realm in which her rage, her shame, her anxiety, her desires, her nightmares and her dreams are projected onto and evoked via the small but telling details of her life. I look at the female body as a site of abuse that could be physical or psychological, that could escape all but the sharpest eyes and the keenest hearts. Often, in my poems, it is the surface, the skin, that is as much a revelation of violence as that which is hidden in gestures, the silent language of damage. I am interested in the ambiguous ways in which violence is perpetrated and lived with: the nature of our complicity. My protest is against not just the incidents that make the news and raise public ire, but against all those unrecorded unseen unmarked instances of daily brutality that millions of women silently accept and live with.

LIANA JOY CHRISTENSEN

Liana Joy Christensen is an Australian poet whose work has been published in literary journals around the world, including *Prosopisia, Lemuria* (India), *Cicada, Organisation and the Environment, Ascent* (USA), *Tamkang Review* (Taiwan), *Southerly, Griffith Review, Famous Reporter, Indigo,* and *Poetrix* (Australia). She has poems in the anthologies *Science Made Marvellous,* ed. Victoria Haritos (2010); *The Sunlight of Ordinary Days,* ed. John Charles Ryan (2011); and *Fremantle Poets 3: Performance Poets,* ed. Scott-Patrick Mitchell (2013). In 2014, she was shortlisted for the Newcastle Prize, one of Australia's premier poetry prizes. Christensen writes for both page and stage and has delivered her performance poetry in European and Australian venues.

ENTERING THE LAZARUS HOUSE

It's a bad business, only the stern sexton to witness
dirt fall on the empty coffin
Her parents weep silently, each alone in their grief
and she is dead to them and her parish

Two parishes away she stands before the gates
The fat crow priest had shadowed her at a distance
They'd walked by night
He stands at the far fence
making the sign of the cross on the empty air
muttering a sketchy prayer in Latin
before hurrying back for Sunday lunch

She is mute — the dead do not speak
He has no need to wait and see her lift the heavy iron latch
If she does not enter she will be stoned
by grim-faced farmers and lie in an open field
for the crows to eat

There is nowhere else to go
She glances up once to the pure azure sky
then takes her impurity within
the cloister of death in life from which none return

The light in the hallway is dim
She cannot quite see
But a woman comes forth and takes her hand
Takes her hand *willingly*
and leads her across a courtyard
fragrant with herbs

They enter the kitchen and she is given milk
"Now, sit by the fire child.
There's time to watch the bread rise
before you meet the rest."

How could she have guessed?
There might be life yet
Even here in death

THE NETHERLANDS

Women stitch rainwater
Shawls, shrouds, veils
Wait by deathbeds
Look from sea cliffs
Clothed in black

> *Wind gusts from the northwest*
> *send seabirds crying from their nests*

Women are stitched
On cell phones
At airports
Deaths, deals, sales
Wait in windows
Stare from dry docks
Clothed in red

Smoke clouds from their nostrils
draw sailors bloated from the breast

The women please
Do they?

They have learned to relieve
The weight of time
Each stitch designed to sign
A fish-nibbled corpse
Each silver needle like lightning
Finds its ground

CHRISTENSEN: "The Netherlands" directly addresses one of the worst forms of systemic abuse current today: the trading of women and girls for sexual slavery. This trade is an international disgrace that is dependent on corruption and cupidity at all levels of society and requires challenging and dismantling at all levels — and with all the means we have at our disposal. Poetry is one of these means. "Entering the Lazarus House," although absolutely focused on the challenges facing women, is not quite as explicit in terms of current affairs. I wrote it because gender-based violence is a worldwide phenomenon that can only be understood with historical consciousness: the recent outbreaks of extreme abuse are not random. It is very easy to demonize particular cultures and religious groups for having some kind of monopoly on the oppression and abuse of women — but this elides the fact that the issues are a longstanding part of the problems facing humankind in all major cultures.

STEPHEN J. CIPOT

Stephen J. Cipot is a scientist with the US Environmental Protection Agency, a writer, runner, and poet. He has received several awards, including a writing residency from the Edward F. Albee Foundation and a citation from the Town Board and Supervisor of North Hempstead for his poetry and civic works. Cipot assisted the first Dylan Thomas Tribute tour, featuring Welsh poets Aerowny Thomas and Peter Thabit Jones, by organizing venues and providing general logistical support for the New York portion of the tour. His work has appeared in many publications, including *The Paterson Literary Review, PRISM: An Interdisciplinary Journal for Holocaust Educators, LI Pulse,* and the *2014 Korean Expatriate Literature* bilingual issue.

PRAYER FOR MALALA YOUSAFZAI

How do you pray for the sun?
In my dream, you descended from heaven,
beaming sweet prayers for us,
your smile showing the true miracles
deeply rooted in the future.

In the dream, we are the aspirants,
and you are shining an array of brilliancies —
each a necklace that we wear,
helping us to grow beyond our cruel roots.

In my dream, then, it is no longer just a dream,
for you are the beautiful bright butterfly
that took on the dragon and transcended our world,
showing us a better way all the way to Heaven,
and the future now.

It becomes crucial, no ordinary morning,
the blue-on-blue sky so wide and deep.

CIPOT: I was inspired to write a poem for the beautiful smiling brave Pakistani girl, Malala Yousafazai, because of the horribly violent assassination attempt against her young life, and because she spoke out so eloquently for the kinds of things that we take for granted as basic human and women's rights in this country — education, freedom of belief and religion, the right to self-development and self-expression, without overbearing masculine impingement. She was trying to express a wonderful sense of freedom by showing women and children that there is a different path and they should try to achieve their own potential — with their own breath, minds, and voices, spared from dreadful shackles and suffering — and that they should not be defeated. My poem is meant as an inspirational poem (a halo), for Malala Yousafzai. I wish her success, and her family health, prosperity, and peace.

SHARON COLEMAN

Sharon Coleman is the author of *Only What You Need: A Memoir* (Ablet Publishing, 2015). Her work will also be published in the upcoming anthology *Seasons of our Lives* (Matilda Butler & Kendra Bonnett, eds.). Coleman can sometimes be found knitting, reading, writing, designing new things, or home-schooling her four precocious kids, in rural Rhode Island. Sometimes she sleeps.

I NEVER CALLED IT RAPE

I didn't call it rape
It was a digital
Ushering of
The digital era.
I bled.
Then forgot.
Until after the
Dot.com crash
When I
Dotted my 'i'
With that
Soul-less memory.
He opened me with his hand.
I understand
The sorrow following
The birth of my son.
When gloved hands ripped
Me open again.
I am raped but not raped
Because it's digital,
Medical.
I am raped again.
But I don't call it rape,
Because it doesn't hurt.

And I don't say no.
I have no words.
Only
Seagulls and
Bay smells.
It isn't rape
Because he kisses me.
It is over
Before I'm aware
There are words
Behind my teeth.

I am raped again,
But not raped.
Because rape is
Genitals in genitals
And it's supposed to hurt
By my definition.
So I don't call it rape.
Because it's rude
To talk with your mouth full.

And I never called it rape.
Because
I go back
For more.

This time it
Meets my
Definition.
It is his
Thirty-six-year-old
Genitals in my
Fourteen-year-old
Body
And it hurts.

I say "No."
And he says, "C'mon,
Baby, if we had a bed
I'd have you screaming
For more."
Doesn't he know
I am screaming?
But I say nothing.
It is my fault.

Soul Survivor

Souls leave bodies pounded hollow.
They are smarter than we are.

They say, "Hey
I'm not putting up
with this
shit. I'll be
right over there.
Y'all let me know
when you're done."

In corners
in rooms
on boats
in closets
on streets
in cars
the world over
souls sit curled
up on themselves
waiting
for a safer ride.

A THANK-YOU NOTE TO MY RAPIST(S)

Thank you for making me understand
that sometimes the world
can turn inside out
and I will remain.

Thank you for teaching my heart
the hidden corners
where it can lick the wounds clean.
Thank you for making me stronger than
she was.
There is no summit I cannot grow beyond.

Thank you for showing me the deepest places,
so I might learn how high I can soar.

Thank you for teaching me about darkness
so I could learn about light.
Thank you for the litmus test
for the man I would marry.

Thank you for teaching me that addiction
can be conquered,
that birth
can be healing.

Thank you for giving me
fodder for writing.

Thank you for breaking me down.
You taught me to build
myself up with steel.

Thank you for opening my soul.
It left space for me to love
completely.

COLEMAN: I am a survivor of rape. I share a common thread with far too many women of this world. "I Never Called It Rape" is a personal account of my own experience with rape. "Soul Survivor" was inspired by a story from a young African survivor of gang-rape who stated that her soul sat in a corner during the assault, and she has yet to reclaim it. It touched me deeply, in that hers is a very common and incredibly creative coping mechanism, which many rape survivors utilize. "A Thank-you Note to My Rapist(s)" reflects my growth through the process of recovery. I try to focus on gratitude in my life, rather than pain and sorrow. It is a choice I have made toward happiness. I do not believe that being a survivor of rape has to own you.

JENNIFER COMPTON

Jennifer Compton lives in Australia and is a poet and playwright who also writes prose. Her book *This City* won the Kathleen Grattan Award in New Zealand and was published by Otago University Press in 2011. Her book of poetry *Barefoot* (2010), published by Picaro Press, was shortlisted for the John Bray Award at the Adelaide Festival. Compton's most recent books include *Ungainly*, which was released by Mulla Mulla Press in 2012; *Now You Shall Know* (Five Islands Press, 2014); and *Mr Clean & the Junkie* (Mākaro Press, 2015). Her poem "Now You Shall Know" won the Newcastle Poetry Prize in 2013.

THE BACHELOR

He will never marry.
The woman who would have been his wife took one sip at life
and was drowned and thrown in the grave-pit.

He will never have children
so he does not know if he would have reared his daughters
for the comfort of other men

or would have looked the other way as the old woman
set the bucket of warm water at the foot of the bed.
To wash his son, or do the other thing.

He visits the women who belong to everyone.
There is one who leans out from an upper window and laughs
then draws the hem of some cloth across her merriment.

As he walks home alone he speaks to the woman me⌐
She slips her pale hand as small as a child's har '
into his hand and he feels strong.

He can't bring himself to blame her father
for who can afford a dowry and a marriage feast?
The name of his ghost-wife falls off his tongue tenderly.

No one else in the whole wide world knows what she is called.
He summons her,
whispers . . .

COMPTON: I've long been aware of the practice of female infanticide in many countries, and it struck me that trouble was on its way as the gender-imbalanced peer group reached marrying age. You might want, you might need, a son, but you will also want grandchildren. I thought — ha ha, hollow laugh — that this would make women more valuable. As my Australian farming friend said when the drought ended and farmers wanted to replenish their stock, "Anything that has a cunt is valuable." But it hasn't proved to be the case. Women seem to be more at risk than ever from wandering bands of bachelor mobs (as in chimpanzee troops) that know they will never be a part of society or have any hostages to fortune. I was planning to write an elegy called "The Missing Women," but I am a wife, and the mother of a son, and the grandmother of a grandson. I decided to imagine that the men I loved would never have known me because I had been killed. They would not even know my name.

NANCY COOK

Nancy Cook, a resident of Saint Paul, Minnesota, in the northern United States, is a parent, lawyer, teacher, and writer. Her work has recently appeared or is forthcoming in *Adventum, Eleventh Muse,* and *Prime Mincer,* and two anthologies, *The Poet's Quest for God: 21ˢᵗ Century Poems of Faith, Doubt, and Wonder* (Eyewear Press, 2015) and *Rust Belt Rising* (The Head & the Hand Press, 2013). With the help of an Artists Initiative grant from the Minnesota State Arts Board, she is developing a witness project, the goal of which is to enable the narrative development and dissemination of stories of, by, and for populations underserved by the justice system.

MANDATORY ARREST

answer to a friday night call: domestic dispute in progress.
heavy knock. a voice crafted from routinized decisions
requests admission.
no response is noted;
the door blasts open.

a bold opening statement. blue uniforms now scope the scene &
household foes' positions. these men are experts in logistics:
one cop's subtle elbow of command rebuts all
defensive oaths,
moves to compel

compliance. from the cornered spouse springs no true
issue of resistance. soon he is a handcuffed man
secured in a law-enforcement cruiser.
vaguely she believes
relief will be granted.

then a uniform returns. its interrogatory stance demands
disclosure; intensely cool stare conveys expectation, a call
for gratitude undue. burden reinstated. her objection,
felled by privilege,
is not preserved.

truths are forged of compound lies, her silence comes to mean "failure
to state an authentic claim." her horror draws scornful reference to
"her honor," translated as "poor judgment." final verdict: lack of
in personam
jurisdiction.

sober laughter, discharged from the gut of power, escapes indictment, like
adolescent parties given slack. witness the compact gun, well-oiled
& bulleted; chambers summarily emptied. yet there isn't
any record of
its firing.

evidence excluded, no principal to be deposed. case dismissed. the aftermath
a return to prevailing order. a commonplace closed file, its sealed contents
proof enough to satisfy the elements:
blood. steel. heat. the wind from
a slamming door.

COOK: The poem is based on a true incident. I work with students in communi-
ty-based settings to provide legal support and assistance to clients and communities
who, by virtue of poverty or marginalization, have limited access to justice. Last year,
two students were working in partnership with a local coalition against sexual assault
to respond to the incident described in "Mandatory Arrest." The police officer who
raped the woman who had called for help was not prosecuted, nor was he disciplined
by his department. In writing the poem, I used the formal jargon of the legal system
to emphasize the irony and the overall detachment of the "justice" system's shameful
complicity in the perpetration of sexual violence.

CHERYL R COWTAN

Cheryl R Cowtan is a novelist who teaches English through filmmaking, performance, and technology at an alternative school for at-risk students. She lives in "the greenest part of Ontario" with her husband, two children and a menagerie of critters that fly, crawl, swim and run.

THE IMPORTANCE OF MUSTARD

I lift the limp paper towel
And peek under at the sizzling bacon
Just a few more minutes to perfection
I push the 1 on the microwave.

The cracked-wheat bread pops out of the toaster
And I lay it side by side on the beige tile counter
Four thick slices of marble cheddar cheese
Slide off of my knife

I place them on one side of the toast
Parked tightly beside one another like school buses
Then I pick up the tomato
Red and round and firm
I hold it to my nose and breathe in the scent
A smell that was three months in the making,
beneath the sunflowers.

I can hear my sons' laughter as they run to the tomato patch
This traditional searching each day,
To see how many tomatoes the raccoons have left us.
I smile as their joyous cries carry across the lawn.
They have found a red one among the green globes

I slice the tomato delicately, trying not to bruise the flesh.
The slices look like microscope cross sections
Alien pockets of gel surrounded by webbed tissue

Ah! The bacon is done.
I air lift it with my fingernails, sizzling and popping
Down onto the cheese
The hot grease slides onto the rectangular prisms
Melting with contact.

I shake miniature black flakes and clear cubes
Onto the arranged tomato slices
I put on the top layer of toast,
And then I freeze.

Mayonnaise! It must have mayonnaise!
I rush to the fridge, uncapping the jar.
It slides out onto my butter knife
Jiggling on its way to the porous bread.

Perfect. Perfect.
I press down on the toast and slice the sandwich
Into two triangles
He's going to love this.

I start to carry it in to him
But the word "mustard"
Appears in my mind
And stops me.
What if he wants mustard on it?

I stop, waver, return to the kitchen.
Mustard, mustard, mustard.
I walk in a circle, not sure, not wanting to make a mistake.
What if I put it on and he doesn't want it?
Do we eat mustard on bacon and tomato?

Ummmm
Ummmmm

He shouts, "Where's that sandwich!" from the living room.
I jump and bite back the startled noise while it's still in my throat.
I'm surprised to find that I'm holding my finger.
It just started to ache.
An ache from a break,
From the last time I didn't put mustard on his sandwich.

COWTAN: For two years, I worked as a counselor at a local women's shelter, and though I had been trained, and had read the stats, and knew how to identify abuse, I was not prepared for the horrifying lives some women were living. As an educational counselor, my mandate was to educate survivors of domestic violence about the cycle they were caught in. And there was a rotation of consistent behavior that made me think an Abuser 101 class must have taught these abusive husbands how to degrade, oppress, and hurt their wives because the stories were all the same. The tactics were all the same. The comments from the women were all the same. Domestic violence is a cookie-cutter phenomenon in our society. And, as such, it can be fought. Women can be made aware of the patterns, and male abusers can be identified by clear profiles. "The Importance of Mustard" highlights how the normal everyday can quickly and unpredictably turn into a violent incident over something as inconsequential as mustard. The poem also shows how this type of environment can damage a woman's ability to think, make decisions, and stay calm, which are all required in the "leaving" of a violent relationship.

BARBARA CROOKER

Barbara Crooker's latest books are *Selected Poems* (FutureCycle Press, 2015) and *Small Rain* (Purple Flag, 2014). Of her four other books of poetry, *Gold* (Cascade Books, 2013) is the most recent. Crooker's poems have appeared in numerous journals and anthologies, among them *The Bedford Introduction to Literature*, *The Bedford Introduction to Poetry*, and *Good Poems, American Places*, and have been read on the BBC and the ABC (Australian Broadcasting Company), as well as by Garrison Keillor on *The Writer's Almanac*. Her awards include three Pennsylvania Council on the Arts Creative Writing Fellowships and the Thomas Merton Poetry of the Sacred Award.

FOR A FRIEND WHO THINKS ABOUT GOING BACK TO HER ABUSIVE HUSBAND WHEN THE NIGHTS ARE LONG & COLD

On the hill behind our house, a tractor has harrowed
the cornfields, stripped the skin off the land,
turned it inside out, a rich dark corduroy.
And you have turned your life around,
left the husband who beat you
with a wine bottle, smashed the thermostat
to save heat, hit your children
with words, followed us on our weekend runs
in case we met with secret lovers.
You've flown north to New Hampshire,
to the White Mountains, where snow
still blankets the woods,
while here we're stripping for spring.
You've left behind your worldly goods,
tangled in a web of litigation,
but your life is now your own.
Tundra swans stopped here this week
on their way to the arctic, paused
a few days to peck and glean the cornfields.

Soon, they'll spread their wings,
white whistling sails,
fly off to the northern rim of the world.
Now, you fly, stay free.

CROOKER: Most of my work is taken from what's around me, and this poem came out of my friendship with a neighbor and my attempts to help her leave an abusive relationship. Her husband actually came to our house with a gun when she was living in our basement; we called the police, but she wouldn't press charges. I'd like to say this story has a happy ending; she did relocate to New Hampshire, but he followed her there. But perhaps it will help another woman realize that no one should stay in a situation like this, that no one deserves to be abused, whether physically or psychologically. The swans happened to show up in our area around this same time, so I let them also show up in the poem.

STIRLING DAVENPORT

Stirling Davenport is a poet, novelist, and short story writer. She has traveled widely in Asia, and many of her poems reflect her Buddhist philosophies. She spent a year in India, conducting art therapy with Tibetan refugees and interviewing exiled Tibetans for a documentary film. Her novel *The Silver Reindeer* (Noth Press) is a fantasy for young girls, meant to encourage them to have confidence and follow their own minds. An earlier fantasy novel for adults, *The Nightwing's Quest*, is about a world governed by women, and its evolving challenges. Davenport's work explores the differences between gender, race, nationality, and belief, so that each may give the other respect and understanding.

FOR THE SOMALI WARRIOR

A woman rises from her pallet
Sky still charcoal, the air chill
In her cloth too thin for warmth
She takes a calabash
And straps it to her forehead
Makes her way in the gray morning
To the high hill and beyond
To the waterhole where lions come
At dusk, now quiet
She fills the vessel
And strides carefully
Back to her house made of twigs
The house she made herself
Next she starts the fire
Rolls the meal into a flat round
And adds it to the pan
Never taking off the ropes of beads
Around her neck and wrists
Never growing out her black curls
More than an inch

Her man gets up now
Enticed by the smell of food
Lifts his head from the wooden pillow
Pats his elaborate headdress
Wraps his cloth around him
Stands and reaches behind her
Kisses her neck where no bead impedes him
Slaps her bottom where she has not been cut
And where she still feels something
And the woman grabs the hot bread
By the edges with her fingers
Tossing it into the center of a plate
She hands it to her husband
And looks out the door
At the rays of new morning
Dancing on the dusty earth

DAVENPORT: This poem was inspired by the One Billion Rising event on February 14, 2013, a day to end violence against women. I had done research into the practice of female genital mutilation when I got a travel brochure with a photo of a Somali woman, and I became curious about her life. I found that the practice of cutting young girls was widespread, not only removing the ability to enjoy sex, but often creating serious health problems. I wrote this poem to show how a woman's life could be different, if only she were uncut. I think if we are to have a world without violence, we have to envision it first.

KATE BONING DICKSON

Kate Boning Dickson studied poetry with Robert Wrigley at Stony Brook-Southampton's summer writing program in 2012. Her background is in classical piano performance and music education, and her poetry has appeared in *California Quarterly, PPA Literary Review, Clavier Companion, New Mirage Magazine, Whispers and Shouts, Paumanok II: Interwoven,* and *Spillway Magazine.* She is a board member of the Long Island Poetry Collective.

READING INTO IT

freeze when you hear
pencils snap
in the quiet woods
of your mind

when steps
behind you
ruffle
blank journals of air

consider sharpening
the sensible
point
of fear

still how can you
divine intention
from a stranger's
stare

brush aside unease
as poetic invention
as if incongruity
is perfectly fine

ignore the crumpled papers
of his delusion
shrug off his strained shuffle
of esteem and disdain

dismiss
your chary inkling
as a smudge
on a preface page

and yet his seething binding
might come undone —
within that isolation
rips a studied rage

and harm can come
to those who don't know
when
to be afraid

DICKSON: In this poem, I wanted to ask some questions that an unsettling experience with one man raised for me. How does a woman handle someone who sets off her silent alarms? Someone who makes her instincts flare with unease? Is it possible to keep a polite distance? He persists. Holds onto things that belong to her. Gets angry when she doesn't respond to his requests for private meetings. Fluctuating between furious farewells and conciliatory appeals, between extreme compliments and temper bursts, he tries to provoke a response. He'll use any reaction from her as an excuse for his next move. If she keeps neutral and distant, will he tire and leave her alone?

JEHANNE DUBROW

Jehanne Dubrow is the author of four poetry collections, including most recently *Red Army Red* and *Stateside* (Northwestern University Press, 2012 and 2010). Her work has appeared in *Southern Review*, *The Hudson Review*, *Prairie Schooner*, and *Ploughshares*. She is the director of the Rose O'Neill Literary House and an Assistant Professor of Creative Writing at Washington College, on the eastern shore of Maryland.

EROS AND PSYCHE

Sculpture by Antonio Canova, 1787

From a certain vantage point they could be lovers — the
man with his arms encircling my mother, and both of
them gone marble. He has woken her with the sound
of broken wings. Her blanket is polished rock, cold
and weighted to the bed. From this angle the knife is
hidden, although it's there, the way an arrow is always
shooting through this story, desire a dart that finds the
tender spot. Bodies make a space for gods to intervene.
Tonight if there are souls like butterflies, then they have
stilled. If beauty could be bolted in a box, if a deity could
say, Don't open this, then my mother might stay asleep
forever, unbothered by the monument of those hands.

A GROUNDING FOR THE METAPHYSICS OF MORALS

Or perhaps the story starts with books on her table.
When the man breaks in, she's sleeping. Tomorrow: an
exam. Tomorrow: a paper due. She's half-asleep, the
sound of someone in the room soft as turning pages.
First, he tells her, I heard a noise. By he is meant the

handyman. And when there is no noise to hear, he bolts
the door. He grinds her face into the wood. A cardboard
box kicked. A hand bitten. That he will kill her if the
night stays gray too long, a kind of a priori knowledge.
He read Kant in prison, comics too black and white,
dime store pulp too literal in its black and blue. There
is an argument for anything, he says: to drown the small
brown dog, to swipe the wallet, even to unlock the girl's
apartment where she is falling in her sleep.

SCHILLER

> Everything that is hidden, everything full of
> mystery, contributes to what is terrifying and
> is therefore capable of sublimity.
> "On the Sublime"

The man with the knife is capable of sublimity. The man
with the knife is capable. The man is capable of holding
her in place. He holds her in a place called home. In a
place called home, a man with a knife. In a place called
knife, a man. In a place called man, a knife that splits
the home from home. And later, it won't be a home
to her. Will only be the knife, the man who holds the
knife, the knife again. Always the knife again and the
hand that holds the knife. In a place called knife, she's
there, mistaking knife for night, and night for mystery.
Everything a mistake. The shadow-body of a man can
hold a knife. The shadow made by words can hold the
knife, not very long, away from her. Away from her,
the hand. The capable hand. The man in his sublimity.
Away, the home no longer home.

DUBROW: This group of prose poems comes from my manuscript *The Arranged Marriage,* a collection that explores stories about my mother's childhood and young adulthood, which she first told me when I was a little girl. At its heart, this is a book about captivity, about different kinds of forced intimacy and closeness. *The Arranged Marriage* centers on an experience of trauma, looking at what came before, what happened during, and what the consequences were after.

My mother was raised in Honduras, in a community of Ashkenazi exiles from war-torn, post-1933 Europe. Even as my mother's family found a temporary home in Latin America, they remained rootless, living in the shadow of the Shoah. When she was eighteen or nineteen, my mother was held hostage by a man who had escaped from an asylum for the criminally insane and had put a number of women in the hospital before the police caught him. In the aftermath of this trauma, my mother was then forced by her family into an advantageous but ultimately loveless marriage. She remained in the marriage for one year, before divorcing her first husband (in an act of "willful abandonment") and eventually marrying my father.

The poems in *The Arranged Marriage* are written to resemble newspaper columns; they attempt to represent trauma through a series of fragmented, often nonlinear, stories. They avoid the use of first-person, so that the poet-speaker recedes into the background, allowing the mother figure to become the focus of the narrative. And because the poems resist the "I," they move toward a more detached, clinical voice, one that allows me to avoid a language that might glorify violence or suggest any possibility of redemption through suffering.

MARY DUDLEY

Mary Dudley completed an MA in American poetry at Stony Brook University, then moved to New Mexico, where she earned a PhD at the University of New Mexico in psychological foundations of education in early child development, across cultures. She has written about, and worked with, young children, their families and teachers, and has published three chapbooks of poetry. Dudley won first prize in the Albuquerque "Poetry on the Bus" contest in 2009. Her poems have appeared in the *Albuquerque Tribune; Friends Bulletin; A Good Place to Stumble Upon: Traditional Haiku and Senryū Poems* (2011); *Sin Fronteras; La Llorona; The Rag;* the Albuquerque Center for Peace and Justice Newsletter; and on the *200 New Mexican Poems* website.

CAN YOU EXPRESS YOURSELF BY BECOMING INVISIBLE?

Look how she has
made herself invisible;
how he takes up
so much space
beside her
on their small settee.

His arm stretches out behind her shoulders,
the other extends beyond the
edge of their little couch.

He spreads his legs.

He smiles.

And she?

She has made of herself
a symbol of Islam, he says.

She is there somewhere
hidden within
her black burqa.

She is a shadow beside him.

She disappears even in daylight.

She is a secret
she will tell no one.

PASHTUN POET

Because I am a girl,
no one knows my birthday.
Afghan poet, age perhaps 17

Because I am a girl
I only speak my poems in secret.

I hide them from my family
and whisper them
when it is safe.

It's never safe.

My poems were found
and I was punished.
My brothers beat me.

Because I am a girl
my words cannot be written.

They must be spoken
only when no one is listening.

Because I am a girl
my life is not my life.

My dreams alone are mine.

Because I am a girl,
My dreams are only dreams.

Listen!
If no one is listening
I will tell you my dreams.
And if you are safe
live them
for me.

DUDLEY: I wrote "Pashtun Poet" after reading about the group of very young Afghani women who write poems in secrecy, in fear of the severe punishment that would follow, if they were discovered (*New York Times,* April 27, 2012), and I wrote "Can You Express Yourself..." after reading (also in the *Times)* about renewed fundamentalism among young Islamic people. The article was accompanied by a photograph of a woman sitting next to her husband. She was small, completely draped in black, and she seemed to me to be a shadow. Her husband spoke for her in the interview. After reading these pieces, I realized how little I know and comprehend about what it can mean to be a woman in the Muslim world.

BAISALI CHATTERJEE DUTT

Baisali Chatterjee Dutt, a former columnist and agony aunt for *Mother & Baby* magazine and contributor to *Parent & Baby*, compiled and edited two volumes for the "Chicken Soup for the Indian Soul" series, *On Friendship* and *Celebrating Brothers and Sisters*. Her latest book, *Sharbari Datta: The Design Diva* (Niyogi Books 2015), is a biography of India's first *haute couture* designer of ethnic-wear for men and a *kantha* revivalist. Dutt continues to write for various magazines, but poetry and theater are where her heart lies. Born in New York and schooled in Bangalore, she attended college in Delhi and now lives in Kolkata with her husband, sons, and in-laws.

A FEW THREADS

Oh maa, is this new sari for me?
Look at the colors,
feel the texture,
the embroidery is so fine
and delicate.
These threads
speak in tongues
and carry tales
I want to sing;
I want to wrap their softness
and many-colored moods
around me
                  and float like a feather
as it free-falls through the air
on its way towards a head-on collision with the grass.
Yes,
my Diwali looks brighter already.

Oh papa,
the cold is setting in;
jeans, sweaters
and multi-colored scarves

will have to warm me now.
I'll match my earrings
with my scarves —
who says a polar bear can't look pretty?
I'll carry your bear-hug with me as I go,
wherever I go,
papa —
they're the warmest memories I own.

Tell me again, nani,
what exactly did Draupadi pray to Krishna
as her soul was being stripped
of every dignity she possessed
in front of the eyes of a blind court?
Did she howl in pain?
Did she beg for a few strands
to cover her modesty,
her breasts
her pussy?
I did,
you know.
I prayed to every God I knew,
using up the mantras of my childhood memories;
the agarbatti smells of your daily worship,
maa,
I used them to numb my senses
as I screamed
while the beasts tore into my body with savage glee.
I howled in pain and shame,
papa,
as they ripped apart my gut
and clawed off my breasts
and bloodied the nation with gore.

And I begged
and I begged

and I begged
for a few threads
on my back
as I lay shivering in the cold
on the road.

Nobody stopped,
nobody cared,
many people looked,
but no one bothered
to throw a few threads
of dignity my way
along with their
looks of pity
and fear
and horror
and shame.

Maa,
you cover me with sheets now,
and there is newsprint
where my gut once used to be.
I've lost the name you gave me,
but I have a few fancier ones instead.
I can hear loud words, maa,
angry words;
words of rage
and pain
and protest
being yelled out
in one big collective wail
of rage
and pain
and protest.
Or maybe that's just the morphine talking.

Papa,
I believe we're in Singapore?
How many boxes of dreams
did you help load on the aircrafts
to fly all the way here
without ever knowing
that one day,
you too
would be here with me?
Is Singapore beautiful?
Is it everything you dreamed of
and more?

It's okay.
Don't tell me.
I can see for myself now.
I can see these tall skyscrapers
and trains speeding through the skies
and women wearing the most fashionable threads
I'd only ever seen in movies
and magazines.

I...
I don't know.
I don't know about castration
or death by hanging.
I don't know about lethal injections
or shoving iron rods up their asses
and scrambling their intestines.
I don't know about lynching them
or feeding them to hungry hyenas
or to an angry mob.
All I know
is that I wanted to live...

I can hear the voices
of my sisters in pain
screaming "Enough is enough!"
but
enough of what?

Today,
my two-year-old sister
died with me,
leaving another scar
on our Motherland's face.
Did she get a name?
Wasn't she a laadli,
a shona,
a pari,
a rani,
like I was once,
before becoming a Damini,
an Amanat,
a Nirbhaya?

Scream away my sisters.
Scream till the blood gurgles out of your throat
staining our corridors of power.
Scream till we change our herstories,
our laws,
our brothers' mindsets,
our daughters' lives,
and
our freedoms.

As for me,
I'm off to have a word with Draupadi now.
I need to know
why her prayer for a few threads of dignity
was far greater than my own.

AMI KALI

I know what it is.
I know why you hate me.
It's because
you
are
afraid
of
me.

Think about it.
You do.
You hate me,
because you're afraid of me,
and because you're afraid of me,
you want to control me,
and dominate me,
manipulate me,
oppress me
and beat the hellish shrew out of me
until I am tamed.
Or dead.
After all,
shall ye not conquer
that which ye fear?

You label me weak
and proclaim to one and all
that I need your protection.
And yet,
you share me with your drinking buddies
and bash my head in when I protest
and fuck me with beer bottles
for good measure.

I am a vamp,
you say,
and I tempt you with my body.
The elbows sticking out as I walk the streets,
or the books I hold in front of my breast,
are actually code for,
"Come a little closer, stud,
And pinch me till I bruise!"
Because you,
you understand the language of vamps!
You say,
that though my mouth screams,

        yells,

        cries,

        begs,

        pleads
"NOOOOOO! NOOOOO! PLEASE!!
NOOOOOOOOOOOOOOOOO!!";
my eyes actually say, "Yes! Please!
Fuck me harder with those iron rods!"
You poor little dears, you,
incapable of rational thought
        and simple comprehension,
you have no control over your urges,
so obviously,
I must bear the blame.

And whenever my sisters and I
have shown the slightest hint
of being smarter than you,
you proclaimed us to be
the Devil's whores
and burned us en masse
at the stake.
Or hanged us.
Or drowned us.

Or shut us away in darkness
deprived of food,
> water,
> human touch.

You're afraid of us,
because,
in the deepest,
innermost core of your heart,
you know that we are goddesses.
We can stand on our husbands' chests
and say "Ooops!"
or sit by their side
in deceptive,
beatific serenity.
We can copulate with them too
and allow ourselves to be set in stone,
to be worshipped forever
in an unapologetic image
of orgasm and cum.
We can also chop off our own heads
and drink our own blood
and quench the thirst of two other
naked goddesses
with
our
own
blood.

We're goddesses.

We bleed once a month
and you call us moody
and mirthless.
We multi-task
every day,

day to day,
day in, day out,
and you wonder why
your daily bread
is a little burnt today.
And,
in a glory of flesh,
       pain,
       blood
       and tears,
we birth your babies,
your heirs,
while ripping our bodies apart in the process.

Don't pour your oil-like judgments
upon my ocean of bubbling anger,
because
I'm warning you,
you won't be able to clean up your mess.
There'll be no Nilkanth*
to swallow your poison,
but Chamundis aplenty†
to suck out your blood.

DUTT: December 16, 2012 is a date that will forever remain etched in our collective human psyche. Jyothi Singh Pandey's brutal rape and resultant death is one that still

---

* "Nilkanth" is another name of the God Shiva. one of the Holy Hindu Trinity. Legend has it that when the ocean was being churned by the Devas (gods) and Asuras (demons) for Amrit (the Nectar of Immortality), one of the early by-products of the churning was a terrible poison that threatened to choke and suffocate everyone. They all prayed to Shiva to rescue them. Hearing their prayers, Shiva scooped up the poison and swallowed it and it turned his throat blue, thus giving him another name, "Nilkanth" which literally means "the blue-throated one."

† "Chamundi" is another name of Kali, the Dark Goddess of War. She was bestowed with this name when she defeated two generals of the demon army, Chanda and Munda.

makes us shudder. This poem was written on the day she died. Jyoti Singh Pandey's rape was horrific. All rapes are. But somehow, this girl became a part of our lives, and we watched and prayed as she battled during the last few days of her life, wanting to survive... but failing. The day she died, I went numb. And soon after the news of her death, I read about the death of the little girl who had been raped in Bhopal. "A Few Threads" came gushing out.

In this poem, there is a stanza where I address my father: "How many boxes of dreams / did you help load on the aircrafts...." This is a reference to my father's job as an aircraft loader. The stanza that begins, "Today, / my two-year-old sister / died with me..." refers to the two-year-old victim from Vadodara who had been raped by her uncle on December 26, 2012, and succumbed to her injuries, a few days before Jyoti passed away. The words "laadli" (darling), "shona" (gold), "rani" (queen) and "pari" (fairy) are all Hindi terms of endearment that parents and elders use for their daughters / wards.

A couple of weeks after I wrote "A Few Threads," "Ami Kali" poured out, because the stories of our goddesses have never failed to move us. Our epics and myths have always inspired me to think, question, write and transcreate. "Ami Kali" is Bengali for "I am Kali." The title of the poem is the only phrase in Bengali. The rest of the poem was written in English. The poem describes Kali in some of her many and fiercest avatars.

JUDY DYKSTRA-BROWN

Judy Dykstra-Brown lived in South Dakota, Australia, Ethiopia, and elsewhere, before moving to Lake Chapala, Mexico, in 2001. She was a semifinalist in the *Atlantic* international poetry competition and first place winner of the Tennessee Writer's Alliance National Poetry Prize. In addition to her poetry, short stories, nonfiction, memoir, and children's books, she maintains a daily blog and is also a three-dimensional artist, specializing in *retablos* and found-art collages. Dykstra-Brown's work has appeared in such journals and anthologies as *New Poets in Los Angeles, The Sculpture Garden Review, Mexico Insights,* and *Ojo Del Lago.* Her books include *Prairie Moths: Memories of a Farmer's Daughter* and *Lessons from a Grief Diary.*

ZAUDITU

I am the storyteller
who lives by the well.
For a coin,
I offer the use of my cup;
and for another coin, its story.

Mine is the cup the young girls choose to drink from —
those who come
more from a need to hear my story
than for thirst.

Often, they choose to tell me their own stories
after I've told the story of this cup they drink from.

This is the cup that he held out to me on the long march.
I was in the middle with my clothes torn.
He was on the side, in his uniform.
I returned the cup that he held out to me
and he did not, for once,
ignore my torn fingers.
This time he dipped the cup again and drained it
from the place my lips had touched.

He palmed me once a new radish
that I ate behind my hand with the loam still clinging to it
as he did what the watchers expected him to do.

He was not the first
plunged into me,
only the first with eyes and hidden fingers
that stroked softly in another language
from the stabbing that I couldn't even feel.
I was that frozen to the tearing —
ice that couldn't melt.
All of me gone from it.
All of me in his fingers
trying
to learn their message
as he, too, raped the prisoner.
He didn't want to do this.
That was the difference.
Of the one hundred seventy-four fuckings
I was the stage for,
I was the stable floor for,
he was the only one bearable.
He didn't want to do it.

This is how removed I was in that place.
I listened for his voice
at night, imagining
four pairs of hands in line in front of him,
then his hands. Something different.

After I was freed,
the men of my village carried me
to Nata's house, and the women
probed to remove the crabs and lice —
scratched to break the crust
and stuff me with the steaming poultices

that made me cry out because
I felt like I was melting
and losing my protection.
As they scraped and
as they scrubbed all from my skin,
they removed the sheared-off clump of hair
from where it had been caught by my collar
and found the new birthmark
on my neck —
a port wine stain
with a fingerprint in it.

"It is an omen," said Aznogitch.
"Some man in all
those devils
has left
his mark on you, Zauditu.
Zauditu."

In their eyes were cravings
for one story that it was even possible to tell.
They needed to be able to
hold onto some rescue
even in this.

At this point, it was more terrible for them than me.
My eyes were closed the two days that it took for them
to purge the cell dust and the pus and crust and blood and puke
and shit and vermin and the salt and clay and food.
In places, my clothing grown into my skin.

I gave my body to them. It was easiest of anything
that I have ever done.
It was as if it was
my profession —
what I could do well —
stepping out of my body and surrendering

to whoever needed it
for whatever purpose.

"What was it like?" they want to ask.
This is exactly what it's like.
I find an unattractive corner to curl up in —
one where there is no need for anyone to go —
some corner with no orifice or swell of flesh.
Some corner so small that it can't be pushed into very far.
Some nook.
Some ledge.
The inside of a rib might do.
The hollow of the foot I used often until
The new colonel found it to be his favorite spot
for relieving himself.

I moved around. It became a type of journey,
finding the hidden places — a game of hide-and-seek
where no one ever found me. Except once.
Four fingers.

I do not tell them all of this.
I do not tell them anything at all.
They see how I am gone when they raise my legs.
The grandmother in me to her wrist,
washing the poultice from my cave
that they will never get tidy
again, no matter how many crushed leaves
sour milk poultices.
Never get my odor back there.
I have finished producing odors.
All my juices have been squeezed.
I have gone from frozen to dry.
Parched.
I pucker so painfully
that I can't sit for long
ever again.

Grandmother smears her finger with animal fat
and slides it into me.
"I am sorry for this,"
she says, each time,
as she spreads my knees;
and she never meets my eyes,
ever, in eight years before she dies.

My father
sees my flinch
as he tries to set his hand on my arm
and it is an embarrassment that is between us
until I leave the village
to make my way away from it.

I know the world, Father.
I know more of it than you.
I have proven what
you always feared.
I have proven you right, Father,
and I am sorry for this.
Now there is nothing left here.
All hands in this place know me too well.
How can I walk a street of uniforms?
My father sits on his hands,
both lips in his teeth.
His eyes clench
and his spine begins to curve
and never straightens.

When he comes to say good-bye,
his left cheek
is pressed to my left cheek
and I put my hand up,
cup his ear;
and I remember

not to pull away
until he has pulled away.
My mother tells me in a letter
that he is trying
and I say that I am trying, too;
but I am dry.
So dry
that I need a river —
another hand that I am looking for.

At first, I looked for the man
who held a cup
and palmed a radish —
four pairs of hands in front of him,
then in his hands, something different.

But now, for my whole long life since then,
I have been looking for a man
who has learned
not to do
what he doesn't want to do.

I am Zauditu, the storyteller,
who lives by the well.
For a coin, I offer the use of my cup.
For another coin,
the story of the cup.

DYKSTRA-BROWN: I wrote this piece as though it was being channeled, then did several rewrites in the years afterward. Having traveled widely, I have been witness to the nearly powerless existence of women in many Middle-Eastern and third-world countries. A number of my Ethiopian women friends had suffered the barbarities of female circumcision, and when another Ethiopian friend left her husband, she had to leave everything: house, car, clothing, and all personal property. But worst of all, she had to leave her children. Unmarried, she had no power and no life. Present nightmare stories of the execution of women who are the victims of rape, as well as situations of young girls being held as sex slaves within my own Mexican community, add to my need to do what I can to try to end such barbarities. Perhaps by telling some of these stories, I will contribute a small bit to the eradication of such atrocities. A personal abduction experience in Ethiopia and another in Wyoming (luckily, in both cases, I was able to escape) were further contributors, I think, to the horror of this piece. I hope that this poem, although fiction, tells the truth

MEG EDEN

Meg Eden received the Henrietta Spiegel Creative Writing Award in 2012. She was a reader for the *Delmarva Review*, and her work has appeared in a variety of magazines and has been nominated for a Pushcart Prize. Her collections include *Your Son* (winner of the Florence Kahn Memorial Award), *Rotary Phones and Facebook* (Dancing Girl Press) and *A Week with Beijing* (Neon, 2015).

CHILD EXPLOITATION

Lovely window girl with your smeared eye
shadow, puffed red lips — you wouldn't win
any kid pageants, but can I ask —
how many men have bought you tonight?

You look too real, too fake — like a doll
tossed in the sand and aged. Like the kind
in antique shops, used and discarded.
The glass makes you look afraid, even as
you stand upright and defiant. You look even more doll-like
in your encasing.

If men weren't hunting
for your child body, I'd say you look
beautiful, maybe — like a girl preparing
for a ballet recital, who stole her mother's
make-up, trying to be what the magazines say
girls should be.

I want to be the mother who wipes
the blue from your eyes, the rouge from your cheeks,
You don't want that nasty stuff on, I'd say, cleaning
the remnants of man off your legs.

But first, I'd take a rock from the ground,
tell you to step back. I'd shatter your case.

Funeral Pyre for Late Abuser

When her husband died, she lifted
his cold wet hand and cried,
No more will this hand hit a woman!

If she could, perhaps she would mount
his hand on her wall as a testament
to the power it no longer holds.
Or would it be more satisfying
for her to watch it burn?

As she held up his flesh, did other women
also lift the corners of their head scarves,
only to acknowledge similar bruises
and commune in their common history?

Or did the earth stay silent
as another hand rose to replace
the one that had fallen?

Eden: For the past three years, I've been working on a poetry collection on sexual and religious persecution. The poems are inspired by accounts I've read, or photos I've seen, the stories that are often, horrifyingly, overlooked. Through writing poems, I can respond to the accounts I hear, and I can raise awareness of the women who have gone through unimaginable horrors. Through writing these poems, I'm also humbled by my own experiences and reminded that, in having the voice to speak, I must be bold to speak, on account of those who cannot speak for themselves.

THERESA SENATO EDWARDS

Theresa Senato Edwards teaches and tutors at Marist College and is a scholar-facilitator for the New York Council for the Humanities' Conversations Bureau Program. Her books include *Voices Through Skin* (Sibling Rivalry Press, 2011) and *The Music of Hands* (self-published, 2012). The title poem of her 2012 collection *Painting Czeslawa Kwoka: Honoring Children of the Holocaust* (Unbound Content), a full-color collaboration with painter Lori Schreiner, won the Tacenda Literary Award for Best Collaboration in 2007 and was nominated for a Pushcart Prize; the book itself received the Tacenda Literary Award for Best Book in 2011. Edwards' short stories have been published in *The Mosaic* and online in *Fiction365* and *Foliate Oak Literary Magazine*.

BATTERED

No man who shared his sex with me
    broke me.

Hotel room:
refuge from close quarters

he, pretending to be Scarface,
vigilante, he —
womanizer,
he showed me
on used sheets
washed, dried, stretched, molded into
stark space.

Bathroom   faintly lit.
From behind, he —

rammed it in.
"A wife's punishment," he said.
I looked left.

Wall shadows.
Butter-
colored background
silhouette ass
rod hidden.
Forced flesh until climax.
— *I remember being 26.*

EDWARDS: When I wrote "Battered," I had the rhythm of Gwendolyn Brooks's poem "The Pool Players. Seven at the Golden Shovel." — A.K.A. "We Real Cool" — in my brain. I loved the way Brooks read this poem, using that staccato "we" at each line ending, and how her lines enjambed so effortlessly and rhythmically. With "Battered," however, because of its unpleasant content, I realized that the rhythm had to emphasize the lines ending with "he" in the poem. So instead of enjambing those lines, I end them with an em-dash to elongate the pause. I also vary the sound of "he" but include it throughout the poem, writing through a memory of a frightening night of sexual abuse that was far from memorable.

JANET EIGNER

Janet Eigner has had the good fortune to study with Carolyn Forché, Jane Hirshfield, Eric Pankey, Natalie Goldberg, Joan Logghe, Miriam Sagan and the late Donald Finkel. Rebecca Seiferle has been her editor for the past decade. Five years ago, Eigner and four other poets formed a small publishing group, Black Swan Editions, which brings out books that feature a blend of artwork and poetry. The BSE catalogue already includes several award-winning chapbooks and full-length books. Eigner's own chapbook, *Cornstalk Mother*, was published by Pudding House Publishers in 2009. Her book-length collection *What Lasts Is the Breath* (Black Swan Editions, 2013) was the winner of the 2013 New Mexico-Arizona Book Awards.

SOMETHING TO DO WITH HUNTED ANIMALS

She asks if I would care to see something
she does with the animals she has hunted.
Holds out an exquisite deer foot — curved
ebony hoof, warm tan fur, three inch
carpentry screw where the shin bone was.

Takes a shy pride in her skill, a tender
reverence in work she does for those she loves.
*If you strap 'em under right away, they dry
in this shape. You use 'em to hold up a gun rack.*
She followed her father everywhere.

As a child; learned man things
but never perfectly. Grew up playing
hardball with neighborhood boys.
Many times a big boy grabbed her
from behind, twiddled her privates,

threatened to kill if she told. She backed off
from men, lifted weights, ran, starved herself —
hunched over, shuffling, a defeated workman,
pinched face green under a heavy tan.
I, who will not own a gun

or eat another mammal,
stand in awe at the exquisite grace of her gift,
the pulsing life still given off by this stump,
stare in grief at the fixed curve of the hoof
repeating the hunch of her shoulders.

EIGNER: I've been a psychologist for 30 years and am now retired, but I still write
about dance and writing, and still publish my poetry with a small Santa Fe press,
Black Swan Editions. I work for social justice and gun safety. My own five years spent
in psychoanalysis, with an excellent clinician, uncovered enough nonverbal imagery
and sexual inappropriateness toward me, on the part of a close relative, to solidify my
sense of self, save my marriage and, eventually, my children, from my anxiety and
confusion. Before I became a psychologist, I did years of work to resolve issues relating
to multi-generational Holocaust survival, sexual abuse in my infancy, and physical
and emotional abuse in my family. Then, in my 30 years of therapy practice, I worked
with both genders on their trauma-abuse issues, combining updated psychodynamic
training with Dialectical Behavior Therapy, the therapy proven in clinical trials to be
most effective with abuse survivors and survivors of war damage. What a constructive
world this would be without the numbing and PTSD that results from, and affects,
every aspect of our lives and the lives of the world's population, not to mention how
that numbing of vibrant, exuberant life affects Mother Earth.

Writing "Something to Do with Hunted Animals" came from psychotherapy work with
a woman who was so deeply disturbed by sexual trauma that she self-mutilated and
starved herself. After working with her for several months, I was moved and repulsed
by her gift to me of deer antlers from one of her own hunts. The poem helped me
to understand my own feelings about the antlers, which still pulsed life, as did this
intensely distressed woman.

SUSAN ELMSLIE

Susan Elmslie's poems have appeared in several Canadian journals and anthologies and in a prize-winning chapbook, *When Your Body Takes to Trembling*. Her first trade collection of poetry, *I, Nadja, and Other Poems* (Brick), won the Quebec Writers' Federation A.M. Klein Poetry Prize and was shortlisted for the McAuslan First Book Prize, the League of Canadian Poets' Pat Lowther Award, and a ReLit Award. Elmslie's poetry has been supported by Canada Council for the Arts grants for Professional Writers, and she has been a poetry Fellow at Hawthornden Castle, Scotland, and a winner of *Arc*'s Poem of the Year contest.

IF THERE'S A WOMAN ON THE STREET

"I told Blanchette, 'If there's a woman on the street, I'll grab her.'"
— Jean-Paul Bainbridge, convicted for his role in the rape and murder of 22-year-old music student Isabelle Bolduc on June 30, 1996, in Sherbrooke, Québec

Let her have her hands
on useful instruments: stitch-
ripper, nail file, stiletto. Her voice
a needle to puncture ears.
Let her know how to snap
a kneecap like a lobster.
Let her know how to kill.

If there's a woman
she has rehearsed her fear; she has
feared the hearse inching up behind her
between the bus-stop and home.
She has filled her lungs with fire
to shout *Fire!* like she's been told.

In her nightmares, she has split
a head like a *head*
with an axe like her hand.
She has suspended herself in high places,
spewed lava. There is no such thing —

Sputtering. We don't help
her. Give life-25
to the hands that drag her by the hair
smash her head with a pipe
drop her in a ditch at our feet.
There was a woman on the street.

ELMSLIE: I am a Canadian poet and college professor. Violence against women and children is an important subject for me. It is a hard subject to write about, I have found, and, in my experience, also one that journal editors tend to shy away from. In fact, my poem, "If There's a Woman on the Street," was rejected by the American feminist literary journal *Calyx* for being "too shrill." It strikes me as ironic that some powerful canonical works of poetry by men, "Howl," for instance, are celebrated partly for their sense of outrage. A small note about my poem: the phrase "life-25" refers in Canada to the maximum life sentence (Canada does not have the death penalty).

CARRIE ETTER

Carrie Etter has published three collections of poetry, most recently *Imagined Sons* (Seren, 2014), and edited *Infinite Difference: Other Poetries by UK Women Poets*. Her poems have appeared widely in such periodicals as *Boston Review, The New Republic, New Statesman,* and the *Times Literary Supplement*. Originally from Normal, Illinois, she has lived in England since 2001 and has been a member of the creative writing faculty at Bath Spa University since 2004.

AFTER THE ATTACK

I hinge one of my ribs
to either side of the doorway.
I stir my father's muscles into mortar.
I carry my mother's eyes in my palm
to set in stone above the entrance.

I am building a house for Joanna, my youngest sister,
designed to protect her.
I regret its late construction —
I had thought, *She is only thirteen,*
believing she had a few more years of safety.

I walk to the nearest hill and look back.
There is no house, there is no sanctuary.
There are bricks I want to heft.
There is a sharpened pole
where I want to place his head.

ETTER: I wrote this poem when I learned my youngest sister had been attacked. She and my family were in my hometown of Normal, Illinois, while I had been living in California for five years; that distance increased my sense of helplessness.

TRISH FALIN

Trish Falin's poetry has appeared in the journals *Soundings, Penumbra, Welter, Dash, Askew,* and others. A former news reporter and editor, Falin earned her MFA in Creative Writing (poetry) at Antioch University. The nonfiction work she's published includes travel books and textbooks for carpenters.

THE RAPE

after Rene Magritte

When he looks into my eyes
he sees breasts, pupils
wide and black, nipples —
dark areolas staring back.

He eats my sight,
devours the day, the sun,
the green grass, the flower.

My nose is his belly,
umbilical uncut; his cord
ties us together.

I cannot cut him loose.

I smell his sweat —
the sting of it burns
inside my nostrils —
rancid breath invades my belly,
weighty as an arm
pressing down a chest.

He takes my mouth
makes it into his cunt,
fucks my voice until I am
silent.

FALIN: René Magritte's painting "The Rape" was used as a writing prompt in a presentation by a fellow graduate student. The image stirred a long-buried memory of a night I was raped by two men. At fourteen, I had no one to go to for help and lived in a community where I would be blamed for the incident. Magritte's painting portrays the impact of rape in a nonverbal way: turning the face into a body conveys how the sense of self is crushed.

My current life is very different from where I started but, at times, the past comes back full force.

CHARLES ADÈS FISHMAN

Charles Adès Fishman is the editor of *Veils, Halos & Shackles: International Poetry on the Oppression and Empowerment of Women.* His previous books include *The Death Mazurka*, which was nominated for the 1990 Pulitzer Prize in poetry, as well as *Chopin's Piano* (2006) and *In the Language of Women* (2011), both recipients of the Paterson Award for Literary Excellence; the revised, second edition of his anthology *Blood to Remember: American Poets on the Holocaust* (2007); and his volume of selected poems, *In the Path of Lightning* (2012), the last two from Time Being Books. Fishman is poetry editor of *Prism: An Interdisciplinary Journal for Holocaust Educators.* He lives in Bellport, Long Island.

A DANCE ON THE POEMS OF RILKE

> *I remember a Czech dancer who danced on the poems of Rilke.*
> — Stennie Pratomo-Gret

In the particular hell of Ravensbrück
where Gypsy girls were sterilized and babies
were drowned at birth   where dysentery
lung cancer and typhus   took life after life
and grotesque experiments in the inducement
of infection and pain were cultivated as a fine art

where women of every European nation slaved
for Siemens   through endless moonless nights
and cut trees   dug pits   loaded and unloaded
railway cars and barges   where abortion was
inevitable   and sexual cruelty the rule   and where

a woman could be duly tortured for using rags
as tampons   or merely for adjusting her dress
a certain Czech woman who knew every word
danced to the poems of Rilke   moving sinuously
to each of his Orphean sonnets   bowing gracefully
with the first notes of each *Elegie*: she felt the dark music

of Rilke's heart   each soaring leap of the spirit   each lunge
toward grief   Though she is long gone   and we
no longer know her name   she is the one who showed
even a halting step could be a triumph   and a dance
on the poems of a dead poet   might redeem

TÁHIRIH: THE SEVENTEENTH DISCIPLE

for Fátimah Baraghání

I.

You were born into a family of Islamic clerics
and your father, Muhammad Salih Baraghání
of Qazvin, a writer of praise songs for the Qur'an
and a jealous guardian of punishments,
named you Fátimah.

It's true that you were allowed to pursue religious
studies and that you quickly distinguished yourself
as a gifted explicator of Islamic law; nonetheless,
your father married you off to a cousin when you
were just fourteen. In due time, you gave life
to two sons and a daughter, but your marriage
was an unhappy one.

Soon you began to correspond with leaders
of the Shaykhi movement, which flourished
in Shi'a shrines, and it was Sayyid Kazim Rashti himself
who gave you the title Qurratu'l-Ayn, Consolation
of the Eyes. It was no surprise that you became estranged
from your husband.

At Karbala, your genius was recognized,
though you were permitted to teach Kazim's followers
only from behind a curtain.

When you were not yet thirty, you took Ali Muhammad
of Shiraz, the *Báb*, as Mahdi and became his seventeenth
disciple, and the only woman. You never met this man
you dedicated your life to, yet surely you were his crown jewel —
so eloquent, devoted, and beautiful that no one who heard you speak
could turn away.

II.

In Karbala, your fierce teaching of the new faith rattled
Shi'a clergy, who arranged your deportation.
What else could be expected but that you would soon
be escorted to the Persian border, with sincere importunings
that you not return?

Unfortunately, you were not a good fit in Kermanshah
either, and with the complicity of your father and brothers,
were brought back to Qazvin, to your husband's bed.

Many flights and betrayals followed, and in the end,
you broke with family, home, and sect forever.
You rallied Bábi leaders to break with Islam
and appeared in Badasht, without the veil,
to demonstrate that Sharia law had been abrogated
and that a Bábi woman was not promiscuous,
a demon, or a hater of God, but free.

Law that does not respect women is the tool of misogynists
and tyrants. At the moment you removed the veil in public,
you were fully Táhirih, the *Pure One*, but your death
had drawn near.

III.

Even while you were under house arrest in Badasht,
people came to listen. Women, especially, were moved
by your voice, which was like a hand of fire
that reached out and touched them.

They could feel their skin respond to every word,
and their minds and bodies awakened. With each syllable
you uttered, centuries of oppression peeled back
like scorched bark from a tree. They began to see
the green center of your vision and knew
that a living force spoke through you.

But you remained imprisoned. You had grown up
with your father and knew your punishment would be swift,
that there would be no amnesty, and so you fasted
and recited prayers and, dressed in white silk,
embraced your death.

In the garden of Ilkhani, in Tehran, you were strangled
with your own veil, which you had chosen for that martyrdom.
But before the silk could tighten around your throat, one
who observed from the shadows heard you cry out, *You can kill me,
but you can't stop the emancipation of women!*

TWO GIRLS LEAPING

They have a favorite color — this one:
this chlorinated aqua, this womb lunar blackness
drawn wholly into the light. The depth of the pool
beguiles them, the weight of their own bodies.

Mother is not near, so it is easy to jump in, to test
themselves against the cold liquid fire of the violently
blue water, to attempt flight, hands linked in a joyous
failure of suicide.

They wear no caps: dark hair spills black puppy tails
along their small tanned necks. Time lunges ahead, eternity
passes. A hundred leaps cannot tire them. They live
to jump: the heart of the water's coolness pulses in them.

In what way are they innocent? *The fragrance of unawareness
stays on them:* their fearful certitude about all things
perturbs the slow dark pools we swim in. In their nonstop
gab, the world's extravagant newness stings and clashes.

They are giddy with the ordinary, laugh in its cold blue
stranger's face.

Becky is still laughing, gliding like a seal
in her favorite aqua water; she is giggling and splashing;
but now Mother is here, now Mother pulls her, goose-bumped
and dripping, from the ice-blue pool; now Mother slaps her,

slaps her again, again slaps her.

And Jennifer has seen everything. Watch how carefully
she moves, how cautiously she holds her tingling body.
"Let's see who can go slower," she says, "Let's see who goes
slower."

The pool is empty now, a liquid rectangle. Water has its
own life, its own candor. Step back. Take a running start.
Now tell me: *What is your heart' desire?*

FISHMAN: "A Dance on the Poems of Rilke" was prompted by my many years of work on the Holocaust and, in particular, on the poetry of the Holocaust (see, for instance, *Blood to Remember: American Poets on the Holocaust*). It was also a way for me to acknowledge the strength, resilience, and courage that many women demonstrated during the years of the Shoah, despite the always cruel and often vicious deprivations and mortifications women suffered at the hands of both male and female guards and other tormentors.

In 2011, I was working on my collection *In the Language of Women*. My sister, Harriet, who is a regional leader of the Baha'i faith in America, knew about my project and asked if I would write a poem to commemorate the life and death of Táhirih Baragháni, an early leader and martyr. I had written poems for my sister before and decided to accept her challenge, which was also a very special gift. In part, my writing of "Táhirih: the Seventeenth Disciple" prepared me to take on the larger challenge of co-editing *Veils, Halos & Shackles: International Poetry on the Oppression and Empowerment of Women*.

"Two Girls Leaping" is the word-video of a scene I witnessed one summer day when I was visiting my parents at a low-income seaside retreat on Long Island, where they stayed while they were not in Florida.

I believe that these very different poems share a theme: that human beings crave dignity and freedom and, insofar as they are able to, resist efforts to chain them or beat them down.

CHRIS FRADKIN

Chris Fradkin is a former beet farmer now living in Brazil. His prose and poetry have appeared in *Monkeybicycle, Thrice Fiction,* and *Thrush Poetry Journal,* and his songs have been performed by Fergie, The Plimsouls, and The Flamin' Groovies. Fradkin's sound-editing for *The X-Files* won an Emmy Award.

SUZI AND THE BOOB JOB

Her daddy'd paid the bill but charged her interest in return. In the family room, while mom was upstairs sleeping. His hands would trace the lines along the scars beneath her breasts. "You can barely see them," he'd say to himself. She'd close her eyes and count back from a thousand every time. When she'd reach 500, most nights, he'd be done. She'd grab her panties then and race upstairs into the shower. She would stand beneath the faucet until dawn. And there her mom would find her, with the water dripping down. And her daughter sound asleep beneath its fall.

FRADKIN: This chapter in *The Saga of Suzi — A life and work in progress* was inspired by a court case in New York. The battle over custody was ugly. In the end, the daughter ended up going home with her mom, but the father hadn't played his final card. As he stood up in court, he requested from the judge compensation for his daughter's surgery — the breast-enlargement surgery he'd financed for her birthday. If he wasn't going to see her, as the court had so decreed, he figured that he shouldn't have to pay.

MARISA FRASCA

Marisa Frasca is a poet, translator, and essayist, whose work has been published in *5AM*, *Adanna Journal*, *VIA*, *Philadelphia Poets*, *Sicilia Parra*, *Feile-Festa*, the *Sweet Lemons II* anthology, the *Embroidered Stories* anthology, and other literary journals and anthologies. Her first collection, *Via Incanto: Poems from the Darkroom*, was published by Bordighera Press in 2014. Frasca holds a BA from the New School's Riggio Scholar program and an MFA in poetry from Drew University. She serves on the boards of the Italian American Studies Association and the Italian American Writers Association, and on the advisory board of Arba Sicula. She was born in Vittoria, Italy, and her immigration experience informs much of her work.

LICKING SARDINES

I.

I was never beaten when I looked up at the sky
Never walked with black shawl over my head — black drowning my eyes
Never mended socks with fingers bloodied by thorny fields
Never sucked flat caps before they'd toss sardine skeletons to lick
Never was forced down on four legs so I couldn't kick, tied like a sheep
Was never beast with ripped hind
Never had ribs cracked when I was swollen with child
Never cleaned dirt floors with my hair — kid hanging on teat
Never saw my kid whipped with oxtail dipped in salt and fat.
Why is my soul trapped in my mother's Sicilian hell?

II.

Listen carefully, my daughters:

this is a photograph of my great-grandmother Catena. Her name
means Chain. She sits on a caned chair in front of our door on Via Bixio.
She sits like the palest wash of stone shrouded in black,
cleaning sardines. How does she emit so much light?
We must all know ourselves through our known

and unknown mothers strapped to our chests.
In the 21ˢᵗ century we look men in the eye — we work
for pay and buy and fry sardines
from Portugal, sit round a table and nod
to each other. We work and buy and tend
house with its flower garden, and the fig tree survives.
We birth, nurture, pass our clipped wings
to you —

> Listen carefully, American daughters: stay
> in school, join us when these old
> tambourines coax our fingers to play —
> Black Madonna of Tindari
> drawn on the drum, release Raffaela, Giovanna,
> Maria, Delizia, Catena out of Siculo Inferno —

> Drum, beat, drum the *pizzica pizzicata,*
> sting *tarantula tarantata tarantella* tracking our cries,
> shaking our voices — dissolve, devour evil spirits.

Our stolen spirits, white skirts, red sashes with eyes ears mouth, feet
and hands do a little fancy dancing. In whirlwind
fury and sound, in conversation with death,
through faith, winds of spirits exit. Enter the force —
the dance — dance to tarantula poison. Get *out*
of our blood, enemy and accomplice.

We work and buy and stuff whole sardines
Sicilian style — *beccafico* — breadcrumbs, raisins,
lemon rind, pinch of sugar, spoonful of vinegar,
bay leaf between each one — round our table
we nod to each other — and we laugh
when Catena says maybe those men
needed to eat more sardines.

FRASCA: Our souls and their sensibilities are not merely made by personal history, but by a collective and sometimes difficult ancestral past. I personally have never experienced physical violence, but I was born and raised in Sicily, as were my foremothers, and Sicily is a place that has been cursed and blessed by the many foreign powers that have inhabited the island because of its fertile and desirable geographic location. Sicily has a history of war, including the raping and ravaging of the land and its women, as well as its men.

My mother has told me stories about her grandmother, Catena (the name means "Chains"), and the abuses and hunger Catena and her eight children suffered in their lifetimes. Two thousand years of greed and colonization have given the island a history of oppression that has not left the bones and psyche of modern Sicilians. The black shawl some women still wear is a custom left by the Arabs — who also brought olive trees and citrus groves to the island. The Greeks, Romans, Normans, French, Spaniards, and countless others who took turns ruling the island, left beautiful temples and mosaics, but they have mostly left the island poor and its people hungry and ignorant. The unemployment rate currently borders on 40%. The vast majority of women do not work outside the home. Poverty and ignorance have plenty to do with violence against the most vulnerable in society, women and children.

Many of my poems speak about violence against women in Sicily because that is a topic and a place I am most familiar with, but I feel linked to all women who live with brutality. Violence against women is a universal problem. I trust image and music to expose and bring attention to this issue. With language, I try to draw from harshness to sustain the beauty of women. I also write these poems because, in doing so, I am not powerless.

BRONWYN FREDERICKS

Bronwyn Fredericks is an Indigenous Australian who advocates on issues of concern to Indigenous Australian women and has published in community and academic journals including *SIGNS: Journal of Women in Culture and Society*; *Outskirts: feminisms along the edge* (Volume 23); *Cultural Studies Review; AlterNATIVE;* and the *Journal of Australian Indigenous Issues*. She led the development of the National Aboriginal and Torres Strait Islander Women's Health Strategy (2010) and is a member of the National Indigenous Research and Knowledges Network (NIRAKN). Fredericks is a Professor, the Pro Vice-Chancellor, and the BMA Chair in Indigenous Engagement at Central Queensland University, Australia.

RECLAIMING

Clap, Clap, Clap
The sound of the clapsticks,
more than 2 sticks,
more than two hands,
more than the air in which they are hit,
they hum, vibrate,
the sound moves through me,
pulsing through my body,
stirs my blood,
stirs my energy,
wakes me,
reminds me,
sings to my spirit.

Clap, Clap, Clap
Women of long ago,
women of today,
women of long ago,
women of today, witnesses of time,
contained in the body,
within the deepest memory —
I am this woman before you,

I am of the past,
I am of the present,
I am of the future.

Clap, Clap, Clap
Experienced and witnessed,
pain, tears and hurt,
blood spilled over,
more than womanhood,
more than childbirth,
blood spilled over,
anger, power, violence,
murder and rape,
the blood of women,
spilled on the earth,
woman to mother,
beyond mind and body,
beyond the sacred.

Clap, Clap, Clap
darkness brings the moon,
night brings the stars,
some think romance,
some feel fear,
fear of domination,
loss of control,
personal invasion,
need for safety,
checking and re-checking,
wide-angled vision,
shadows that hurt,
light brings the need to be clean,
bruises like rainbows.

Clap, Clap, Clap
Witnessing through the years,

generations,
memories of what happened,
to us and to others,
memories are still being made,
this second, this night,
memories that make us weak,
that make us strong,
that make our spirits cry in pain, and loss,
memories that make us ask —
will we ever be free?

Clap, Clap, Clap
In uniting together,
we become stronger,
we demand to be free,
to walk the earth,
to be mindful of ourselves,
in our very being,
women of the past,
women of the present,
women of the future,
we claim our sacredness,
we reclaim the day,
we reclaim the night.

FREDERICKS: "Reclaiming" was performed with clapstick accompaniment at
the Reclaim the Night Rally, 27 October 2000, River Stage, Rockhampton, Central
Queensland, Australia. Clapsticks are a form of percussion instrument and are used
to keep rhythm with Aboriginal Australian songs. They are struck on one another and
not on a drum or other object. The work connects the past, the present and the future,
the earth and people. It describes the pain and suffering of women and asks that the
violence towards women stop, to allow women to live free from violence and to be
themselves as women.

Susan Gardner

Susan Gardner is a poet, painter, photographer, and literary editor. Her first poetry was written in Japanese calligraphy, later followed by works in English and Spanish. She lives in Santa Fe, New Mexico, and is principal editor and co-publisher of Red Mountain Press. Her book *To Inhabit the Felt World* was awarded the 2013 Eric Hoffer Book Award honorable mention for poetry and was a finalist for the Da Vinci Eye Prize, and *Drawing the Line ~ A Passionate Life* received the 2011 Eric Hoffer Book Award honorable mention for memoir. She also has a bilingual book of poetry, *Box of Light ~ Caja de Luz*. Gardner's most recent collection is *Lifted to the Wind Poems 1974-2015*.

Each One

I.

Men drive the jitney buses.

Bus girls collect tickets
    clean the buses
    perform other services.

They come from poor farms
    to help their families through hard times
    or just to escape.

In the city, they live in a company dormitory,
    each room with sixty girls,
    each paid the lowest wages
    for six-day weeks and ten-hour days.

On the buses: constant abuse from riders,
harassment from drivers, sexual favors demanded
    or taken
    right on the rubber-matted floor.

Kept uneducated, they become rough-spoken, dirty,
        unwilling, unpaid prostitutes.
After five years, at eighteen or nineteen,
        they wait

for the bus company
        to provide a dowry
        for their entry into marital
        servitude.

II.

A summer afternoon at the YWCA: sixteen women
        in pale, starched, linen dresses,
        meet in a bare, dusty room.
        Sun slants through open windows.

Folding chairs in a circle,
        we eat watermelon,
        suck ice,
        ask

who are these girls?
what do these ragamuffins
have to do with us?

Yet we know the sorrow of
our younger sisters.

Each one does one thing
to assuage our outrage,
to quiet our shame.

Each one is our sister.
        Each one grows
        one iota

toward a free life

GARDNER: The events of "Each One" took place when I was living in Korea in the 1960s. The city of Kwangju was at the leading edge of development, changing from a southern, rural, agricultural center to the modern city it has become. While I lived there, I saw the first sidewalk, the first traffic light, and the first western-style hotel built. Television arrived. Many rural people came to the city, hoping for a better life.

The women concerned with the bus girls' situation formed a committee through the Kwangju YWCA. They were the comfortable, educated elite, most with university degrees, in a city where the average girl did not finish high school. My part was small and I am glad I was there to do that little bit. Over months, not years, this group of women overturned the system, and a little humanity crept into labor conditions. As this campaign matured, our understanding of our roles as women and members of the community was evolving as well.

CHRISTINE GELINEAU

Christine Gelineau is the author of the book-length sequence *Appetite for the Divine* (Ashland Poetry Press, 2010) and *Remorseless Loyalty* (Ashland Poetry Press, 2006), which was awarded the Richard Snyder Memorial Prize. Her other books include *French Connections: A Gathering of Franco-American Poets,* which she edited with Jack B. Bedell (Louisiana Literature Press, 2007) and a new poetry collection, *Crave,* which will be released by NYQ Books in 2016. Gelineau teaches at Binghamton University, where she is associate director of the creative writing program and coordinator of the Readers' Series. She also teaches poetry in the low-residency graduate writing program at Wilkes University. She is a 2013 Pushcart Prize recipient for her poem "Sockanosett."

LETTER TO MY RAPIST

Wrapped in summer's green-black dark
we slept, lulled to dreaming in
the insect hum, while you unzipped
the dining room window's screen
with the small, precisely sharp
knife you later held to my throat.

Did you see the ground-floor bedroom
where the baby slept, curled in that
high-backed hump, little pulse of flesh,
heart in a box of bars? Was it
the hatch of crib bars in the night
light's glow that kept you clear of her?

Why didn't even the dogs awaken
in their crates? confined, contented
in their molded-plastic dens, while
you mounted stair by stair to where
I slept on the side of the bed
Stephen would use if he'd been home.

The first flash of knowing may have been
the worst, your hands already on me
in a sudden end to dreams. Was that
the instant that satisfied you most?

How orderly it was.
How well we understood
the way things would unfold.

You burnt off my sense of touch,
of smell, of self, with the hot metal
of your hands, the acrid smelt
of your sweat and sperm, the mutilation
of your knife where only lovers
and infants had come before.

This need not have happened
to have happened: you wait for me,
for any woman, there
in every darkness.

GELINEAU: The impetus for this poem was to acknowledge that, in some sense, no woman escapes the violence of the threat of rape — that, from preteen to old age, women can never really relinquish the thought that their sense of the world is shaped by their fear. For some of us, utterly shaped by it; for others, less so, but no woman escapes it entirely because it is a violence perpetrated on us merely for being female. I don't claim to equate threat of rape with rape itself, but the insidiousness of how that intimidation trims our lives is not insignificant. "Letter to My Rapist" actually grew out of a workshop I took many years ago with Marilyn Hacker. Each week, we were asked to write a poem in a different received form. When asked to write an epistolary poem, I thought to myself who would I write an undeliverable letter to, and that specter of implied violence that follows every woman, at every age, in every country, down every alley, into any bed she sleeps in, that threat we can never dodge, that menacing male presence, seemed to me the perfect person to address.

JUDITH GOEDEKE

Judith Goedeke became a seeker during a tantrum at age four, and over 60 years of seeking she has figured a few things out. She learned to laugh long and loud, in spite of early trauma. She lives a completely backward life. Saddled with early responsibility, she now plays, explores her creativity, and is unconditionally loved. She enjoys a large circle of family and friends and lives in a posh tree house with Charlie. A semi-retired acupuncturist and former teacher, she continues to devote herself to healing, now through radiant words. Her chapbook, *River of Silver Sky*, was released by Finishing Line Press in 2015.

FIFTIETH ANNIVERSARY

I wished for you a beautiful death
your face would be peaceful
and something of you would lift,
float long enough that I'd know you were okay
then like a dragonfly you would rise and drift away
a nine year old still lives a little in make believe
instead you were leaden and yellow
your breath rattled softly and was still
you just collapsed
there was no beauty
nothing peaceful
none of us was okay

I was sure you would come back
because mothers aren't allowed to die
so I looked for you after school
and at bedtime I stared into the darkness
night after night learning a little more about never
a little more about being alone in the world
a little more about taking care of my little sister
a little more about my tortured father
a little more about making him feel better in bed,
and wondering whether he'd kill me today or tomorrow
all in tiny bits, slowly, patiently

the other day a mouse died in the garage
leaving a single drop of blood on the concrete floor
the next day a baby mouse, one inch of pink and gray softness
lay on the empty spot, breathing hard, looking up at me
nowhere to run

THOUGHTS

it had to begin with a thought
one in a billion ideas just making the rounds
innocent ones and crazy ones, side by side
he rejected it many times before, nothing new
except this time there was
this time he allowed himself to toy with it
the way you do with things you'd never actually do
no harm in it, just a little private pleasure
and after a while he might have said well you've had your fun, that's enough
but this time it wasn't
so he tickled the idea, conjured the flesh of it
until something pricked awake, pranced around
and began slowly erasing his relentless, desperate life
the relief of it seeped in, dulled him, nothing to fear
he stroked it with details, gave himself anything he wanted
collapsed in warm waves of soothing, thrilling comfort
his pulse began to race, that's when it got real
that's when the thoughts began to happen
five
six
seven steps, each one a choice
eight, yes or no
nine to the doorway where his daughter lay sleeping
ten
eleven

GOEDEKE: Anger compelled me to write these poems. The enormous healing potential of the word powerfully spoken compels me to share these poems. The certainty that some of those in great need will find comfort in this volume compels me to share these poems. The certainty that by raising consciousness we draw closer to demanding and receiving effective protective action against repression, genital mutilation, human trafficking, war rape, limited reproductive rights, economic strangulation, and physical and sexual violence, compels me to share these poems.

I write to understand my own human experience more truthfully and deeply. I write in hopes good may come of it in the hearts and minds of others. This project will shine a light into a very dark place.

BARBARA GOLDBERG

Barbara Goldberg has authored four prize-winning poetry books, most recently *The Royal Baker's Daughter,* recipient of the Felix Pollak Poetry Prize. Her latest book, *Scorched by the Sun: Poems by Moshe Dor,* contains her translations of one of Israel's foremost poets. She and Dor also edited and translated three anthologies of contemporary Israeli poetry, including *After the First Rain: Israeli Poems of War and Peace.* Goldberg's work has appeared in *Paris Review*, *Poetry*, and *Best American Poetry.* Among her honors are two fellowships from the National Endowment for the Arts. A former senior speechwriter at AARP, she currently is Writer in Residence in American University's MFA program.

AFTER BABEL

One summer night a man burst into my room
brandishing a knife, looking for Sukie,
that "bitch with the big tits" he'd hitched
a ride with that afternoon. Odd that I
remember her name (it was long ago, I was in
another life). He was drunk, thick of tongue,
slow-witted. "I'm Joan," I lied, a simple
sound he could retain. But more. If I kept
my name from him I'd have something
he couldn't touch. It seemed to gentle him.
He settled on my bed, in for the long haul,
and with slurred syllables he rambled on about
a car, his new Trans Am, black and sleek,
it could do 170, 180, "Zoom," he said, his arm
slicing the air between us. Did I want to
ride in it, test it out?
                              It was raining, ziggurats
of lightning split the sky. I was more afraid
of breaking into pieces than of what he might do
then and there. I said no. "So, Joan," he said,
"Wanna fuck?" No, I said again, but he could
hold my hand, which he did, babbling on. He was

so difficult to understand; his speech
had no hard edge to it, no plosives, only
vowels flowing into each other without
restraint. Something about a mother
turning away, a father, a belt.
            We spent
hours like that until a wan sun seeped
into the room, I could see the dim
outline of his face, the scar zigzagging
across his chest, me stroking his hand, fatigue
taking hold. It gripped him too. We made
a date. He left.
                    Terror when it strikes, strikes
(it was long ago, it was night) first
in the bowels, then snakes up to lodge
in the throat. It burrows in. It has
a taste. It leaves a taste. Does he
remember what wasn't my name?

ALBANIAN VIRGIN

> *If a girl of the Klementi tribe fiercely objected to the proposed marriage, a blood*
> *feud could only be avoided by her swearing an oath that she would never marry.*
> *Such a woman was called an Albanian Virgin and ranked in the tribe as a man.*
>
> — Carolyn Heilbrun, *Reinventing Womanhood*

1.

The way he caught that horsefly
midair, the way he grinds his heel
into the dirt, taking pleasure
in the spider's slow death, the way
he throws a look at me as though
he already owns me —
I do not consent.

I shall smoke with the men.
I have seen them in the greying
light, their weapons close
to them always.

2.

The day is hot. My hair
is cropped. It is so still
I hear the bells clank
from the field. I swear the oath
before twelve witnesses
to forsake the intimate gestures
of all men, to remain chaste
as an unfreshened goat.

This night spent in solitude
on a rush mat, alone with the gravity
of my own body.

3.

I have learned to clip
the horns of goats, to slit
the throats of sheep
so the warm blood bathes
my fingers and the animal feels
no pain, so sharp is my blade.

I am carried by dreams to the field
where I lie on the earth flanked by goats,
push a pale wet form from my loins.
It struggles to rise on its spindly legs.
I look deep into my goat-child's eyes.

4.

I eat with the men.
I chew charred slabs of meat
with the men. We smoke together,
my rough trousers chafing
the flesh of my thighs.

I gaze at the women who sit
in tight circles, pounding
pestles into stone bowls.

My lungs fill
with harsh, comforting smoke.

GOLDBERG: Some years back, I won a poetry contest. The "prize" was a free weekend at an artist's farmhouse just outside Washington, DC. The farmhouse was lovely, in a shabby kind of way, large and airy. The artist was there when I arrived, as were a few other poets. The next day, she and the others left, all except one who was staying in a geodesic dome on the property. The next night, I was alone in the house. Because my room was bright in the mornings, I went to sleep with a long black sock around my eyes. Suddenly, I felt a presence in my room and ripped off the sock. A strange man, tall and drunk, stood by my bed. My first impulse was to soil myself. I saw he had a knife. I feared he would cut me up so badly that no one would recognize me. I thought of my two children growing up without me. I believed I would die.

He sat down on my bed and asked if I had a match. I actually did, but told him to look in the kitchen downstairs. Off he went, and I frantically looked out my window to see if I could crawl out to the roof, jump to the ground, and hide in the bushes. It was raining torrents and it was pitch black outside. The roof was steep and slippery. The jump itself could lead to serious injury. I ruled out hiding in the house because he might find me and become enraged. He returned with a lit cigarette and sprawled out on the bed, his knife visible at all times. He began talking about his father, his new Trans Am. He asked me my name. It turned out he was searching for the woman he had given a ride to that afternoon, the one staying in the dome.

Time passed. My goal was to keep him talking. I asked a lot of questions about his car. I could tell he was slow-witted, yet excited to be with a white woman from the city.

He asked if he could fuck me, but I suggested we hold hands instead. I was astonished when he agreed. I began to think I might live. He grew tired. I suggested we meet for a "date" the next afternoon and that he should dress up. He left at dawn without physically harming me.

I filed charges and appeared twice before a grand jury. They first dismissed all charges, claiming I had "seduced" the man. The second time I appeared with unwashed hair and baggy, outsized, clothing. I cried all the way through the questioning – on purpose. This time, there was a more favorable outcome. Why? Because clearly I was a helpless woman. And because of my tears.

The first poem to emerge from this experience was "After Babel," which describes in a precise, dispassionate, voice what happened. Later, I wrote more overtly about my anger, but disguised in the voice of "The Albanian Virgin."

SUCHI GOVINDARAJAN

Suchi Govindarajan works as a technical writer for an Australian company and also writes a monthly humor column for *Deccan Chronicle / The Asian Age*. In her spare time, she pretends to be a photographer and dreams of becoming an artist. Poetry is her first love. She hates brinjals (eggplants).

IN GOOD FAITH

The minister looked up from his porn video
To say the girl's character was in question
And so it was unfair to target the man
Who'd maybe broken a few laws
And just been violent.
(When were men ever the problem?)

The minister who was driven everywhere
By her coterie of security guards
Said girls should not go out after 7 pm —
Where was the need, anyway?
It's not like they needed to work
Or study, or live a full life.
(That was men's work.)

At the shop, the man was surprised
That the girl in pants spoke Kannada.
"If you are real Kannadiga," he said,
"Why to dress like Westerner?"
(And then he sat back in his Allen Solly shirt
And Park Avenue pants.)

"We are implementing dress code —
Indian wear for girls, Western formals for boys,"
Said the college professor,
"Because Western wear corrupts girls

And jeans corrupt everyone."
(And then she calmly collected bribes
From a trail of greedy parents
Who all agreed.)

The moral police broke into pubs
And hit women who were drinking,
Women who thought they were free.
"They are an insult to Hinduism," the police said,
"Unlike the sadhus at the Kumbh,
Who stride about naked
And smoke marijuana."
(They only bring Hinduism honor.)

And muftis and imams muffled girls' voices —
Apparently god had made a mistake
Handing out voice boxes and long hair,
And various other body parts,
To women, and it was imperative
That god not be reminded of it.
(Why rub salt in god's wounds?)

At a temple in the south,
The priest rubbed his bare tummy,
Folded his dhoti up, then pointed to a girl
And swore: "Tie up your hair. It is vulgar."
Then he turned to his flock and said,
"Don't focus on superficial things.
Try to live life with kindness."
In the movie, the famous star
Had a funny speech about rape
With references to women's body parts.
It was so funny that families
Roared in laughter and let their kids see it.
(Misogyny is best started early.)

Then, years later, the same star
Led a crusade on TV for women's rights
And cried when the women spoke of violence.

At the home, the woman was beaten
By the husband who said,
"She dominates me too much."
And her relatives agreed.
"Don't break up the family for your ego,"
They said to her "Think of the kids —
Isn't it better they have a father?
So what if they see violence every day?
At least they will have good Indian family values."

Meanwhile, on a street somewhere,
A banner flies in the air.
"Happy Women's Day," it says.
Up to 50% discount on all atrocities.
(Offer open while stocks last.)

GOVINDARAJAN: On 24 January 2009, a right-wing Hindu group called the Sri Ram Sena attacked girls in a pub in Mangalore, India, and claimed that the women were violating traditional Indian values. In December 2012, a woman was gang-raped in Calcutta, India. In response, Trinamool Congress MP Kakali Ghosh Dastidar dismissed the incident as "a misunderstanding" between "a woman" and her "clients," thereby suggesting that the victim was a sex worker. In February 2013, the Grand Mufti of Kashmir issued a fatwa against Kashmir's first all-female rock band, Pragaash, which maintained that music was un-Islamic. Pragaash was forced to disband. Lastly, the "Kumbh" refers to the Kumbh Mela, a mass Hindu pilgrimage, distinguished by the presence of many naked ascetics. Smoking marijuana is also common. Pictures of these men are widely circulated — this in a country where women are often accused of being immodest and succumbing to Western sins like drinking and smoking.

I wrote this poem a day before Women's Day, on 7 March 2013. My email inbox had been flooded earlier that week with discount coupons for handbags and dresses. Meanwhile, as a nation, we were still coming to terms with the rape that had happened in December 2012. I was troubled by the hypocrisy I noticed around me, in the things being said in public, and in private, about women. A small incident earlier that year also rankled. I had been on a photography tour to the temple-town of Melukote. We had stopped at a shop to buy some local delicacies, and the shopkeeper was taken aback that a woman in our group spoke Kannada, despite being in what he called "Western" clothes. He made a few sly remarks. It did not occur to him that he himself was also in "Western" clothes. It seemed to me to be indicative of the double-standards and hypocrisy in Indian society, when it came to women. And so I decided to take the subject head-on and write about it.

DEBBI MILLER GUTIERREZ

Debbi Miller Gutierrez is a poet, singer-songwriter, and children's-book author living in rural New Mexico. She is also treasurer and webmaster of the New Mexico State Poetry Society and vocalist/guitarist for the band Dog Star. Her first CD, *Anywhere but Where I Am,* is a compilation of 12 original songs about "trains, dogs, and other people's lives," and is available at CDBaby.com. Gutierrez's children's books (*The Pinecone Problem, Why Baby Sister Woke up from Her Nap,* and *Cactus Factory*) can be found on Amazon.

COLD AS A STONE

A Song for the Rain

He emptied his glass as the rain filled the sky;
becoming a gleam in the dark of his eye,
I desperately searched for a safe place to hide —
but I never cried. I went cold as a stone,
and then I sat quiet, wishing that I
was alone.

Two small hands clasped tightly in prayer;
his hands were tangled up in my hair.
My heart fled away so that I couldn't care —
but I never cried. I went cold as a stone,
and then I sat quiet, wishing to die
all alone.

The years waxed and the years waned;
love never came to me without pain.
The gleam in his eye burned a mark on my soul,
and I pray that someday I'll be whole.

I heard his last days passed in terrible pain;
the nothing I feel's not too hard to explain —
I'm empty inside and as dark as the rain —

but I never cry. I'm cold as a stone,
and now I sit quiet, wishing my heart
would come home.

GUTIERREZ: As a teen, I had a close friend whose father had molested her when she was young. The damage to her self-esteem was vast, but the "nothing" she felt upon her father's early and painful death did not fully resonate with me until I became involved with the CASA (Court Appointed Special Advocate) program many years later. The volume and gravity of the sexual, physical, and emotional abuse and neglect suffered by so many girls and young women, in just my little part of the world, spurred me to write several poems and songs, some of which I was asked to perform at program events. "Cold as a Stone" is one of those pieces, one that always elicits a hushed but deeply affected response when it is performed.

JOHN GUZLOWSKI

John Guzlowski's writing appears in Garrison Keillor's *Writer's Almanac,* the anthology *Blood to Remember: American Poets on the Holocaust, Ontario Review, North American Review, Salon.com, Rattle, Atlanta Review, Crab Orchard Review,* and elsewhere. Guzlowski's poems about his parents' experiences as slave laborers in Nazi Germany appear in his award-winning books *Lightning and Ashes* and *Third Winter of War: Buchenwald.* His first novel, *Suitcase Charlie,* about a serial killer in a neighborhood of Holocaust survivors, is available on Amazon, and his latest book about his parents, *Echoes of Tattered Tongues: Memories Unfolded,* has just been released by Aquila Polonica Press.

MY MOTHER WAS 19

Soldiers from nowhere
came to my mother's farm
killed her sister Genia's baby
with their heels
shot my grandma too

One time in the neck
then for kicks in the face
lots of times

They saw my mother
they didn't care
she was a virgin
dressed in a blue dress
with tiny white flowers

Raped her
so she couldn't stand up
couldn't lie down
couldn't talk

They broke her teeth
when they shoved
the dress in her mouth

If they had a camera
they would've taken her picture
and sent it to her

That's the kind they were

Let me tell you:
God doesn't give
you any favors
He doesn't say
now you've seen
this bad thing
but tomorrow
you'll see this good thing
and when you see it
you'll be smiling

That's bullshit

GUZLOWSKI: In 1942, German soldiers came to my mother's village in Eastern Poland and killed many people. A number of the women in my mother's village were raped. Those who survived were taken to concentration camps in Germany to work as slave laborers. My mother spent almost three years as a slave laborer. For most of her life, she would not talk about what happened, but toward the end of her life, she told me to tell people and to make sure they understood that she was not the only one this happened to.

RASMA HAIDRI

Rasma Haidri is an American writer living on the arctic seacoast of Norway. Her poetry and prose have appeared in many literary journals and anthologies in the United States, as well as in Norway, the UK, Canada, India, and Hong Kong. Her work has received the Southern Women Writers Association creative nonfiction award, the Wisconsin Academy of Sciences, Arts and Letters poetry award, and other recognitions.

ATMA ADITI ACHUTA

India is a woman
with bangles of gold, yellow silk
draped over a bronze arm
fingers elegant and long
at the end of a hand
lying in the dust, chopped
so the bangles fell off, one by one
bloodstained like fetters.

India is a woman
with slender long limbs
sheathed in folds of softest cotton
that lift and stretch and bend
as she steps into a rickshaw
where two men already seated
smile and wag their heads
and make room for her
between them.

India is a woman
partitioned by a retreating army
into East and West, Us and Them
split along the red rape line
where her blood, like a river,
would have carried sons into the world
and daughters.

India is a woman
who trusts the strength of men
put in position to protect her
but again and again she is flung
like pieces of meat between them
her golden brown body devoured, ripped
by their white gnashing teeth.

A SHORT HISTORY OF LOVE

I came black-eyed
out of the stairwell
but the parking attendant
wasn't looking
and all the windshields
were blind

later in my room
of cement
in my whirligig
chair
I hunched
over the page
pencils loaded
aimed
shooting you
full of lead
     pow
          pow

that first winter
in White Sands
the dunes were snow
a wedding cake
meringue

where you crossed
and re-crossed
on spindle legs
trudging my name
in the sand
we didn't wait
to see the letters
crumble

we negotiated the moon
craters of Texas
in love
in a rental car
moving toward a threshold
a passage
but El Paso
was only a bridge
that went both ways

there were combs for my hair (mother of pearl)
a statue of Mary (mother of God)
and a rug
graven with Justice
or Aphrodite holding her children
Eros and Anteros
the firstborn and the afterthought
the give
the take
the me
the you
it was a blanket
a thing to own
to roll a laughing child in
or keep the wall
where we hung it
warm

in Wisconsin
they make you wait seven days
to buy a gun
three days to get married
they check your blood
they show you his penis free of germs
they show you the dotted line
they put the dripping nib
in your hand
you write
your crippled name

we sat in the car
our seatbelts buckled
the parking lot
abandoned
I abandoned
he throwing spittle words
a policeman knocked
on my glass
    ma'am?

           ma'am?

there was ice
it was a frozen country
everything was fine, fine

HAIDRI: Because poetry can name and speak for what is most hidden, I have written these poems. It is a silent language that can be heard when you are in a situation where words fail, when there is just the emotion and the awe or horror or shock, all of which make up the poem you try to write and sometimes succeed in writing, in part. It is never a whole, just a glimpse, and so you write again, something else, something more. Each poem releases a small notch of the jaw, the locked language of experience.

Along with the rest of the world, I was stunned, then outraged, at the rapes in India in 2012. My father was from India and I have a strong affection for and identification with the country, its glorious past and its shattering fragmentation in the wake of colonialism. The poem's title is composed of three female names that are not those of the rape victims but, instead, have a symbolic meaning: Atma is the soul or self; Aditi signifies consciousness, the past-future, and fertility; Achuta is another name for Sri Krishna, and it means imperishable.

The other poem is perhaps a bit awkward because it is more personal and difficult, a piece I honed as if attempting to crack a polished crystal façade with a toffee hammer. That, too, is a type of poetry.

MARY HAMRICK

Mary Hamrick was born in New York but moved to Florida when she was a young girl. Her writing often reflects the contrast between her Northern and Southern upbringing. Her work has appeared in a variety of publications, including *Blast Furnace, decomP, Mad Hatters' Review,* and *Rosebud Magazine.*

GINETTA'S SECRET

Stan swats his girls
five shades lighter than blueberries.
His secret history — a shameful thing.

Sometimes my lips swell like Brazilian cherries
and I swivel away from him. I swivel toward him,
burnt useless under his gaze.

And sometimes by 1 am, he's whittling notches into this tropical body,
so I come around to *his* way: his drive, his wish, his craving.
Nasty blood vessels pop on his forehead —

Must I beg again?
My body is a quiet room of imperfection:
Strip off the skin and look for yourself!

Late morning, Momma visits and says,
*Ginetta, you have dark silent-movie eyes
that sing ballads of last night.*

Huddled in the kitchen, kneading flour into dough,
I see that my womb is exposed on a long, powdered table
that fingers are pinching as they crush, lift, slam — vigoroso.

Tired limbs slip down onto a chair that is all-knowing
and full of devil details. Momma sits like a man.
Her long cotton dress is open wide; her floured apron

reeks of citrus fragrance. Let's see, Momma —
how can I describe pain? My small mistakes will resurrect
hands that knuckle the body sticky-sweet.

Old woman, let me tell you the secrets of each night
that shies and smalls a woman,
how after the evening meal, he will holler, *Lay down!*

Whey-faced, I will smell like almond milk;
my lips will swell like Brazilian cherries
as I slide into place under the slope of Stan's bony body.

HAMRICK: I was once asked this question: Should poetry upset or soothe the reader?
My answer was that it depended on the mood of the poem. I prefer using the word
"rouse" over the word "upset." Although, when it comes to politics or abuse, the word
"upset" might prevail. At times, it is correct to move the reader with a poem's cruel mouth.

"Ginetta's Secret" is based upon two women I once knew. A middle-aged co-worker
was shot by her husband after years of abuse, but she fortunately survived the gunshot
wound. The other woman was a next-door neighbor at an apartment complex. We
were both married and in our early twenties, and she felt confident to ask this favor: If
you ever hear anything out of the ordinary, please call the police. I felt a kinship with
my neighbor because I asked her to return the favor.

PATRICK CABELLO HANSEL

Patrick Cabello Hansel was one of four poets selected for the 2008–2009 Mentor Series by the Loft Literary Center in Minneapolis, and he was also a 2011 Minnesota State Arts Board Artist Initiative grantee. His poems have appeared in *Hawai'i Pacific Review, Painted Bride Quarterly, Parachute, Turtle Quarterly, Main Channel Voices, Passager, The Cresset, Perfume River Poetry Review, The Meadowland Review,* and other journals. Hansel has studied with such poets as Philip Schultz, Ed Bok Lee and Jude Nutter, and his novella *Searching* was serialized over 33 issues in *The Alley News* in Minneapolis.

SALVADORAN STORY

We sit on sacks of corn
donated by
The People of the United States,
and listen to the woman
tell how her daughter
and her daughter-in-law
were *disappeared.*
When she went to the police,
they took off her blouse,
heated their machetes
in the fire
and held the tips
under the folds
of her breasts
until they were done,
and then they sent her home.

DON'T KIDNAP MY MOM BEFORE
MY FIRST COMMUNION

for Janette

She crouches behind
the stove on the 4th floor
of a building with no elevator,
no front door, no smells
but rum, urine, frijoles,
flowers, fried fish,
t-shirts and pork.
She breathes as softly
as her mind will let her,
with knocking at the door.

Who could it be?
A machete?
A tiny telegram from Tio?
An angel whose face
is on backwards?
The little peephole
is a magic pipeline:
good things come in small packages
and bad things, too.

Her body is twelve, skinny
enough to squeeze behind
the stove, tight enough
to attract mustaches,
fingertips, *maldiciones.*
Her eyes are mousetraps
being nibbled.

She prays with her thumb,
her nightgown, the stuffed
bear she thought
to bring along.

She remembers
the story from First Communion —
the five thousand fed,
five little breads,
two small fish
given by a young boy.
"But it could have been you,"
the pastor said. "It could have
been your hands
holding up the miracle."
She looks at her hands,
browned like stove grease,
white knuckled, red
in the creases.
I will be bread, she thinks.
I will be a fish:
a tiburón, a shark,
something that is
difficult to catch.

FREE TRADE, CUERNAVACA, APRIL 2007

The older one is still in her school uniform,
green plaid jumper over a white top.
It is a size too small, and dust rides
up from the hem like a tongue of flame.
The younger girl crowds into our talk, all
elbows and eyes, scent of corn and wasted gum.
Thirty necklaces hang over the shoulder flounce
of her faded coral dress and flap at us
like sea urchins. She is too large for her skin.
She pounds the moist air into our faces:
Buy a ring, una joya, necklaces
Solo 50 pesos, dos por 80, cómprame más.
Even when we buy, it doesn't stop her plea:
Otra, otra, otra más.

I show her my wallet
with pictures of my wife, my teenager,
and my first grader, a year or two younger
than her, smiling in school. She grabs it up
as if it were a fish about to jump
out of her boat. For a second,
there is parity in our hands. Free trade.
Miraculous catch. *Daughter,*
sister, stranger, let go of my faces.
When I ask her name, she drops her head
and mutters into the paving stones long ago
pressed into the burnt earth by Cortés
and his gang of gods.
For a wounded moment,
she stops talking, and we each look
down at our feet. If I were Jacob, and she
my heaven-sent adversary in the desert,
would we wrestle to the end? Would her
words put my hip out of joint? Would she

lift up her head and float like a cloud? No.
We buy. We sell. We part. We leave
the plaza with its memory of Aztec stones.
The girls spread their eyes for customers,
shoes slipping over rocks still dripping.
Their socks have all but forsaken them.

HANSEL: During the past thirty-plus years, I have worked as a pastor in poor neighborhoods in the Bronx, Philadelphia and Minneapolis, including many immigrant communities, where women and girls are especially vulnerable to violence and oppression. These three poems relate to actual people I have known: a Salvadoran woman who was tortured during the military government just for asking about her "disappeared" daughter and daughter-in-law; my goddaughter, whose mother was kidnapped in the Bronx to "settle" a drug debt incurred by an uncle, and whose family lived under constant fear; and two girls selling jewelry to tourists in the old city center of Cuernavaca.

JANINE HARRISON

Janine Harrison is a poet, fiction writer, and nonfictionist, who teaches creative writing at Purdue University, Calumet. Her work has appeared in, or is forthcoming from, *A&U*, *CREDO*, and other publications. Indiana Poet Laureate George Kalamaras selected her poem "Weight of Silence" for inclusion in his 2014 National Poetry Month spotlight on Indiana poets on the *Indiana Humanities* website, and she was also a featured reader in his Five Corners Poetry Exchange. Harrison leads the Indiana Writers' Consortium, is a teaching artist and arts activist, and is currently finishing her first poetry collection, *Weight of Silence*, about Haiti's history, issues, and promise, and her experience teaching there.

As It Bloomed

First slate-gray hair
first under-eye furrows
mile markers already met.
I was ready.
"Love your belly,"
advised a friend.
And I did.
But he did not.

As it bloomed
I rubbed it like
I was my own Buddha;
I read it bedtime stories,
Snow White and *The Hobbit*.
I sang it
the "Alphabet" song,
my voice nearly on key
perhaps for the first time.

As it bloomed
His eyes hollowed.
I ingested vitamins;
he inhaled
from a glass pipe.
And came home to us
without himself.

As it bloomed
I intuited *it* was *she.*
I loved her,
journaled to her,
dreamt and planned
our span ahead.
I pried open spaces,
inserting peaceful thoughts
to send to her.
But as she bloomed
He withered.
His full lips
encompassing
my left breast,
he sucked her milk
hard,
yelling,
"That's how you
suck my cock,
bitch!"

As she bloomed
I remembered my name
and found her one,
origin, the same:
Grace.

She bloomed
despite his poison
saturating soil
otherwise rich.
She bloomed
despite his threat,
"I'll kill you
and the baby
right now!"

Six years later
He struggles
in parched dirt.
She is still
blooming.

HARRISON: In her essential volume *On Lies, Secrets, and Silence: Selected Prose 1966–1978,* Adrienne Rich states, "When a woman tells the truth she is creating the possibility for more truth around her." Even though we address violence against women in more direct and active ways than we did several decades ago, the same issues persist across the globe. We need work such as *Veils, Halos & Shackles* to add to the truth, to help more women become empowered to voice their truths. Only by continually adding evidence to the existing body can we illustrate the continued prevalence and relevance of the problem and have it taken seriously and addressed.

In Fall 2012, I went to Haiti to teach English as a Second Language, and as I was researching the country, I learned about the rampant rapes occurring in the remaining earthquake camps — homeless women being impregnated — and was sickened. On a much more personal note, I was physically abused by my alcoholic father, molested by my eighth-grade science teacher, physically abused by an alcoholic boyfriend, and physically and sexually abused by another man, who was addicted to drugs. Those experiences, cumulatively, have extensively affected my life, causing considerable pain, anger, and sorrow. I want a better world for the generations to come.

RACHEL HEIMOWITZ

Rachel Heimowitz is the author of the chapbook *What the Light Reveals* (Tebot Bach Press, 2014). Her work has appeared in *Poet Lore, Spillway, Crab Orchard Review,* and *Prairie Schooner,* and she has been nominated for the Pushcart Prize. She is currently the editor of *arc-24*, the literary journal of The Israel Association of Writers in English, and has just received her MFA from Pacific University.

NANAA AL GENINA

> *"I own my body; it's not the source of anyone's honor."*
> — Amina Tyler

We refuse to stay
wrapped away,

inside stone walls,
under a dry sun.

The garden calls us,
nanaa al genina —

the smell of spearmint
and sweat tickles

our noses, lifts
the tips of our breasts;

lemon verbena
and cool air

drift to our lips;
our hands reach to crush

the supple mint
under our fingertips. We

can't help ourselves,
so determined are we

to discard these crow
clothes, uncover our faces,

step into the garden
without looking back.

And if this means you will raise
your hand against us

and our names will become
emblazoned

across some woman's bare
torso, then so be it.

Come, sister, feel
the spark in our hips

as our breath mists —
shway, shway — slowly

into the garden's
climbing green. We

can open ourselves
like the twang of the oud

opens to the ney,
deep in the shadow and shade,

na, na, na'ana,
nanaa al genina.

PURE WATER POURED

In memory of Ruth Fogel, d. March 2011

Three women move together without
words, light candles, fold sheets, fill

pail after pail with water.
They sing psalms, voices

weaving through the candlelight.
Ruth, on the table, her hair,

the hair he would push back
from her face, ten fingers splayed

like a comb, now falls, full and brown,
down the sides of the table, her body

straight, breasts still round
with mother milk. The women

gently comb her hair,
clean her feet, wash

the gashes on her face,
her arms, the bullet hole

in her chest; her wounds
bathed until they stand,

jagged and white in candlelight.
The bloody washcloths

folded carefully, stacked
together with Ruth's

blood-scabbed nightgown,
the bathroom carpet,

three teeth that scattered
like beads; now gathered

to be buried with her. Pail
after pail of pure water poured.

The women chant and sing.
They dress her in hand-sewn shrouds,

stiff and white. The avnet
is tied around her waist

and, like an enormous hand,
the blue and white tallit

covers her: no casket, her body
returned to the land.

HEIMOWITZ: "Nanaa Al Genina" is actually the title of a Sudanese love song, "In the Mint Garden." This poem came about when I saw a picture of a beautiful, bare-breasted woman, holding up her fist with a slogan written across her chest and an old man coming up behind her to give her a kick. The article was about a young Tunisian woman, Amina Tyler, who had joined a radical feminist group from the Ukraine called the Femens. The Femens protest for women's issues throughout Europe, often posing topless with their slogans appearing on their bodies. Though Amina was from a Muslim family, she had posted a picture of herself topless, and across her chest, written in Arabic, were these words: "I own my body; it's not the source of anyone's honor." Though I am not a radical feminist, I understood that what Amina was trying to say was absolutely right. Each woman needs to have the freedom to dress as she wants, the freedom and right to do what she wants with her own body. After the picture appeared, Amina disappeared and the Femens demanded her release. That was what I saw in the picture. I took the poem one step further. Centering the poem around a romantic song about lovers meeting in a mint garden was a good choice for two reasons. First, I love the song, but when I wrote the poem I used both Arabic and Hebrew words, and many words that appear in both languages (Nanaa — *mint* in Arabic — is Na'ana, *mint* in Hebrew). I wrote the poem specifically this way because I believe this is a Jewish as well as a Muslim problem.

"Pure Water Poured" is about the religious preparation for burial of the body of a woman who was killed in a terror attack in the town of Itamar in 2011. Ruth was the mother of six children and a teacher. She and her husband were strong members of their community. The attack occurred on a Friday night, which is the Jewish sabbath, a day of peace. Two young men, 18 and 19 years old, entered the house. Using knives, they immediately killed Ruth's husband and three of her six children, including her four month old daughter, whose head was left attached only by the skin at the back of her neck. Ruth fought the terrorists alone, sustaining multiple wounds before the terrorists finally shot her with a gun they had stolen from a neighbor's house. The three children who survived did so because they were sleeping in unexpected places. One boy was asleep on the living room couch. One was in bed with his brother, hunched under the covers. The third was their eldest daughter, 12 years old, who was at Scouts when the attack occurred and was the one to find her family when she got home. In the poem, I tried to demonstrate the beauty of the religious beliefs and practices, as well as the love and connection between women. I felt very close to Ruth, though I never met her in life. I too have six children and raised them here. Ruth is me. I have written many poems about her.

TAMARA L. HERNANDEZ

Tamara L. Hernandez was born and raised in El Paso, Texas. She earned a Bachelor of Arts degree in Psychology from Texas State University in San Marcos, Texas, and is working on a Master of Arts in Interdisciplinary Studies with concentrations in Communication and Leadership from the University of Texas at El Paso. The unique social position of growing up along the US/Mexico border has given Hernandez a vivid understanding of the difference an imaginary line can make in terms of quality of life. As a result, she has developed a deep and compelling interest in border issues, border culture, and border life.

GARDEN OF ROSES

The dying garden
of Roses
near
the cemetery   hides
its rows of   rose
roots
and   bones
no hope
seeks
to find
the weeds
overly   grown
violently
uncontrollable
hidden killers.

Each   and every
flowered   petal
laid to rest
     lost within
its shadowed
darkness

and
quiet
of a silenced crypt.

Each   and every
Flower picked
beaten   broken
and   bloodied
ripped

                            apart
stained

                            in pieces
smothered by a
fatal carpet
of dirt.
We watch
each and every
thing
weakened
as they wilt
                            withering away.
Death turned   dust
to ashes
in our mouths.
And   the garden
it
grows
with new rows
of   each and every
flowered

                            dying
Rose.

HERNANDEZ: "Femicide" is the mass murder of women simply because they are women. It is the term that has been coined in response to the murders of nearly 400 young women on the US-Mexico border in the city of Juárez, just across the border from El Paso, Texas.

Regarding the femicide in Ciudad Juárez: In the early 1990s, Ciudad Juárez, a large Mexican city that borders El Paso, Texas, began to see a sharp and sudden increase in violence against women. Women began disappearing at alarming rates, only for their bodies to be found later, often sexually assaulted and mutilated, near public areas or in empty desert lots on the outskirts of the city. It has been determined that the majority of these women lived in poorer areas of the city and were traveling to or from work at the time of abduction. Most were young, pretty, and had similar features. Some were pregnant (in Juárez, it is not uncommon for girls as young as 15 or 16 to get pregnant, especially those living in the impoverished areas of the city). While it is difficult — if not impossible — to find statistical information on the exact number of women who have been murdered in this brutal fashion in Ciudad Juárez over the past 20 years, most publications estimate that number to be more than 400.

Many argue that despite the magnitude of these atrocities, the Mexican government has failed to provide an adequate response to these ongoing murders. The general consensus is that the murders have been seemingly dismissed by authorities, the crimes poorly investigated, and the victims typically blamed for their ill-met fates. This alleged failure can be demonstrated in the fact that these femicides have remained prevalent in the region for nearly twenty years. The murders have never been solved. The ongoing femicide has gained world-wide notoriety, inspiring the creation of numerous documentaries, a major motion picture, books, news articles, and advocacy organizations. This topic is incredibly difficult for me. It always has been. And, to write this, I must ignore the black smears of wet mascara on my fingers as I try to wipe the stinging pain, anger, and frustration away.

Almost 10 years ago, I became obsessed with the stories of the murdered women of Juárez. I drowned myself in books about them. I pored over articles in newspapers and magazines and lost myself in countless documentaries. I used my research to write papers for classes, exploring different ideas and theories that could explain the social circumstances that would allow these murders to continue so openly, with such obvious impunity. I had recurring nightmares of dark, empty, desert fields lined with pink crosses and plastic flowers. Scholars have termed this phenomenon "femicide" or "feminicide," but I always thought the terms never truly described the murder of women for simply being women that is really a barbaric atrocity. What other way is there to describe a society that continues to allow the brutal, savage, slaughter of innocent girls, young women — our mothers, daughters, sisters?

I realize that, in addition to being human and being female, my personal background is a major component of my inclination to identify with the women of Juárez. After they were married, my grandparents migrated to El Paso from Ciudad Juárez, in search of better work and a better life. I often think about what my life might have been like if this hadn't happened. Who would I be if my grandparents had stayed in Juárez? Would I be working in a maquila? Would I be one of *them?* What about my mother, daughter, sister?

This poem is for these women. Each and every one of them.

WILLIAM HEYEN

William Heyen, a former Senior Fulbright Lecturer in American Literature in Germany, has received NEA, Guggenheim, American Academy & Institute of Arts & Letters, and other fellowships and awards. His work has appeared in hundreds of anthologies and magazines, and he is the editor or author of more than thirty books, among them *Crazy Horse in Stillness*, winner of 1997's Small Press Book Award for Poetry; *Shoah Train: Poems*, a finalist for the 2004 National Book Award; and *A Poetics of Hiroshima*, a Chautauqua Literary & Scientific Circle selection in 2010. Three new books of poetry and the first two volumes of his journal appeared in 2012 and 2013.

MOONLIGHT IMPERATIVES

Consider the plantation mistress who knows her husband lusts for
 & seeds their slaves.

Consider the mistress whose husband releases himself in her after re-
 leasing himself in those, & vice versa.

Consider the mistress watching her husband return in moonlight
 from their slave quarters.

Consider the mistress whose newborn is attended by her husband's
 mulatto daughter.

Consider the mistress who maintains her face in the face of other mistresses
 who keep their faces

while tea & honeycakes are served by slaves sired by her husband
 &/or son.

Consider the mistress's emotions when the master's bastards
 are auctioned off,

when money from these sales buys her lace, silver, porcelain, her livery
 which will never

take her where she needs to be even if she prays for absolution.
   Consider the mistress

who every morning whipped Araminta Ross, a girl whose hair
   had never been combed,

who had to scutch flax, who had to wade into waist-high water
   to remove muskrats

from traps, who put on thickest clothes to try to protect herself
   from the mistress

who wielded that whip as though she were breaking silence with
   her iniquitous husband

for what he'd inflicted on her. Consider the muskrat's sodden fur & its blood
   & intestines in Araminta's palms,

its fetid smell, its eyes & snout, & the snapping turtles' work, the leeches,
   & the trap's teeth to reset, to reset.

To reset, understand the mistress watching the master return in moonlight
   to their slave quarters.*

HEYEN: "Moonlight Imperatives" came to me in a rush years ago. Since writing is a process of discovery, I didn't know what-all I intended, except that I wanted to reach out to that abused girl within that dangerous forced misery of removing dead muskrats from traps. And reach, too, that vindictive slave-owner's wife who takes out her husband's iniquities on a child. I'd read this story of heroic Araminta Ross/Harriet Tubman somewhere, considered it for a time — is my poem's speaker telling not just his listener but *himself,* eight times, to consider the degradations of slavery? — and realized that the girl's travail here was the epitome of such systematic violence against other human beings. *This* was reality, not that most romantic of all themes, plantation moonlight, that repulsive swoon-song of the Old South.

---

* In 1849 Araminta Ross escaped from slavery and changed her name to Harriet Tubman (1820–1913). Tubman became one of America's greatest abolitionists.

As I read it now, "Moonlight Imperatives," as it challenges us to understand/imagine the ramifications of rape, as it tells revolting stories, is a faithful poem, believes in poetry's potential to help us "reset" ourselves toward the evocation of our better angels.

Romi Jain

Romi Jain is a writer, Indian art designer, novelist, and vice president of the *Indian Journal of Asian Affairs*. Her creative works include *The Storm Within* (2008; 2011), *Poetry! You Resurrect Me* (2011), and *Voices of Rocks in the Dusk* (2012). Her poems have appeared or are forthcoming in such anthologies as *Family Matters* and *Poems from Conflicted Hearts,* and in such literary journals as *Off the Coast* and *Munyori Literary Journal.* Jain is a recipient of a research grant award from the Gerald R. Ford Presidential Foundation, has contributed articles on China to refereed international journals, and has published in *Asia Times Online* and *The Diplomat.*

Acid Attack

Such an innocuous thing frightens her.
A plastic bottle!

She used to take it to school carrying lime juice
which when emptied would look helpless
when a whiff of wind would knock it over
and in her bag she would give it refuge.

To some men, it's a rifle
in which to load bullets of acid,
whose phosphoric masculinity tells them:
"Go, disfigure her, how dare she say 'no!'"

And they invade as barbarians,
ravaging a land they can't conquer!
Buildings are re-built, we know.
Plain structures brought down to zero ground
can dream of appearing as magnificent palaces.

But ask a girl who has been abandoned by dreams,
whose life
scars have swallowed up.

When you find her laughing heartily,
do you find her laughter genuine?
Her laughter is the wavering steps of someone
marching toward an abyss.
She realizes time and again
that a life of love and kids is not for her.
And the contorted mouth that she would enjoy
using to tease her friends
has become the permanent imprint on her face
that teases her devilishly.

Ask a girl who fears passing by the *Mohar* street
where she grew up watching pretty ladies
buy ornaments and cosmetics. This is the street where
she first became shy of men who turned around to see her.

Ask a girl who perfectly matches the darkness of her mind
with the darkness of the night, in whose union
she keeps tossing in bed, crying. When she dozes off
fortunately and eventually, dawn comes to rob her of peace:
she wishes to run away to a place where nights prevail
and no brightness exists,
where she doesn't see herself, nor do others see her.

They, the celebrities, now pat her on her shoulder
praising her courage that she survived.
She's expected to smile to be an inspiration to those
who dislike their lives.

She's expected to appear cheerful,
to lift her family out of trauma.
She's expected to scold her tears:
"Come on, by now you should have dried!"
She's expected to tell her pain:
"Like a dark sheet that is supposed to fade
in the sun of time, you must subside!"

And they, her attackers, have settled into their lives.
They nonchalantly go about in their lives.
They have daughters, I've heard.
But their consciences refuse to rise.

JAIN: An acid attack is a horrifying act that not only damages a woman's face or body but leaves a deep scar on her mind and life. She not only undergoes tremendous physical pain but suffers from immense mental agony over the loss of normal or beautiful looks and the ruined prospects of marriage and a good job. Acid attacks have been common in South Asian countries, though developed countries are not completely untouched.

SHENIZ JANMOHAMED

Sheniz Janmohamed is an author, spoken-word artist, and freelance writer, based in Toronto, Canada. She is the founder of Ignite Poets, a youth spoken-word initiative with an emphasis on social awareness. Her work as been featured at the TedX Youth Conference (Toronto, 2010), the Indian Summer Festival (Vancouver, 2012), and the Jaipur Literature Festival (2013). Her book *Bleeding Light* (TSAR, 2010) is a collection of English ghazals that explores a woman's journey through night. *Bleeding Light* has received international praise and has been taught in numerous Canadian academic institutions, including York University and the University of Toronto.

KALI MA

for Jyoti Singh Pandey, the Delhi rape victim

You break the bones in the body: The body who breaks the bones of women.
Your black milk flows into the mouths of men who dare to trample women.

Queen of the night: you have birthed dusk from dawn, coal from diamond.
You carry the weight of life, breathing fire into the breasts of women.

Your trident is our spine. Your hue is the bottomless ocean in our wombs.
Every strand of your hair is a quill, pricking the wells in the hearts of
     women.

Oh, three-eyed warrior, fierce and loving. You see everything beyond sight.
Your necklace clanks with skulls. You are the Dark Mother in all women.

We embrace your ebony shadow. Our skin gleams black, like hematite.
Bleeding with rage and renewal, we rewrite stories men have written for
     women.

Change your clothes. Keep your eyes down. Stop tempting men with your looks.
We reject poison from their foaming mouths: tar that once stuck to the ribs
     of women.

Kali Ma, your tongue hangs from our tongues. We refuse to sew our lips
  shut.

Israh* will scream until her throat burns: *We were not born to simply
  woo men!*

JANMOHAMED (ISRAH): When I heard about the Delhi gang rape, I was furious.
I vacillated between extreme rage and deep sadness. For days, I couldn't make sense
of what happened, or why. One evening, I was sitting at a dinner table with friends,
and the news of Jyoti's death flashed across the screen. Tears welled up in my eyes,
my throat burned, and I was stunned into silence. For the next few days, I sat with
the images of Kali Ma, and read about her powerful, fierce compassion. Despite the
hellish appearance of Kali Ma, she is also known as the "Mother Goddess." Kali Ma's
dual nature of wrath and compassion resonated deeply with me and echoed many of
the sentiments of the women around me. We wanted to protect and nurture, but also
to find justice. Many protesting women and men in India and around the world were
tapping into this *Shakti.*

"Kali Ma" is an invocation to Kali Ma and a call to women and men everywhere to
reclaim their strength and stand for justice and equality. I mention men, too, because
they are also rediscovering this sacred feminine principle.

I read "Kali Ma" for the first time at the Jaipur Literature Festival in 2013, a little over
a month after the Delhi gang rape took place. Every time I peered into a dimly lit bus
on the roads of Delhi and Jaipur, I was reminded of Jyoti.

---

* "Israh" is the author's pen name.

JENNIFER JEAN

Jennifer Jean's debut poetry collection *The Fool* was released by Big Table Publishing in 2013. Her poetry chapbooks include *The Archivist, Fishwife,* and *In the War,* and her poems have appeared in such journals as *Drunken Boat, Denver Quarterly, Caketrain, Poets/Artists,* and *Tidal Basin Review.* Jean is co-director of the Morning Garden Artist Retreats, poetry editor at *Mom Egg Review,* and administrative editor at *Talking/Writing Magazine.* She also leads Free2Write poetry workshops for sex-trafficking survivors and is on the advisory board of the Massachusetts Poetry Festival.

TRAIN

We're not like them. Phone-sex girls tease
men on the wire
for nickels on the minute,
for fractions of a penny on the word.
Their masterminded words
like vaginas, like wormholes, like succubi,
like the fingers of the animated
dead pushing men in little wagons
over a little hill. The men give a weak *weeeeeeeeeee.*
Then crawl out the transport
still lonely. *We're not like them.*
At least, say the phone-sex girls
about streetwalkers, stiletto-stomping down the block,
who follow through on the threat —
give a B.J. for a 50, a backdoor for a Benjamin —
who choose to quick-kill
desire. They don't know the body
is the soul. *We are not*
like them, whisper the streetwalkers about the slaves
brought up from Tenancingo, from Odessa,
from Portland. Tricked
and trafficked, locked up by fist,
by force-fed dope,

by "mamchkis" or "boyfriends" or blockbusters
like *Pretty Woman. We're not like*
them, think some old slaves
about those tight slaves
pimped by parents,
the little girls ripped
apart. The daughters who moan, *Mommy…*
while a "train" of men shout, *Shut your fucking mouth.*

JEAN: This poem is from my manuscript on sex-trafficking in America — tentative title: *Object.* I chose this title because it works on several levels: first, as an indicator of what buyers think they're getting when they purchase a human being; second, as an indicator of the trafficked person's ignored or violently silenced NO; and third, as a plea to readers to say NO to objectification and all forms of trafficking

As for why I'm writing about this — I've met many modern abolitionists who tell the same story I tell: I was at church one Sunday and heard a sermon about a grisly encounter with trafficking, about trafficking stats and survivor stories; I was so horrified and full of sorrow that I knew instantly I had to do something proactive. Yet, as I've interviewed survivors for a blog run by Amirah (a survivor advocacy group), I've realized that my life has been riddled with my own encounters with objectification — that there are experiences that I haven't processed, and certainly haven't written about, that give me the foundation to talk about this scourge of the 21st century, which is rightly called "slavery."

Some things to know about "Train": Tenancingo (in Mexico), Odessa (in Ukraine), and Portland, Oregon (in America) rank high on the list of cities where sex-trafficking occurs most often in the world; "mamochka" is what a female pimp or second-in-command manager is called if she's from a Slavic country like the Ukraine; and, finally, a "train" is a forced initiation into prostitution. Usually a pimp will lock an unsuspecting girl into a room with ten or more men who rape her one by one. Soon after, she's sent out to troll the streets for "clients."

MICHAEL LEE JOHNSON

Michael Lee Johnson lived ten years in Canada during the Vietnam era. Today he is a poet, freelance writer, photographer, and small-business owner in Itasca, Illinois, who has been published in more than 850 small-press magazines in 27 countries. He edits ten poetry websites and has released *The Lost American: From Exile to Freedom* as well as several chapbooks of his poetry, including *From Which Place the Morning Rises*, *Challenge of Night and Day*, and *Chicago Poems*.

BATTERED BEHIND DARK GLASSES

An otherwise beautiful lady
with eyes matted and closed
is not exactly sleeping.

The trouble goes deeper,
the doctor has a laser-
light drill penetrating her eyes
that have turned thunderstorm-
black with smudges of red and pink.

She tells herself this will never
happen again, there will be no
rebirth with him.

In idle hours she self-nurses
a cave of hurts. The lights are off;
her eyes are bruised and burning.

In the morning, still in bed, she looks in a mirror,
her face thickened with puff and irony.
She weeps splintered sounds.

Above her head on the lamp desk the alarm clock keeps ticking,
across the room, around the corner, the refrigerator keeps humming.

The man who had his way is dark in her, like distant echoes embedded in a memory or shadow.

She owes him nothing. He hears none of her sounds.

JOHNSON: "Battered Behind Dark Glasses" is a reflection on domestic violence over the ages. Only recently, under duress of penalty and law, has this trend started to subside in some countries. This poem is a personal reflection on years and days passed by... the 1950s, the 1960s and, unfortunately, even today. My goal is to reflect social conditions and stories of the now, the past, the present.

ELIZABETH D. JOHNSTON

Elizabeth D. Johnston teaches writing, literature, and Gender Studies at Monroe Community College in Rochester, New York. Her poems have appeared, or will appear, in *The Muse: An International Journal of Poetry, Organs of Vision and Sense, Trivia: Voices of Feminism, Yellow Medicine Review,* and *B,* a collection of poetry inspired by Barbie. Her poetry is influenced by her scholarly work in Gender Studies and tends to center on issues of women's experiences. When she is not teaching or writing, she facilitates community writing workshops for breast cancer survivors and survivors of sexual assault.

DEAD IN ABSENTIA

*for Natalee Holloway, vanished in Aruba May 30, 2005;
declared dead in absentia, January 12, 2012*

What did you know of life's meanness?
In gym chosen last? Beloved cat
killed by car? Boy
who didn't call?

Dead in absentia, and only sixteen.
What did you know of regret?
Of shame that cocoons
you in bed for days? Guilt
you live with and reframe?
You made only one mistake worth counting.

Dead in absentia
you don't get to earn
forgiveness, the redemption we grant ourselves
as years lapse into decades, and decades
into perspective.

You won't grow old
counting wrinkles, lamenting
foolish youth, tears you wasted,

beauty slipped like dandelion snow from your hands.
You — hollow stem,
unbranched and leafless.

Dead in absentia
you are always liminal —
tease of smile, glimpse of shoulder.
We crane our necks to see
outside the photo's frame —
the danger you did not expect,
the threat we know to look for.

Grown wise, we keep our heads raised,
dip only hands to drink.
But you were dizzy with life's pleasures,
gulping noisily from its cup,
celebrating the breath, and blood, and body you believed
belonged to you.

Mothers know better, warn daughters:
live quietly.
Gods and men have lustful eyes.
Now another is in the water,
absent as spring.

You had yet to learn:
it is no love song the ocean murmurs,
unrolling his wine-dark tide at your feet,
wrapping his fingers around your ankles,
and, while you are dancing,
stealing you under,
rolling you back into his dark and quiet bed.

THE STONING

"Each Hurt Swallowed Is a Stone"
— Rita Dove, "Promises"

"a woman's body / is a grave; it will accept / anything"
— Louise Glück, "Dedication to Hunger"

The woman with cancer watches the news
in a paper gown on a plastic chair in a lobby beside strangers.

Somewhere far away
someone's daughter
is being stoned.
Buried in sand to her neck,
veil ripped away,
she bows her head low,
hair scraping the ground like the boughs of an olive tree —
the weight of shame.
Fathers, brothers, sons crowd in,
fists gripping rocks,
grim reapers all.

Western viewers cannot bear
        these horrors —
so a reporter tells the story,
shakes her head and sighs.
Though her face is veiled,
a curl escapes,
reckless
writhes and dances in the desert air,
glinting gold.

The woman with cancer thinks of snake charmers,
how men make snakes safe
by stitching closed their mouths;
she reaches, fingers
her scarf, remembers

hair falling to the shower floor,
petals from a wilting stem.

Still she can spare no sorrow.
Her life has been a stoning,
swallowing of all things hard,
mouthful of rocks
shredding her throat as they sank,
her belly full of stone like the wet-jawed wolf,
like the poet whose words won't come,
hungry, and heavy, and drowned.
But she says nothing,
takes it in,
toes the line,
eyes on the summit,
though rock piles on rock, crowds every crevice
and she hardens from the inside out,
and her fingertips stiffen
and her joints crunch when she walks...
One morning she tastes gravel
and coughs up blood and stone —
litter of rock to mark her passing.
Hard lot for living softly.

Yet even now she is a pillar —
drives to the hospital alone, waits in the hospital alone,
bears the weight of each test
        alone.
Her husband, sons are grateful,
celebrate her strength,
at night recite the eulogies they'll write —
their heads are in the sand.
She has lived her life a statue
And, dying, hates them all.

How durable women's worshippers,
their houses built of sand and glass,
a stone in every hand.

JOHNSTON: "Dead in Absentia" is a poem that I began in 2005 while pregnant with my second daughter and on bed rest; confined to the couch in my living room, I found myself watching a lot of cable news, including the frenzied news coverage of Natalee Holloway, an American citizen who disappeared on a high school trip to Aruba. She was last seen on May 31, 2005 leaving a nightclub with Joran van der Sloot. Her body was never recovered, and though Van der Sloot was arrested, he claimed innocence and was never tried. Five years to the day after Natalee's disappearance, van der Sloot killed a Peruvian woman. He was found guilty of that murder and is serving 28 years in a Peruvian jail.

A survivor of sexual assault, I was struck by Holloway's mother's grief and horrified by what seemed to me to be the misogynistic news coverage of the missing girl and her grieving mother, and the culture of victim-blaming. When Holloway was finally declared dead in absentia in 2012, I unearthed the poem I had begun seven years earlier and finished it, knowing I wanted to write about absence — all the ways the "real" Natalee was absent from the stories the media told about her, and even those her mother told, replaced by a flattened-out characterization of her as just another beautiful blonde stolen too soon. I also wanted to give Natalee some kind of voice and to grant to her mother some reprieve from the media's intrusions.

When I first wrote "The Stoning," I imagined a woman in her mid-fifties sitting alone in a hospital room, convinced that the cancer that is killing her is a corporealization of the hurts she had swallowed throughout her life. As I saw her sitting there, I followed her eyes to a television screen and, on it, the story of a woman in the Middle East being stoned. It was almost as if the woman in the hospital wanted me to tell both their stories and, in so doing, to draw connections between all the ways in which women are alienated from one another, shielded from the truth of other women's experiences, systematically silenced as a community, and subjected to very different kinds of gender-based violence. The idea of "stoning," then, becomes a metaphor for the ways women are reduced to objects; internalizing societal expectations, they become monuments or, rather, shrines for male desire.

My poem is also in direct conversation with poems by Rita Dove and Louise Glück, writers who have used poetry to challenge misogynistic policies and practices. When I was in my early twenties, I read Dove's collection *Thomas and Beulah* and was struck by a line in one of the poems, "Promises": "Each hurt swallowed is a stone." Later, I read Glück's poem "Dedicated to Hunger" in *Descending Figure,* and her lines "[A] woman's body / is a grave; it will accept / anything" reminded me of Dove's poem. Both poets allude to the idea of women's swallowing of words, and, in turn, to the way we are consumed by our own silences. These lines have stayed with me for years, as I studied English literature and took courses in Gender Theory and as I dated, married and had my own daughters. Raised in a deeply conservative, fundamentalist home, I knew much about what it meant to be silent, to swallow words, to feel those words sink into my stomach like stones.

For me, writing poetry has been a way to break open these silences and to give voice to the voiceless. The characters who emerge in my poems show up in my mind as if they've always lived there, just waiting their turn for me to tell their stories. There is always an inherent danger in trying to represent the voices of other women, real or imagined; the danger, of course, is that we might misrepresent those voices or allow our own biases to misshape their stories. Therefore, I humbly offer these poems to this collection not as "truths" of what women really feel, but as versions of truths, as a means by which to populate the world with more stories told by women.

ADELE JONES

Adele Jones lives in Queensland, Australia. She has a professional background in science and writes young-adult and historical novels, poetry, and short inspirational and fictional works. Her first YA novel, *Integrate,* was awarded the 2013 CALEB Prize for an unpublished manuscript. Jones draws inspiration from her passion for family, faith, friends, music, and science.

SEVERED

She is crouching, rocking,
staring at the crude dirt floor
of her mother's hut. Agony burns hot
like the sun,
no less than the moments
of her attack.

She was pinned down,
her secret place exposed,
torn beyond repair.
No crisp, white sheets.
No highbrow doctors.
No pungent antiseptic stinging the air.
Just a rust-dulled blade in
mutilating hands.
The frenzy has passed,
but still her pulse pounds
like a village drum.
Throbbing.
Relentless.

What was her crime?
Dare a girl child presume
rights — to choose pleasure
instead of pain?
The bounty?
Her womanhood.
Stolen
before she had scarcely
learned to count.
The offending breach
stitched tight.

Though she cannot see beyond this haze,
in time could she be
drawn by love's sweet perfume?
Will she feel the
thorn of its embrace, then mourn
the promises of intimacy?
Lost.
Forever.

My own daughter
is asleep in her bed.
She is snug
between freshly washed sheets,
dreaming of being a princess,
of making castles with sand
until her prince comes.

Carefree days of girlhood
beckon.
Unblemished
golden rays
shimmer
on the horizon.

Though dawn will break over Africa,
a little girl will never be
the same.
And no one
     did anything
         to stop it.

So she crouches and rocks
while blood drips from her wounds
into the dirt at her feet.

JONES: Violence against women impacts us all. Whether one is a victim or is affected indirectly through another's experience, these violations must be exposed to elicit change. These oppressions take many forms, with age and culture no discriminator.

The poem "Severed" adopts a child's perspective of female genital mutilation (FGM), while encompassing my own response to an article detailing the experiences of a human-services worker who spent time with villagers in a particular region of Africa. This account briefly mentioned a young girl who had suffered FGM, and the reference impacted me deeply. At that time, our daughter was similar in age to the featured child. It broke my heart to think of a small child like her being subjected to such treatment. Writing this poem articulated my objections, whilst personalizing the plight of the assaulted girl.

PRIYANKA KALPIT

Priyanka Kalpit is a Gujarati dalit poet. She has published two collections of poetry in Gujarati, *Hanshiya Maan Hoon* (*My Self in the Margins*, 2001) and *Ghasarko* (*Gash*, 2011), and has been awarded the Dr. Ramanika Gupta Award by Gujarat Sahitya Sangam. Translations of her work have appeared in *Indian Literature, Muse India,* and many other journals. She is currently working on her third collection of poetry. Kalpit lives in Mehsana, India.

ગાંઠ

મારામાં
વકરી રહી છે
પરંપરાની રોગષ્ટિ ગાંઠ.
તેઓ જાણે છે
એટલે
ધીરે ધીરે
પણ
મક્કમતાથી સારવાર આપે છે
આ ગાંઠને,
એ પૂરેપૂરી પાકીને
ફાટી ન જાય
ત્યાં સુધી...

TUMOR*

The malignant tumor of tradition
festers within me.

They know this
and treat the tumor
slowly and steadily
till it ripens
and explodes —

KALPIT: Expendable and disdained, in a divisive and exclusive Indian society, women
are thrust to the margins and, even within these lines, cannot be safe. Ossified traditions
have turned into angry, cancerous tumors. These tumors will grow and then explode.
And the victims, Indian women, will also be destroyed. Despite knowing this truth,
most Indians accept the situation readily because the establishment has its punishment
mechanisms, its conventions and moral codes. Its methods are sugar-coated. In this
poem, I have attempted to present the predicament of Indian women who find them-
selves being annihilated under the code of endurance and suffering.

---

* Translated from the Gujarati by Gopika Jadeja.

BREINDEL LIEBA KASHER

Breindel Lieber Kasher was born in New York City and has lived more than half her life in Israel. She is a documentary filmmaker and published poet. Her work has been translated into Hebrew, Polish, and German; it can be found in *Midstream*, *Prism: An Interdisciplinary Journal for Holocaust Educators*, *21ˢᵗ Century Journal*, *Cyclamens and Swords*, *International Poetry Journal*, *Poets West*, *Seventh Quarry*, and *Palabras*. Kasher has twice won the Reuben Rose Prize from Voices Israel.

THE RABBI SPEAKS

At the community meeting
The rabbi speaking said:
Look what happens
To our daughters
Who do not
Keep the Sabbath

And that is how he
Justified the rape
In our village

Everyone kept silent

KASHER: I have 4 children. My poem was written after my youngest daughter was raped. To be 100% supportive of my daughter, to stand by her through those trials and tribulations, came naturally to me, as it does to a mother cat. I knew how to do that. I would walk to the ends of the earth for my family.

What I didn't know was how we, all my family, would suffer so deeply. When I spoke to the rape-crisis clinic they would say "What about you, how are you holding up?" and I would answer, "It isn't about me, I just want to be there for my daughter," but the process of falling apart happened, despite my mighty-oak self-image. I began battling an entire community — friends I had for 30 years, people who didn't want to deal, people who used the words "alleged rape," people who found ways to justify what happened, people who remained friends with the rapist, who lives in our village. I thought the people of the village would tell the rapist he was no longer welcome here, but that never happened. It was a 5-year process of breaking down, breaking ties, friends no longer friends, day after day breaking, and then enduring the court's decision to let the predator go because "there was not enough evidence."

What I learned, what I would like to pass on to other mothers, is yes, be there 100% for your daughters, but also be compassionate regarding your own pain. To see your child suffer is excruciating, devastating; nothing prepares you for that. I felt helpless and furious, and, for the first time in my life, I felt I could kill. Therapy, time, family power, and the love we have for each other helped us survive. We will never be the same, but we find the strength, and even the courage, to help others, and that is a good thing.

J. KATES

J. Kates is a poet and literary translator who lives in Fitzwilliam, New Hampshire. He co-directs the non-profit literary publishing house Zephyr Press and has published three chapbooks of his own poems: *Mappemonde* (Oyster River Press, 2001), *Metes and Bounds* (Accents Publishing, 2010), and *The Old Testament* (Cold Hub Press, 2010), as well as *The Briar Patch: Selected Poems & Translations* (Hobblebush Books, 2012). A former president of the American Literary Translators Association, he has translated a dozen books by Russian and French contemporary poets and co-translated four books of Latin American poetry.

THE WOMAN IN MY BED TALKS ABOUT HER CHILD

The woman in my bed
talks about her child.
At first I think she means
her adolescent son
clambering in the Rockies
even as we kiss.

But no. It is a girl
cowering in a barn
among the dairy cows
unwilling to look twice
at her uncle's milky legs
and hairy underparts.

This happened more than once.

The child is three. She is
also twelve years old,
then fifteen in the stripes
of a hospital volunteer
who can't endure the sight
when an old man's johnny rides
too high up on his thighs.

She will not be a nurse.
She tried to be a wife,
feels guilty as the mother
of that adolescent boy
camping in the mountains.

She flinches from my touch.

Around this little girl
is wrapped a grown-up woman.
Around the grown-up woman
is wrapped a silent man
listening to a woman
talk about her child,
as humble as a husband
in a birthing-room.

DONNA KAZ

Donna Kaz is a multigenre writer and activist based in New York City. Her dramatic work has been seen at Harlem Stage, the Edinburgh Festival Fringe, the Spit Lit Festival/London, the International Women's Arts Festival/UK, the Women Playwrights International Conference/Sweden, the City of Women Festival/Slovenia, and Lincoln Center in New York. She has been published in *Lilith, Turning Wheel, Trivia: Voices of Feminism, Western Press Books, Hawai'i Review, Mason's Road,* and *Step Away Magazine,* and has received the Ian MacMillan Award and a Pushcart Prize nomination. For her activist art, she has received the Yoko Ono Courage Award for the Arts, the Skowhegan medal, and an Elizabeth George Foundation Grant. Kaz's memoir, *UN/MASKED,* will be published in 2017.

COUNTING

for Ruby

I struggle to picture you safe, but
you remain standing at the kitchen door
asking to borrow a loaf of bread
and a quarter for the phone.

"Use our phone," my mother says.
Caught between the screen door
and the phone on the wall
I see you shake as you grab the receiver,

put a chipped red nail
into a number on the dial,
terror coming out the tip of your finger
in a jerk and poke. I hear my mother

counting to ten, ask you to count
with her, and together you recite
a simple math lesson, some kind
of grown-up trick I don't understand.

The next time I hear you it's the middle of the night.
You rouse me from a child's dream
as you scream for help from outside
on the street. I wonder if you are counting now,

hear a gun go off three times.
The next day I watch them take you
out of your house in a body bag, remove
the bloody sofa pillows wrapped in plastic,

see your three small children
stand together clutching themselves
by the throats before someone comes
and leads them away.

When you died you must have curled up
inside of me, lain there sleeping for years
until the night I too ran down a street
screaming, trying to save my own life.

Waking just in time to teach the simple exercise
my mother taught you, I hear you count to ten,
hear you ask me to count with you,
like magic, open my mouth and let you out.

MY ASSAILANT

Lives in Europe with two daughters,
his three sons left behind,
their only memories his open hand,
his open mouth, his tears.
Has a French girlfriend,
is wealthy, is sober;
passes by expensive wine shops
without even a sniff of regret.

Reads the newspapers in another language,
meets a few friends in small cafes,
speaks with passion of his dreams.
Sleeps in a tiny bed of wrought iron
on a hard mattress, peacefully,
but not for very long.
Takes long walks along some river
no longer recognized by passersby,
his chiseled face framed
by the turned-up collar
of his starched white oxford,
his receding hairline invisible
under a brown leather cap,
his eyes squinting at the sun.
Is captured one day in the background
of an international news program on TV
buying cheese and meat from a street vendor
while the foreign correspondent
speaks of a terrorist attack, a bombing.

KAZ: In 1992, I was living in Los Angeles and decided to volunteer to answer calls on the LA rape-and-battery hotline. At the first training session, all the volunteers introduced themselves. As each woman before me stood to speak, she said her name and then added that she identified as a survivor of sexual assault. After three or four women spoke, it hit me for the very first time — *I had been a victim of domestic violence and was also a survivor.* For 13 years, I had downplayed and denied the abusive relationship I had once been in. The supportive women of the LA Commission on Assaults Against Women (now Peace Over Violence) helped me to work through what had happened to me. Writing about an intimate and personal perspective of terrorism was a part of that process.

When I was eight years old, a mother of three who lived on my block was shot while running down the street in the middle of the night. My younger sister and I were the only witnesses. Her husband, who had just been released from prison, was arrested and convicted of the crime. Her three young children were taken away. Her house was put up for sale and the crime was soon forgotten. But I couldn't shake the memory of Ruby, a young African American woman, who my mother had befriended. Ruby would often come to our house and ask to use the phone. I now realize she needed the phone to call the police.

When I graduated college and moved to New York City, I became involved with a man who beat and abused me for three years. It was only while exploring volunteer work with battered women that I realized and accepted the fact that I was a survivor of domestic violence. I will never forget Ruby. In many ways, my memory of her has helped me in my recovery. I dedicate this poem to her.

SUSAN KELLY-DEWITT

Susan Kelly-DeWitt is a former Stegner Fellow and the author of *The Fortunate Islands* (Marick Press), eight previous small-press collections, and three online chapbooks — most recently *Season of Change* (*Mudlark* No. 46); her work has also been included in many regional and national anthologies. Kelly-DeWitt is currently a member of the National Book Critics Circle, a contributing editor for *Poetry Flash,* and a blogger for *Coal Hill Review.*

MY MOTHER AT THE MUSEUM OF BOUND FEET

Golden Lotuses
like toddler booties —

    "cranes for long life,"
    silvered wings where

    bones were broken:
toes, young child-soles

folded under. From her
wheelchair my mother

    points to a dime-sized
    peony embroidered

    in gold: *"wizard stitchery…"*
— She can't speak;

half-blind since
her stroke, she's often

    confused; the nerves
    on her right side

dead but, born in 1919,
a year before suffrage,

her outrage
can still spark.

    Everything she has
    left tingles with it.

PAINTING CLASS

Deborah is a bee this morning: she stings
her boy Luther with the hard, flat back
of her hand. She pounds the table

twice with a cross-boned wrist, flashes
a tattooed wrist knotted with inky
lassoes. Nairobi is not going

to have any of it. She pounds
the table back — harder — hurls
four-letter words like live bait.

She is boldly beautiful in a cobalt
pique sundress that bares
a puckered constellation of scars

across her arms and chest.
(Her face is untouched except
where kerosene lit

a pink ragged moon in one
shined cheek.) She'd like to peel
off the crosshatched lizard skin

and fold it away, permanently
creased. Misty Lavender is mute
since her rape. She gets shaky

and afraid whenever Deborah
and Nairobi start to fight. Today
she crayons a purple scallop

of cloud in a choppy lemon
sky, and dangles a neon zigzag
cord from it — a rescue

helicopter's waxy rope
but no rescuer to slide down
with hope-burned palms.

SATI, 1987

for Roop Kanwar, in memory

*On September 4, 1987... a young girl of 18 in the village of Deorala in Rajasthan
was murdered. She was burnt alive on the funeral pyre of her husband. Yet, according
to local tradition, Roop Kanwar had become a 'sati' and had 'voluntarily' immolated
herself.... Two decades later, the problem has not disappeared.*
    — the Hindu, September 23, 2007

1.

They said a hundred hand-sewn butterflies
ignited the gauze filaments
of your veil, that

once, when you fell off
the pyre with plainly scorched
feet, they hurried to lift you

back, onto the fire: *Sati*
                Mata ki jai! Glory
to the Sati Mother!

They said you were struck by
the beauty of the gesture: Your body a lotus
of flame, your soul rising like incense

from its burning stem.

2.

    What do I know,
sitting here, continents away,
weeping?

Weeping for whom?

3.

They said you cradled
your dead husband's head
in your lap as you burned,

a Kali
with one skull —

his.

KELLY-DEWITT: I wrote the "Sati" poem a long time ago, when the story first appeared in the *New York Times* and then in our local paper. I had read Bullmiller's book *May You Be the Mother of a Hundred Sons: A Journey Among the Women of India,* which examined women's disenfranchised roles in 1980s Indian society, and I was, like many of us, galvanized by Kanwar's story. Had she lived, her choices would have been few, but she was not even allowed those choices. At the time, Kanwar's family tried to make everyone believe that she had undertaken this act of her own free will, that it was not murder.

I grew up on Oahu, in the Hawaiian Islands. As a child, I often saw women with tiny doll's feet hobbling around the streets of Honolulu in embroidered shoes. The word "bound" always sounded violent, but no one ever explained to me what that actually meant. As an adolescent, I read a lot about Chinese history and customs, so I learned the gruesome details.

There's also the personal backstory — my mother's patriarchal, Portuguese Catholic family and stories about my grandmother's and great-grandmother's powerlessness, their dictated subservience and sometimes violent abuse. All of this led to my writing "My Mother at the Museum of Bound Feet."

I've worked with many different populations, including an arts program for homeless and low-income women called the Women's Wisdom Project, which I helped start up in 1991. As the first program director, I developed a curriculum that included painting classes, poetry workshops, and an artist's cooperative. In the early days, I also taught most of those classes. I heard a lot of disturbing stories and met women who had endured tortures. In "Painting Class," the names have been changed, but the stories in this poem are real.

DIANE KENDIG

Diane Kendig has worked as a poet, writer, translator, and teacher for 40 years, and she has authored four poetry collections including *The Places We Find Ourselves*. A recipient of two Ohio Arts Council Individual Artist grants, a Yaddo fellowship, a Fulbright, and an National Endowment for the Humanities fellowship, she has published most recently in *J Journal, Wordgathering, About Place,* and *qarrtsiluni*. Kendig taught at Bentley University and the University of Findlay (where she created its creative writing program), including 18 years at the UF Prison Program, and now is writing in her hometown, Canton, Ohio.

ON THREE PORTRAITS BY MARÍA BLANCHARD

Her curator calls these "execution of duplication."
Watching her students, she'd sidle up,
say, "C'est fini; n'y touchez plus,"
and if they would protest they weren't finished,
they wanted to improve it, she'd say,
"Then take another canvas and go further
with the same subject."
Not just for beginners, but her own practice,
as in her fourth decade she produced these three
whose differences draw me.

i. *Head of a Moor*

In the mustard background of her early painting,
Capricho, she places this portrait:
a dark olive face and hands, deep gray lines
in the headdress and sleeves,
the asymmetric face, eyes a bit out of kilter.
The hijab seems impossibly wrapped,
pinned at the heart by the woman's two
shovel-shaped hands.

She looks the youngest of the three, barely a teen,
like the little girl at the front of the boat
to Algeciras whom I watched in 1971 while dark men
in heavy robes, despite the heat,
were shoved and shouted to the back:
"Vosotros moros! Bah!"

"How can you say there's no race problem in Spain?"
I asked my hosts. "This is different,"
they answered. "Moors are not like your Negroes.
Moors are dirty and lazy and bad."
María's Moorish girl looks out at us,
as astonished as I was.

ii. *Figure of a Girl*

Chalk, loose and free, the hijab
now wrapped just right, held on the opposite shoulder,
by hands that looks handier. The eyes still seem off,
the nose and mouth, centered.
She looks older to me, about twenty-one,
and her robes are whiter.
This is the one the critics prefer.

iii. *Figure of a Girl / Head of a Moor*

Two titles, as though she can't decide,
and the hijab, the same in our time as then.
So France passes "the veil law." I can't decide either.
On my American beach today, a husband
in white short shorts and t-shirt, led his wife,
in long slacks under her long-sleeved dress,
wearing her hijab in the 8 a.m. already-90-degree day,
through a series of calisthenics: running
backward, sit-ups in the sand, arm circles in the hot air.
I want to support her right to wear what she wants,
but it's hard to uphold in this heat.

This painting is most stylized, the folds in the robe
as sharp as the angles of Blanchard's many
cubist still lives, curving in counter-position
to the erect face and torso. For all the style,
she moves me most, her straight-on stare
sadder than the second take, and calmer,
the mouth a thick slick of lips with slight downturn,
eyebrows as defined as over-waxed ones today,
the skin much darker, the face most symmetrical,
all very neat and troublesome.

I ask the woman seated next to me on the T,
her head wrapped in a hot pink scarf,
laughing with her, and her daughters
complain they can't hear their Kindles
because of our noisiness.
"For respect," she says, pointing to her head,
"yes, but not too much," and she motions
over her face as though putting on purdah
and throwing it off: "No, no. Too much."

KENDIG: I have been writing biographical and ekphrastic poems on the Spanish artist María Blanchard (1881–1931) and her paintings since 1986, after coming across a mention of her by Federico García Lorca. When I began, it was very hard to find information about her or images by her, but I proceeded with what I had and, in each poem, I included a quote from someone and some piece of my own biography. Then around 2005, a lot began to happen. I found a 746-page catalogue of Blanchard's life and works at the Reina Sofia Museum in Madrid, which features her magnificent painting "Woman with a Fan."

When I came across the three portraits referred to in my poem in that catalogue, I was struck by a 1971 memory of being a college student in Spain and traveling by boat to North Africa (for $1!). There, I saw the long-robed Moorish men who boarded being screamed at and shoved to the back. I had never seen racial or ethnic prejudice outside the US till then, and it shocked me. More recently, I had been struggling with the

Muslim women I encountered in the Boston area where I was living, whose clothing struck me as an advertisement for their oppression. Yet in conversation with some of these women, I found that some felt unoppressed, while some were conflicted. As always, I used writing about Blanchard's three paintings to explore her life and work while at the same time thinking about the issues of prejudice, oppression — and clothing. I am pleased to see this poem as part of the larger conversation, which this anthology represents.

ADELE KENNY

Adele Kenny is the author of twenty-three books (poetry and nonfiction) and has had poems published in journals worldwide, as well as in books and anthologies from Crown, Tuttle, Shambhala, and McGraw-Hill. A former creative writing professor in the College of New Rochelle's graduate school, she is founding director of the Carriage House Poetry Series and poetry editor of *Tiferet Journal*. Among other awards, she has received two poetry fellowships from the New Jersey State Arts Council and the 2012 International Book Award for poetry. Kenny has read her work in the United States, England, Ireland, and France, and has twice been a featured reader at the Geraldine R. Dodge poetry festival.

THINGS UNTOUCHED

After he was done, he beat her again and
left her for dead on the bedroom floor.
She doesn't remember his face but can't get
rid of his eyes whenever she closes hers.

Now she never enters the house without
fear — she looks behind doors for a man who
stands behind her in every mirror, whose
shadow hides inside her own.

She hasn't slept in her bed since, though
the mattress has been replaced. People
who don't know her well would never guess
(the secret a dark, still history);

and only her closest friends know that she
still refuses her husband's hands, that over
and over again she says it is only the silence
of things untouched that keeps her sane.

KENNY: In writing this poem, I told the story of a woman I met shortly after my first poetry collection was published. She introduced herself to me at a book signing in a local bookstore, and we met again by chance in a neighborhood park a few months later. We talked briefly about my book, and she said she thought that writing might be healing but that her "story" was too upsetting to put into words. I asked her if it would help to talk about it, and she told me that she had been raped a few years before. She said it was freeing to talk about it to a stranger, someone who didn't know her. I never saw her again.

T A B I S H   K H A I R

Tabish Khair is a poet, novelist, and journalist, who currently teaches in Aarhus, Denmark. He has received the All India Poetry Prize, and his novels have been shortlisted for a variety of major awards, including the Hindu Best Fiction Prize and the Man Asian Prize. He is the author of a critically acclaimed collection of poems, *Where Parallel Lines Meet* (Penguin, 2000), and has written or edited several studies and anthologies, including *Babu Fictions: Alienation in Contemporary Indian English Novels* (Oxford University Press, 2001) and *Other Routes: 1500 Years of African and Asian Travel Writing* (Indiana University Press, 2006). His most recent novel is *How to Fight Islamist Terror from the Missionary Position* (2013).

IMMIGRATION

At the corner her past makes with their future,
across the gleaming metal counter he asks her,
Where's the proof of your being,
the stamp that seals who you say you say you say you are?

Behind him stands, with folded hands,
a matron who seems to have jumped gender,
a few centuries and at least one epic:
Could she be the born-again Dushasana
Shakuntala has been warned of, mythical
bully whose hands pull off cloth like wings
from the bodies of women of color, seeking
in their wombs the deceit of pregnancy?

Shakuntala looks in her papers for the royal
signet ring, she rummages through her leather
handbag bought on Janpath at the last moment,
and just when she thinks all is lost, she finds it:
The letter attesting to her identity and grant. She
produces it with a surge of pride, but it appears
the ring of her achievement is lost: The officer
holds it and her passport as if they were cut
out of the belly of a smelly fish.

Shakuntala leaves, relieved at having escaped
the hands of Dushasana: she has no God
to invoke and doesn't trust the length of her jeans.
But even as she walks the cold corridors
of arrival in this country of old stolen gold,
this palace of freedom slavery built,
she sees suddenly her face reflected
in the faces of women sweeping the floor;
she feels the eyes that stop her at random
and strip her to one more wife of many men.

STONE

The west wind will blow for you, coming, as it does, from the land of the
    living:
It was a prophecy to awaken the dead.

When you turn fourteen your clothes jump two sizes ahead.
It is not just in hopscotch that the flat stone is always in front of you,
And on it you can lay the spread of an afternoon's picnic
There where *sal* leaves went sailing in the breeze and your hair
Was not held firmly in place by *dupatta*, clip, rubber band.

To know when to look, to know when to laugh:
These are delicate knowledges, enshrined in postures of the body
Which have grown into you like the dirt once under your nails.
Your nails started being examined around the time you turned fourteen,
Cleaned, shaped, polished: you were being prepared for something.
You guessed the day your *dupatta* slipped and you heard the crash
Of something breaking that was always too big to mention.

What prophecy this,
where the angel keeps the book to himself?

It was like a storm: the thunder of music, the lightning of bulbs,
The rain of tears that was false as custom and true as parents.
Though you recall the day with the help of smells: the various dishes,
murgh musallam, shahi korma, seekh kabab, pulao, makuti.
And there was something else after it all, but you were prepared:
It was a small price to pay for those dreams of escape.

What revelation this,
where the angel never intercedes before the slab?

Distance and dollars have made the *dupatta* disappear,
But you stay in place behind a table of rubber-bands and clips,
Fake mahogany it is, and marble-topped: polished, flat stone
In its own square in the city of your escaped dreams.

Buzzer, button, shelf, file, computer, Mr. Jacobsen,
A print of nude natives by Gauguin (who had a Danish wife),
An echo of the Scream by Munch (who had a Danish shrink),
And you (with your Danish visa) adding trans-local color
To the true colors of a global office: the perfect frame
Behind which is hidden the ignominy of your arrival, the body
That could not pass through Customs on its own and followed
The stony tinkle of metal. You are here for their sake.
They decided to make your picture real. Yes, Mr. Jacobsen?
These metal slabs to which you were tied by a proud parent
Who had also heard the prophecy and whom no angel stopped,
This game of perpetual movement you play on only one leg:
Can you decipher their secret before closing time today?

The west wind has blown for you, coming, as it does, from the land of the living.
There is no prophecy to awaken the dead.

KHAIR: I grew up in a family that contained many kinds of women. I also grew up in a small town and hence met women from various classes and social backgrounds, including hyper-urban and hyper-rural ones. What always struck me as significant was how the discourse of the emancipation of women gets hollowed out by colonial and "progressive" elements just as often as it is subverted or opposed by conservative and traditional elements. While I believe strongly in equal rights and opportunities for women, I feel that the matter cannot be simplified on the East/West axis. For instance, many illiterate women that I met, with no exposure to the West, were independent working women, sometimes even single mothers. On the other hand, many sophisticated, educated, "Westernized," middle-class women were grossly confined in their family roles, and either did not work or worked only as a "hobby." I think these are the matters that I try to explore in my poems: not just the "veiling" of women in a traditional sense, but also the "shackling" of women in a modern sense, including the immigrant context.

Molly Sutton Kiefer

Molly Sutton Kiefer is the author of the full-length lyric essay *Nestuary* as well as three poetry chapbooks, including *Thimbleweed,* which will be published in 2016. She is co-founder and editor at *Tinderbox Poetry Journal* as well as publisher of Tinderbox Editions. She lives in Minnesota with her family.

At the start of thunder,

I count the triggers until ten and that's when spidering
begins. Does it mean something that the sky sounds
like a hungry stomach?

                    In Africa,
they've started what they call the hunger season,
and women earn rice by carrying stones
from the field in bowls on their heads. Fight back
the Sahara. Veils catch. No matter the slip, the slow terror
of vanishing flesh.

                    Last summer,
my sister got married. Last summer was Texas
with land riddled by eczema. Her skin
was like milk, to match the dress. I kept wanting
to give her a scarf to tie it shut. I was afraid she'd spill
and I'd see.

                    That August,
I fell in love with a faraway baby whose death mask
would blister. These women's breasts dried
into lost walnuts, hard little hearts. They left the dying
as each arrived in the camps, counting fewer each time.
The baby's mouth opened like a cricket's.

My own babe could scorch
a pouch in minutes. She fennels Greek yogurt. Splits peas.
She skims a soup.

At my sister's wedding,
miniature burgers in foil. Croquettes
of macaroni and cheese. She rumples a lace veil,
made lovely. Strings a pearl. Flower dye tinges
vase water blue and orange.

This is the hut with a view:
white-blue sky, a rusted earth. Flake away.
Rosebud mouths clamped shut.

DISPOSABLE WOMAN

> *Kepari Leniata, a young mother, was burned alive in Papua*
> *New Guinea after townspeople accused her of sorcery.*
> (Various news services, February 2013)

The opening wave was the hardest, an unburdening
of flesh. Between her toes, the lint of everyday,

packed tight like tires, wicking away rain. No clothes
left, not a stitch, nothing left but skin, cattle-branded.

How many bottles made it round the circle?
Was there singing? What witch is dead?

Throat wide open, deep enough for sky, for hen-feathers.
Her, tarred; her, burned neatly.

Eight months before and she'd thrust a body like hers
into the world, little limbs and all suckling. Her teats

were pulled taffy, spun sugar, in a house
reeking of cinnamon and gold.

TRIPOLI

*for Iman al-Obeidi, of Libya, who accused Gaddafi forces
of rape**

That blood, someone's nails pulling runnels in her cheeks,
and her hair, such a muss, and she's saying something,
she is wet with emotion, *wet with it,* maybe foolish too — the men
are having their dinner, they are soaking their bread
in cups of tea. There are others, men whose elbows
bend outwards like sturdy wings, bringing up a singular eye,
the other burrowed, squinting, and the flick of a wrist —

> *They tied me up . . . they even defecated and urinated on me.*
> *The Gaddafi militiamen violated my honor.*

Even the waitresses struck her down. Their hands
plucked at her blouse, rattling her tigress scarf,
the silk too easy to slip through their roughshod hands.
Pots began to spill in the back.

> *She describes being bound, beaten, and having alcohol poured*
> *over her eyes. She also says she was gang-raped repeatedly,*
> *that one of the soldiers sodomized her with his Kalashnikov*
> *while her hands were bound.*

The cameras swelled; scarred and splayed hands
blocked the manicured, the wool coats
and brass buttons, one grasping at a dusty oxford;
then a button popped, fell, and the bespectacled man stumbled —
who were they? where were they taking her?

> *This girl is a prostitute. She has her rights completely, but the girl*
> *is not what she pretends to be; this is her line of work.*

---

* All italicized lines are based on Huffington Post articles, March–April 2011.

We see her own bird-arms, a tissue in a clutch, and she's
still speaking, she's desperate, and a man's hand slides
over her mouth, then holds it still. There's a car waiting
for her, white, dark windows. She's sealed into the lip,
and we cannot see her now, what she's done with her hands.

They drive away too quickly. What they've done with her hands.

KIEFER: It's hard to pinpoint precisely how my poetic interests veered into this arena: I could start by explaining how, as an undergraduate, I was involved as a producer of *The Vagina Monologues* through the V-Day movement, which raised over $100,000 for local women's shelters and organizations, and how this exposure rooted me deeply in the activism aspect, but that might not be quite accurate.

I found myself writing close to the body not long after I was diagnosed with an infertility condition, one that could be treated, and I began to examine the body as a medical object. Since writing my first full-length collection, *Tethering*, and since giving birth to a daughter and a son, my stance as a feminist has drastically changed. After having Maya, I began to write fiercely about a kind of alternative hero — the strong woman in many forms. I have published poems about trans beauty pageant contestants and roller derby champions and cowgirls and Hillary Clinton meeting Aung San Suu Kyi. Not all of the women win, though — and I began writing about them, too. About Henrietta Lacks. Another on a Holocaust survivor.

I wrote "At the start of thunder," when my daughter was still breastfed and I'd been shattered by the 2011-2012 crisis in the Horn of Africa. How does one contend with plenty when other women are walking towards camps, risking rape and loss, just to save what they can? Perhaps this is where it started, that summer of the famine, the one famine that made me realize I needed to begin to understand a wider world, one in which my daughter (and my son) would live.

DEBORAH KAHAN KOLB

Deborah Kahan Kolb was raised in Boro Park, Brooklyn, and currently resides in Riverdale. She earned her BA and MA degrees in English/Creative Writing from CUNY–Queens College, where she minored in Jewish Studies, served as editor of the *Queens College Journal of Jewish Studies*, and was the recipient of the James E. Tobin Poetry Award, the Lois Hughson Essay Prize, and the Essay Prize in Holocaust/Genocide Studies. Kolb earned her MS in school administration and supervision from Touro College before serving as principal of a private school for Jewish children of Bukharian descent. Her work has appeared in *Poetica* and *Voices Israel*.

ELDEST DAUGHTER

For the first twenty-one years of her life,
She made herself into the quintessential conformist,
Toeing the line as parents and neighbors and rabbis demanded,
Even though it killed her.

When they led her into the elegant living room in March of her eighteenth
        year
And introduced her to the boy she would marry later that summer,
Quick on the heels of her high school graduation,
She smiled at them as her heart splintered into a million shards.

When she cried, they took her into the dark den with its imposing paneling
And opened ten different yellowing tomes and pointed,
Trying to convince her, first subtly then severely, that it would be best to do
        as they said
Because love is overrated and contentment will come in time.

When her son was born she was eighteen and she hated him for stealing her
        youth,
As she hated her father for stealing her hair that they forced her to shave
After the wedding, as she hated her mother for wielding that razor and not
        fighting
For her, even though she knew her mother had survived the same charade.

When she craved a college education, she took a receptionist job instead,
And she envied other women behind the wheel while they forbade her a
    license,
And she hid the TV in the microwave box so no one would see how
    wayward
She'd become, and she did everything they told her with gall in her gut.

When she wanted some independence, they forced her onto her back
Because they wanted babies. And so she had three and loathed the entire
    messy business,
And they thought her tears were from the onions she dutifully grated for
    every Shabbos kugel,
And they thought the knife nicks and cuts among the potato peelings were
    all incidental.

But when her sister approached her eighteenth year, snarling and spitting,
Tossing her glossy tresses, fighting back fiercely, then driving off
Into freedom, she swallowed the little white pills
That finally killed her.

KOLB: A Hasidic community is no place for a woman. That is, a woman has her place. A woman should know her place. And that place is invisible. Secondary. At best, a woman is an afterthought. At worst, she is a target of the vitriol of men. What Hasidic men cannot control, they seek to oppress.

Such has been my experience growing up in Boro Park, Brooklyn. The poetry included in this anthology illuminates for the world at large what is for many Hasidic women a life not worth living: their identities so marginalized, their thoughts, feelings, and desires so inconsequential, that the bottle of pills or the high-rise ledge can become, eventually, the ultimate escape.

ZOE LAMBRINAKOS-RAYMOND

Zoe Lambrinakos-Raymond is a poet who currently resides in Montreal. While most of her free time is taken up by her obsessive need to take pen to paper, she also enjoys sculpting, musing over philosophy, and anything having to do with T. S. Eliot. Lambrinakos-Raymond is pursuing a double major in Liberal Arts and Creative Writing at Concordia University. Although aspiring to be a poet in the twenty-first century seems a daunting and almost foolhardy ambition, she cannot imagine any other future for herself.

FOR RENT

For once it's not black
as He sits me in the Room,
tells me bitter-sweet
half lies and wipes wet
from my cheeks. The door cracks
open as He lets go of my hands

and passes me into new Hands,
that brush my thin black
hair out of my face and run their fingers over my cracked
lips. The light in the Room
gets turned off and I hear the wet
sound of freshly licked lips and smell my own sickly-sweet

perfume in the dark. "You're like fresh, sweet
honey," these new Hands
tell me, right before I feel wet on my neck. I shut my eyes against the black;
I want the Room
darker. I want to not hear the bed creak,

but I still hear myself crack,
break. And the sweet
words wither in the Room
as the new Hands pin my own hands,

feel up and down my black
silhouette, let their wet

mouth trace mine. I feel warm, wet
as they get off me, their lips a cracked
Cheshire-cat smile glittering in the black,
laughing as they still spit sweet
words at me while the Hands
do up their belt. They leave the Room

and then He comes in. Now it's just Our Room
again, and He tells me to get cleaned-up, get the wet
off my thighs and hands.
He holds me, stops me from cracking
in half, pieces me together, calls me sweet-
heart, kisses my eyes, freshly black.

In the bathroom, the cracked
porcelain sink is wet as I rinse make-up and sweet-
smelling soap. It runs down my hands and turns the sink black.

LAMBRINAKOS-RAYMOND: The topic of rape and violence against women is never easy to talk about. I myself have been faced with situations that no prevention campaign could ever have prepared me for and that no form of counseling could have helped me recover from. Poetry is a path that I stumbled upon that allowed me to have a voice when I couldn't imagine speaking out. The reason I wrote "For Rent" was to allow others to also have a voice. Although not everyone who reads this poem will have had the same experience, or type of experience, I hope that the words on the page are able to reach out and help one person.

Aggression against women is a horrible reality of the times we live in. However, I am an avid believer that the most beautiful art, the most healing art, can come out of the most horrible of realities.

GAYLE LAURADUNN

Gayle Lauradunn has published poems in numerous journals and anthologies, and some of her poems have been adapted for the stage. Her first book, *Reaching for Air* (Mercury Heartlink Press, 2014), was named a finalist for the Best First Book of Poetry award of the Texas Institute of Letters and her manuscript "All the Wild and Holy: A Life of Eunice Williams, 1696-1785" was awarded Honorable Mention for the May Sarton Poetry Prize by Bauhan Publishing. From August through December 2015, her poems "High Desert," "Lavaland," and "Dichotomy in Bhutan" were part of the exhibit "Dirt: Scientists, Artists, and Writers Reflect on Soil and Our Environment" organized by the library at the University of Puget Sound.

TELLING

Sometimes I think I made it up. Try to convince myself that
        he didn't hurt me
that mother didn't turn on me, didn't yell to a five-year-
        old "How could you let him do that?"
or the old man didn't exist, or the old man didn't do it.
I remember my lack of fear, the pleasure, telling
        mother.
He could have been 40 or 70. A deaf mute who must have
        wanted to experience as much of life as possible.
        Being left out of sound.
But, no, he was really just a dirty old man.
I only remembered this experience again after many years
        and now it won't leave me.
That old man's face haunts me. I see it even with my eyes
        closed. I couldn't have made it up.
He was tall and slender, almost thin, and wore khaki work
        shirt and pants with a brown belt, wide leather
with a gold buckle. The shirt had seven buttons down
        the front, tan buttons.
His hands were large, square with thick hair on the fingers.
        His finger warm and gentle inside my panties.

His face had deep lines, the flesh leathery. His
       thin hair black.
He hurt me. He wasn't gentle. But, no, mother stops him.
She stops him just as he reaches under my dress. No, she
       stops him just as he pulls down my panties.
She grabs his arm, jerks it away. Screams at him. He runs
       away. He is back
with his hand between my legs, his fingers digging.
       His fingers inside me and I am laughing.
I am daddy's Baby Doll. I am crying. I am pushing against
       him. I am running.
Every man I meet has a lined face. Every man I bed has hairy
       fingers.
I laugh, cry, with every man. Mother, where are you? No.
       This scene is all wrong. It is a hot July afternoon.
The old man sits with my baby brother asleep in his lap. I
       am five.
No one else is in the house. The doors and windows open.
       Light is everywhere in my grandparents'
house. He is granddaddy's cousin. He wanders and works
       where he can in his boots,
high topped, laced around the ankles. He is quiet. He grins.
       A Halloween mask. Some teeth
stained with tobacco. Outside, the windmill creaks.
       No. It wasn't a dress.
It was a pinafore with large ruffles on the shoulders. A
       blue pinafore with white eyelet trim
and white buttons. I was five. He motioned me to him
       pointed to the baby asleep.
He pulled up my dress, put his hand in my panties.
       No. We were outside,
down the hill in the woods behind the house. I followed
       him out into the wavering heat.
I wanted to know his silence. The baby wasn't there. My
       dress was yellow.

It was my panties that were blue. His belt was drawn tight
          around his waist, his pants gathered.
It was there in the dry grass that he did it. Yes, I'm
          sure.
I'm sure. I was wearing a blue and yellow check sunsuit
          and my panties were white. White.

LAURADUNN: For years, I told myself that this event didn't happen, but it haunted me. As the media began to report on more and more "forgotten" rapes and molestations, I listened to other women's stories and realized that a five-year-old can be confused by such an event and blame herself for its occurrence. My mother, who I expected to help me, instead blamed me. That was a shock, and I've spent my life trying to understand and forgive her.

WAYNE LEE

Wayne Lee is a Canadian/American who lives in Portland, Oregon. His poems have appeared in *The New Guard, Sliver of Stone, Slipstream, Pontoon,* and other publications. Lee's awards include the 2012 Mark Fischer Poetry Prize and the 2012 SICA "Poems for Peace" award, and he has been nominated for a Pushcart Prize and three Best of the Net awards. His collections include *Twenty Poems from the Blue House, The Underside of Light* (a finalist for the 2014 New Mexico/Arizona Book Award), and *Googling a Present Participle: Poems, Prose Poems, Bogus Monologues & Fraudulent Artifacts.*

CAMP FIRE

She twists a linen napkin in her hands
looks down as she sips her Riesling
a twitch in her upper lip
whispers to her son something about
an incident at summer camp
how she left the sunset fire circle
to fetch a sweater from her cabin
got snatched by the maintenance man
dragged into the storage shed.

She kept it sealed
a burning ember inside her
simply straightened her shorts
rejoined the other girls to sing
"What a Friend We Have in Jesus"
and roast s'mores.

She asks *how could he have done it*
such a nice young Christian man
always so polite.

She takes another sip of wine
fingers trembling
rosacea cheeks tearstreaked now
wonders aloud if that one vile act
had changed her life
thinks it might explain the failed marriages
hopes it didn't make her a bad mother
that *God will forgive her*
and that nice young man.

She leans across the table for a hug
sighs *I'm tired now*
wants to go home to her dark apartment
knowing nothing can extinguish that fire.

LEE: I wrote this poem for my mother and sister and for all other women who have been sexually victimized by men. My sister was sexually molested for years by her father, and my mother was raped — twice — as a teenager. The first rape was committed by a church-camp employee when she was only 12, the second by a group of three close high school friends in a car after a basketball game. Those crimes have caused my mother, who is now 90, to live her life filled with shame, always believing that she was somehow responsible. It also might explain why she was married seven times.

DANIELLA LEVY

Daniella Levy is a writer, poet, translator and self-defense instructor for women and children. She is also training to be a childbirth educator. She was born in the USA and immigrated to Israel with her family as a child. She currently lives in the Judean town of Tekoa with her husband and three sons. Drawing on her spiritual roots as a religiously observant Jew, she strives to connect women with their inner power, both in self-defense and through empowered choice in birth.

STOCK-PHOTO WOMAN

I have always wondered why
Next to every news item about sexual violence
There's a stock-photo woman hiding her face
Crouching in a corner somewhere
With jarringly perfect hair
Where are her eyes?
Where are her angry, smoldering eyes?
Where is her sweat, her tears, the blood of her soul
He spilled out and greedily drank?
Where is her victory in that she
Survived?
Where is her courage in that she takes
One
More
Step,
Every
Single
Day?

No. All they want you to see is shame.

And what about him?
Where is his shame?
Where is the blame?

Where is his slumped-shoulder frame
Surrounded and neutralized, cuffed and chained
Disgraced and downtrodden, caught and contained
By the system that claims
To protect us from this kind of pain?

I wait
For the day we'll see her
Chin high, chest forward
Jaw set in defiance and pride
Because she had the courage to step forward
Because she had the courage to be seen
Because she has the power in her body and soul
To stand up in her brokenness,
In the name of those who did not survive
In the name of those who suffer still
In the name of those whose voices are silent
And those who still crouch in the corner
Hiding their faces
With anything-but-perfect hair.

LEVY: I chose to write about this subject because it has always bothered me to see the same style of stock photo used to "illustrate" news items about sexual abuse or violence. I believe that the way the news reports these incidents both reflects how society conceptualizes them and perpetuates those conceptions. In my mind, these "illustrative" images speak far louder than the factual, objective words used to report these incidents. They project a very disempowering concept of what it means for a person to be subjected to sexual violence, and perpetuate a message of victimhood and shame instead of survival, empowerment, justice and courage. As a self-defense instructor, I believe that these concepts are not only wrong — they are dangerous. The more women see that they are powerless in the face of this phenomenon, the more they will believe it and, worse, the more their potential perpetrators will believe it. I hope that the day will come when the stock photo chosen to illustrate such news items will show an empowered, strong woman, rather than a woman crouched in a classic pose of fear, shame, and helplessness. And I believe that when that day comes, the world will be a very different place.

DIANE LOCKWARD

Diane Lockward is the author of *The Crafty Poet: A Portable Workshop* (Wind Publications, 2013) and three poetry books, most recently *The Uneaten Carrots of Atonement* (Wind Books, 2016). Her previous books are *Temptation by Water, What Feeds Us* (winner of the 2006 Quentin R. Howard Poetry Prize), and *Eve's Red Dress.* Her poems have been included in *Poetry Daily: 360 Poems from the World's Most Popular Poetry Website,* Garrison Keillor's *Good Poems for Hard Times,* and other anthologies, and in journals including *Harvard Review, Spoon River Poetry Review,* and *Prairie Schooner.* Lockward's work has also been featured at *Verse Daily* and *The Writer's Almanac.*

THE MISSING WIFE

> *Wife and dog missing.*
> *Reward for the dog.*
> — bumper sticker on a pickup truck.

The wife and the dog planned their escape
months in advance, laid up biscuits and bones,
waited for the careless moment when he'd forget
to latch the gate, then hightailed it.

They took shelter in the forest, camouflaged
the scent of their trail with leaves.
Free of him at last,
they peed with relief on a tree.

Time passed. They came and went as they pleased,
chased sticks when they felt like chasing sticks,
dug holes in what they came to regard
as their own backyard. They unlearned
how to roll over and play dead.

In spring the dog wandered off in pursuit
of a rabbit. Collared by a hunter and returned
to the master for $25, he lives
on a tight leash now.

He sleeps on the wife's side of the bed,
whimpering, pressing his snout
into her pillow, breathing
the scent of her hair.

And the wife? She's moved deep into the heart
of the forest. She walks
on all fours, fetches for no man, performs
no tricks. She is content. Only, sometimes
she gets lonely, remembers how he would nuzzle
her cheek and comfort her when she twitched
and thrashed in her sleep.

LOCKWARD: As indicated in the epigraph, "The Missing Wife" was inspired by a bumper sticker. On my way up to the Frost Place in New Hampshire one summer, I noticed those words on the vehicle in front of me. I wondered what kind of a slob would put that on his car. I wondered about his wife, how he treated her, if he treated her like a dog. That bumper sticker got under my skin and stayed there. Eventually, it led to the poem.

When I was revising this poem, I realized that the ending was a bit ambiguous. Who is the "he" — dog, or husband? I thought about how to fix that but then decided to leave it. It seems to me more suggestive and interesting than it would be if I specified which one I meant. It's a case of Will-the-Real-Dog-Please-Stand-Up. I think the wife now misses human comfort and companionship, but not her husband's. That she prefers her furry dog is suggested by her walking on all fours. The wife has found a more genuine self and life in the forest where she "performs no tricks." Because the husband treated her badly, the wife could bear his touch only by making herself emotionally dead. For me, the saddest line in the poem is "They unlearned / how to roll over and play dead." I wouldn't go so far as to say that the wife is happy now, but she's found contentment. She's lonely, but she's no longer afraid.

GLENNA LUSCHEI

Glenna Luschei grew up as a corn and bean farmer in Iowa and is now an avocado rancher in California. She was named Poet Laureate in San Luis Obispo for the year 2000. Luschei's newest book is *Zen Duende*, a collaboration with Eric Greinke, publisher of Presa Press.

MEN WITH THEIR SECRET GARDENS

There is always a man
who brings me back from Santiago
when I have barely met Gabriela Mistral.
Even at the prison
there is a man who pushes open
the turnstile.

I carry a man on my coattails
until he conquers me,
undresses me,
saves me in distress.
A man will impregnate me
at the moment I am due to make a discovery.
My champions were men.
I bore sons. Now they drive me
to the homestead where I climbed
the apricot tree.

When I walk around the block
where I memorized the cracks
picked blue flax,
they step on the gas. They honk
when I stop at the library where I checked out
Jo's Boys when I was ten.

Men.
There was always a man to
unlock my cage,

to throw away my papers, to enrage me.
"Man the editor; woman the creator," I wrote.
A man to shoe my horse
a man to operate the buzz saw while I dodge the splinters.
He'll fund my projects, give me money, take it from me,
steal my daughters.

Men cover our fingers with secret
gardens of emeralds.
I wear the engagement rings of my grandmother
and three aunts. "Engaged."
Do you gain the trust of a heifer
to lead her to a distant place of slaughter?
One day I will take off all my rings
and give them to my grandsons,
never know who will wear sapphires for loyalty
rubies for heart
diamonds forever,
only that the veins of my hands sprout potato tubers.
I will remember my happiest hours
(after men grow tired of uprooting me)
digging in my own garden.

LUSCHEI: At the time of my coming out from a brutal divorce, I was fortunate to have a supportive editor, Harry Smith, of *The Smith,* in Brooklyn, who published my book *Matriarch* in 1992, as well as a wise and gentle mentor in Hugh Fox, whose words were always heartfelt.

As a woman and a poet, I want to be fierce and empowered, the way a feral wolf is with her cubs, yet blessed with the tenderness of a lover. Wolves are coming back now from near extinction in California, and women are also coming back from near extinction, with the full range of their emotions and abilities demanding to be expressed.

KATHARYN HOWD MACHAN

Katharyn Howd Machan is a professor of Writing at Ithaca College and holds degrees
from the College of Saint Rose, the University of Iowa, and Northwestern University.
Her poems have appeared in numerous magazines; in anthologies and textbooks, in-
cluding *The Bedford Introduction to Literature*, *The Best American Nonrequired Reading*,
Poetry: An Introduction, *Early Ripening: American Women's Poetry Now*, *Sound and Sense*,
Writing Poems, and *Literature: Reading and Writing the Human Experience*; and in 30
collections, most recently *When She's Asked to Think of Colors* (Palettes & Quills Press,
2009). In 2012, Machan edited *Adrienne Rich: A Tribute Anthology* for Split Oak Press.

LES SALLES-DU-GARDON

And what if you hadn't hit me,
hadn't swung your arm backhanded
against the curve of my eyes and mouth,
your blind father right across the table
confused: what did I murmur wrong?

And again, later, back in Marseilles —
simple candles and the harbor lamplight,
wine in strong clear glasses —
after my broken French had explained
you could never, never do it again,

your rage uncoiled like a creosote rope
within the storm of midnight. What
if you hadn't opened that drawer
and pulled the gun from its careless corner,
in your other hand the unsheathed blade —

you sneered you could easily kill me,
but I wasn't worth it, a woman.
Two weeks pregnant with my daughter of roses,
the child you'll never know we made
because I fled through winter rain

back to America, to silence.
What if you'd hidden the fist
of your laughter till later, longer
in love's warm rooms, and I
had stayed behind time's doors

and learned to believe you were God.

ONCE IT'S BEEN DONE

You walk differently.
Not even once
the pigeon-toed model strut
when you're wearing a short skirt —
if you ever
wear short skirts
again. You move your eyes
side to side, up and down,
always wishing
they could also see backwards
so you wouldn't keep turning
your head. You find breathing
difficult sometimes
and shadows become
cellar entries, bedroom doors,
vacant buses, hard forest moss.
You buy extra lamps.
You pull in your smiles.
You don't tell the story
or you do tell the story,
every word rhyming with *night*.
Once a month you dream your mother
is giving you a birthday party
and all the other girls are in white

while you're dressed in red, a dirty crimson,
cake crumbs spilling in your lap
and ice cream melting everywhere
you try to run, you try to punch,
you hold deathly still, beyond help.

MACHAN: "Les Salles-du-Gardon" chronicles my experience in January of 1988 when the charming Frenchman with whom I had fallen in love the previous summer, and for whom I was prepared to become an expatriate, revealed his violent nature. Fortunately, I was not young (he might have cowed me when I was 20) but a feminism-strengthened 34-year-old with the courage to drive myself hundreds of kilometers away to an airport. He was a charming Beast, but I knew I could not, and would not, be his Beauty. Even if I had then known I was pregnant, I would not have stayed; in fact, I kept my daughter's existence a secret from him until, at 16, she asked me to try to find him for her. I did so, and he eagerly sent her money for a plane ticket from New York, but I made sure to send along a willing good friend of mine as chaperone, as well as my daughter's best friend. Like me, they had to flee from him (whiskey removed his outer guise), but my daughter got to see why I did not stay in France.

"Once It's Been Done" has at its core my older brother's wrong use of me and speaks more generally to all of us who have to work to survive molestation, rape, or any other sexually-connected violence. Even if we are able to speak out or write about it (as I was finally able to do in my late twenties, again because of the literary feminist movement), a shadow of victimization remains part of our psyche.

RITA MALHOTRA

Rita Malhotra is a National Science Talent scholar, National Scholarship awardee, and post-doctoral Fellow in Mathematics (University of Paris). She is also Vice Principal of Kamala Nehru College, University of Delhi; president of Poetry Across Cultures; and World Poetry (Canada) ambassador to India. Her research papers have been published in seven countries, and her literary writings have been translated into Chinese, Serbian, Telegu, and six other languages. Malhotra's recognitions include the Michael Madhusudan Millennium Award; the Visionary Poet Award from WIN, Canada; and the Honour, from the Ministry of Foreign Affairs, Romania. She has authored two books in mathematics and eight collections of verse, among them *I Remain the Ignited Woman* (World Poetry Almanac, Mongolia, 2013).

CHRYSANTHEMUMS

we were brought up
by the rule book
that spelt love for us daughters
as immoral, infidel,
masked, contagious
dreams were cached
within constrained confines
the self remained dwarfed —
bonsai like —
unable to reach beyond its grasp
but a moment of wild defiance
unleashed a tempestuous will
to self-expression
i followed love's trail
scanning the horizon of darkness
to arrive at the moonlit patch
of a perplexed night —
a night that witnessed
love's intimate dance
in the sensual celebration of

intimacy between
soul, mind and body
with the first footfall of dawn
i tore all pages
of the book of norms
made paper flowers out of them
this morning they have metamorphosed
into golden-orange chrysanthemums

MALHOTRA: Women have been marginalized for too long. Their bitterness at being exploited, day in and day out, naturally arouses the woman in me. Poetry is my medium, and I use it to reach out to others and awaken them to a woman's sensibility. So one aspect of my writing is an emotional response to my social thought.

MARIE-ELIZABETH MALI

Marie-Elizabeth Mali is a poet, underwater photographer, and desire coach. She is the author of *Steady, My Gaze* (Tebot Bach, 2011) and co-editor, with Annie Finch, of the anthology *Villanelles* (Everyman's Library Pocket Poets, 2012). Her work has appeared in *Drunken Boat, Poet Lore, RATTLE,* and other magazines and anthologies.

ANGLERFISH

for Iman al-Obeidi

What if we women were anglerfish, our lures
springing from our foreheads, an irresistible
lighthouse of hunger, our giant-toothed jaws
so unhinged we could swallow prey twice our size?
What if our men were small, unable to feed
on their own, equipped with little more
than a powerful nose with which to find us,
starving to death if they don't? When they find us
and bite into our sides, what if they were
to dissolve like angler males, becoming
an ever-ready portable sperm factory
hanging off us, of which we might carry six?
No more forest of barstools to hack through
on a Friday night, hoping to meet a kind
baboon in a clearing. No more detention
at the checkpoint for no good reason, no more
booze poured in our eyes, nose, mouth, vagina,
no more army boots to the head, no more
gun-barrel rapes, no more running naked
down the street begging for help from people
who blame us for our blood-streaked thighs.

MALI: When I read the story of Iman al-Obeidi's kidnapping and escape during the Libyan civil war in 2011, I got angry, again, at the treatment of women worldwide, especially during times of war. I didn't want to write another rant. I knew I needed to find a compelling image on which to hang the poem, one that could carry my anger without being consumed by it. As a scuba diver and underwater photographer fascinated by gender dynamics in the sea, I naturally turned there for inspiration. I'd recently watched a video about the anglerfish, and once I began exploring a world in which the female dwarfs the male in size and power, I found my way into the poem.

SHAHÉ MANKERIAN

Shahé Mankerian's poems have appeared in *Ellipsis*, *Mizna*, *NEBO*, *Riverwind*, and *Spillway*, and he has won both the Erika Mumford Prize and the Daniel Varoujan Award from the New England Poetry Club. In 2011, he was a semi-finalist for the Knightville Poetry Contest, and his recent poems have also received Honorable Mentions in the 2011 Allen Ginsberg Poetry Award contest and the Arts & Letters Rumi Prize for poetry competition. Mankerian is the Principal of St. Gregory Hovsepian School in Pasadena, California, and directs the Los Angeles Writing Project every summer.

PICNIC AT MT. SANNINE

Thirty-seven years later,
I still remember the slap,
the gasp of the guests,
and your wife hiding

her face between her palms.
You kicked the picnic chair
and stumbled away; I stared
at the chopped parsley tucked

between your wife's fingers,
and the beads of sweat above
the bridge of her nose.
No one comforted her;

I wanted to, but I was too young
and had a slingshot
dangling in my hand. She fixed
her apron and added crushed

wheat to the *tabbouleh*.
When she walked to the hillside
well to haul a jug of water,
you managed to lower yourself

and sleep under an olive tree.
There were too many birds
chirping above your head.
I wanted to kill all.

I didn't know if you slapped her
because she forgot to offer
you buttered sesame bread
or place ice in your *arak,*

but you slept comfortably
all afternoon, surrounded
by flowers, as your wife
served us humbly with red cheeks.

MANKERIAN: When I was 12, my family and I escaped the civil war in Lebanon and migrated to the United States. Gradually, my writing became reflective and consumed with tragedies of innocence lost. Somehow, a peculiar episode, tucked in the mountains of Lebanon, kept tugging at my psyche. The story was about a drunkard, his docile wife, and a startling slap. That singular act of crudity resonated for me more loudly than a bomb and struck me as deadlier than a sniper's bullet and more dehumanizing than any checkpoint interrogation. Father later said, "Civil wars make men uncivilized." I thought it didn't take much for men to become debased.

MARI MAXWELL

Mari Maxwell's work has appeared in a variety of online and print publications in the USA, the UK, and Ireland, among them Galway's *Crannóg* magazine, *Boyne Berries*, *Beyond the Diaper Bag*, *Southern Maine Review*, *Maine in Print*, *Coping*, and *Barbie*. Her work was shortlisted in the 2014 Walking on Thin Ice Short Story Contest (a short-story contest where writers fight back against stigma and institutional power) and longlisted in the 2013 Over the Edge New Writer of the Year rankings in Galway, Ireland. Maxwell is a former journalist.

RECOLLECTIONS BY YOUR GRAVESIDE

I.

Down Anglesea Road the roses are blooming
blood red, lipstick pink and Easter yellow.
There's no dying clutch of stem or thorns —
these Dublin roses are here to stay.
But the birch trees along Baggot Street
are dragging barren,
the lower leaves, hangers-on:
maple red, translucent, yellow faded edges in mid-November.
The heady rose scent soothes me, as I bend the stem down,
delighting in the drizzle-coated softness.
Hubby and I breathe deep the wet white petals,
enjoying our alone time and memories of you.
With each step forward, we heal.
I say hello with wet clay trickled between my fingers.
Trees sift raindrops and bird song.
I know you hear me, Mom.
Your voice will ring out.

II.

You speak still in each embroidery stitch
on your wedding dress bodice, tablecloths
and framed work, on chair arms and headrests —
lush cottage gardens, thatched roofs and trailing
brambles, flowers and petticoat shepherdesses —
and in each brushstroke of your paintings of Irish
countrysides, pastoral, winding lanes, bucolic scenes
you savored in the stories of your childhood.

And, Mom, how you sang: lyrical and joyful:
summer evenings around the piano,
trickling glissandi across the octaves,
teaching your children how to sing.
Your son's soprano trilled Scottish highland airs,
your daughter's, Killarney's lakes and fells.
We sang together behind your ramrod spine
as you counted out the beat — One! Two! Three! —
on those ivory keys.

III.

Your youngest may have held fast to your phones,
preventing children and grandchildren from visiting,
intercepted your post and sent letters in your stead,
but he couldn't quash your spirit, Mom.
Those "frequent falls" listed in your hospital notes
only happened in his presence.
It was not your voice telling me to have a nice life
or to stop badgering, nor was it you typing copious letters
vilifying me and your other children. It wasn't you
depleting your bank accounts.

Twice he kidnapped you.

I saw your sorry gaze as he flung the hall door open,
felt the chill in the room
and his rage,
saw that the life in your eyes was gone,
that you were shattered fathoms deep.

We tried to chat and share a cup of tea, but our time together
was annihilated, as he dragged you to his car.
Police were unwilling to hear my voice,
and yours had been silenced by decades of abuse.
At Christmas, in the midst of a family gathering,
he kidnapped you again and tore you
from children and grandchildren.
Your phone was answered by others.
There was no intervention,
only prearranged visits better suited to prisoners
than to a mother and her children.

IV.

Those last days in your home, you were unreachable.
In the wee hours of morning,
you heard his jitterbug dance behind your bedroom windows,
then the smack and clatter of your belongings in the skip below.
Finally, he made an ambulance call
and your heart was restarted,
but children were banned from your last bedside.
There was no cause. He had no right.
How quick he was to say he was your sole caregiver!
On whose authority? On whose say?
In the twisted Irish way where men still speak volumes,
are revered and never questioned,
while women are subservient: the *nothing*.

V.

I'll bet they didn't expect my voice, Mom.
Now I understand what you endured, why the fight went
out of you and survival was the only route left.
For eight short weeks, I was proud to be at your bedside,
your own 24-hour protection vigil.
Together, we watched that birch tree shed leaf after leaf
in the fading autumn. And how you giggled at my outfits.
"That's a lovely shade of teal, Tessie," you'd say,
using my nickname. You'd reach to touch fuchsia
and lemon while I wept within.

In your final year, I was never able to see you,
yet I knew that, face-to-face, mother to daughter,
you would have spoken. He knew the same and kept me away.
Instead, I carry your voice, Mom, gladly:
to ensure justice and retribution,
so that others will know you —
a battered woman, a mother.

MAXWELL: I'm an incest survivor and my mom was a victim of elder abuse. She died in 2010. Many systems failed my mother and continue to fail me as I try to find justice for her. Domestic violence is a huge social issue here in Ireland and remains underfunded and under-researched. There are lots of statistics and reports but little in Irish law to protect battered women. I hope to be part of the change, by bringing domestic violence further into the light and ensuring it is stamped out.

My childhood was a war zone filled with sexual, physical, and emotional abuse in a patriarchal and oppressive society. I returned to Ireland in 2008, 24 years after moving to, and finding healing in, America. Ireland had changed, my school friends assured me. Irish society was now much more open, progressive, and rights and systems were in place to protect women. Witnessing the abuse of my mom, I called in the HSE Elder Abuse service, the Gardai (An Garda Síochána, the Irish Police Force), her GP, her solicitor, and others, an entire year prior to her death. Each failed her — systematically. When she was hospitalized, unresponsive and incoherent — as many family members had predicted she would be — and under highly suspicious conditions while in the sole care of my youngest brother, the police refused to investigate. The elder-abuse service dropped her case because she was no longer in their care. Her GP knew nothing. Her solicitor promised to act for her and to protect her estate upon her death, but crimes and fraud and lies regarding her estate have gone unheeded.

It has been almost four years since my mother's death. I believe my mother was murdered. Even with hard evidence, I have been unable to find any Irish agency, government official, or system that will ensure that these crimes will be accounted for. I live in horror daily, knowing much of the suffering my mom endured. My mom was a battered woman and suffered decades of emotional and physical abuse at the hands of my father and, in her final years, at the hands of her youngest son. And now, I cannot let it go because my mom is dead. My mother deserved so much more, and she was so much more: A painter. A singer. A survivor. A mother who gave it all for her children. She had a zest and exuberance for life that Irish oppression tried to snuff out so often. My mom was about surviving. She knew Irish systems would not help her. I write of her in the hope that someone will hear her voice. I know that without those words, I cannot survive.

MARIANA MCDONALD

mariana mcdonald is a public health scientist who works in the arena of health equity, addressing infectious-disease disparities. Her work has appeared in numerous publications, including poetry in *The Anthology of Southern Poets V: Georgia, Southern Women's Review, Sugar Mule,* and *El Boletín Nacional,* and fiction in *Up, Do: Flash Fiction by Women Writers* and *So to Speak.* She lives in the greater Atlanta area, where she is active in the writing community and the immigrant-rights movement and is also a frequent reader at literary and community events. mcdonald became a Fellow of Georgia's Hambidge Arts Center in 2012.

SWIMMING AT LAKE CABLE

Summer day. Scores of bathers, swimmers, divers
around a crescent beach with withered sands.

A public place for summer swims. Lifeguards lazy in
their towers. Children of all ages splashed and shrieked.

She'd gone too far. Close to the ropes where plastic
buoys bobbed, as if to jeer. Swimming out was easy

with her simple stroke. But now, near those ropes, she
lost her way, began to flail about and sink, could only

think of getting to the ropes or getting help. She saw
him coming, saw hope in his fervent strokes.

He reached for her with hands that she imagined
would shake a friend's hand, or high-five him, flip

a tassel to one side before tossing the mortarboard
into the air. Hands that make funny doodles

in the margins of his math book.
Instead his hands came at her broken into digits —

one or two that entered places she hadn't known
she had, dove into a place where no one,

nothing, yet had passed, not even monthly wages
of a latent womb. Gulps of sandy water

drowned her voice as her final burst of effort
found the ropes at last beside her.

She told no one of that summer day, its lambent skies,
the crescent shore, the violation floating in those waters.

MCDONALD: I have been writing for many years against the violence that women experience because it is unfortunately a constant reality in our lives. I have suffered violence myself, and have seen countless women victimized by it. I hope that by writing about it and bringing the horrific reality into the light of day, we can build a strong and effective movement to end it.

I wrote "Swimming at Lake Cable" in response to the sexual assault of a ten-year-old girl who is very dear to me.

JUDITH H. MONTGOMERY

Judith H. Montgomery lives and writes in Bend, Oregon. Her poems appear in *Ars Medica, Cimarron Review, Measure, Hunger Mountain,* and *Cave Wall,* among other journals, and in a number of anthologies. She's been awarded fellowships in poetry from Literary Arts and the Oregon Arts Commission to work on a new manuscript (*Cicatrix*). Her chapbook *Passion* received the 2000 Oregon Book Award for poetry. Montgomery's second collection, *Red Jess,* appeared in February 2006, from Cherry Grove Collections; her second chapbook, *Pulse & Constellation,* was a finalist for the Finishing Line Press competition and was published by that press in 2007.

AGAINST KNOWING

after "Arab Woman," by John Singer Sargent, 1905–6

    mark   how he's blurred   her face
smudged blue   mute   as he paints

her still   into our rapt   gaze she
    apparently   gazeless   anonymous

    her face   erased   above a body
veiled   head to ankle   arch

aswirl   in cream &   blue-shadowed
    cloth   such delectable   drape

    his paint   containing   what   *what*
as he takes   her measure   as she

braces   against stroke   & sanding
    sirocco   resists as his sable

    brush lays   such caressing   flares
of shadow   sun &   despite the dry

gusts   that press   the robe against
    her limbs   no   *silken tent*   tugging

it threatens   to whip away   revealing
what   *what*   as she faces   faces

down   any eye   never mind how
the lush swath   hides   but does not

hide   her shape   mark   how she
anchors   against knowing

counters   embrace   cloth knotted
tight   in her hidden   hand   she

asks   for nothing   gives away   nothing
apparently   silenced   apparently

anonymous   she speaks   & withstands
by the firm   holdfast of her hand

Her Silence Is

A thin robe, seamless tissue-
of-silver wrapped about her limbs.

Endless linen wound to cripple
her toes, binding ever closer

the voices of her feet.   Her hair
bound in a snood of woven gold.

(Is consequence.   Statement.   Custom.)

Her hips' swash constricted
by panniers' brocade.   Floating

rib removed, the more closely
to corset her waist.   Breath.

(Handcuff.   Straitjacket.   Gag.)

Her stiletto heel.   Hobble-skirt.   Chador
     muting verb and adverb of her stride.

Both bandage and wound.   Glitter
     and mesh that nets her tongue.

     (Calling.   Witness.   Refusal.)

Clitoridectomy: cancel
     cancel the throat of her moan.

     (Shame.   Cinch.   Crib.) Is

fear: of what she might say,
     were she free to speak: breaking

forth from ankle, ear, hair, cheek,
     rib   hand   hip   lip   lips —

from tongue   tongue
                her unbridled tongue.

TETHER

Red silk dress a blur about my knees,
I track him through the crush of satin
camisoles, leather-elbowed Harris tweed,

my ears pricked sharp in costly Christ-gift
diamond — my wrists cuffed in his fine-
beaten gold. I carry my mouth like a net.

His ruddy hand sleeks the mayor's palm,
familiarly grazes my sister's nude
nape. Candles flicker double-mirrored

tongues. Orbiting the alcohol glitter,
our velvet children cruise silver platters,
on the hunt for dainty treats. Caressing

his crystal amber glass, he lifts our ruffled
daughter squealing to the tree. Her Mary-Janes
flutter-kick — some see this as a dance.

He drifts by the bar, liberates a tidbit
to tempt the dean's plump wife. I shudder
full alert when his sly head cocks:

camouflage to banter that bitters from his
lips — *insult, accident.* The woman's red
mouth gapes like a wound. I abandon

my Fumé, I siren mutely in.
AMBULANCE is pasted on my brow.
I pick out bits of shrapnel dressed as wit —

of course he meant . . . I edit him back
into a host. Heavy-sailed in 25-year
Scotch, he watches me proffer gin martini,

olive antidote. When he crooks
his pointer finger to reel me in, I
summon for witnesses my red-oil smile.

He draws me to his hip, crushing scarlet
silk, and spins again that cocktail tale
to his grinning friends. *My wife, she's so*

cute, he seems to say. He strokes my un-
defended spine, so that I must smile.
So I cannot walk away.

MONTGOMERY: I am interested in the silencing (sometimes self-silencing) of women, especially through masks and disguises, as protection against violence and as submission to imposed social roles. Such disguise often manifests itself in the form of clothing or jewelry, as the woman becomes an art object (think Pygmalion and Galatea, Professor Higgins and Eliza Doolittle), a "creation" of the man and subject to his desire to perfect her, to shape her as a creature under his and society's control. *Confinement* and *escape:* our myths and stories, our public and personal histories, are replete with examples. I hope by addressing these in poetry to bring the former to greater light and the latter into the realm of celebration.

MÁIRE MORRISSEY-CUMMINS

Máire Morrissey-Cummins lives in Greystones, Co. Wicklow, Ireland. She is early-retired and has found joy in poetry and art. She has been published in *Every Day Poets, Wordlegs, The First Cut, A New Ulster, The Galway Review, Bray Arts, Notes from the Gean, Shot Glass, A Hundred Gourds,* and in many other online and print magazines worldwide. She is a member of Haiku Ireland and was recognized as one of the top 100 European Haiku writers in 2012.

SHINY RED APPLES

The patter of rain was constant
on the galvanized roof
drowning out the Royal show band
on the radio.
It was a Saturday in summer,
your baking day,
and Sean and I
were on the dining room table,
a sheet of brown paper
and box of crayons between us,
coloring our dreams.

I drew our house
with a curving avenue,
an apple tree
at the bottom of the garden.
Chubby fingers struggled
with a thick red crayon
circling shiny apples on the tree.

I watched you measuring flour,
iron weights balancing the scales.
I could hear the click of the latch
on the door beneath the sink,

twiddling of a bottle top
clink of glass
swish and swallow
in rhythm with the rain.

Caught,
our eyes locked;
your caustic glare
darted to the pit of my stomach.
I clasped my crayon,
gouging the drive to the house.

You snarled my name,
snatched me from the table,
bruised me up the stairs
to my room.

I knew that atonement
would be my only route to your love
and that the path to our door
was not blood red
by accident.

MORRISSEY-CUMMINS: I have written about my mother and her years of alcoholism and mental illness throughout my childhood and into my adulthood, as it was cathartic and important to voice my pain. She is a dry drunk today. I've spent a lifetime wanting a mother/daughter relationship but accept that it will never happen. She labels me "emotional," highly strung, unbalanced, and I seem to bring out the worst in her. It is better to keep my distance and live my life with my loved ones, my husband and children and friends, who know all that I am and who I feel comfortable to be around. I forgive her but will never forget what she did to me. She was a cruel woman.

I was a child soloist in a choir every Sunday from the age of 8 to 12. The church was next to the convent school that I attended. There was a man in the choir who abused me in the music room before mass every Sunday. I used to get sick/faint afterwards, and this developed into a phobia about church rooms, polished halls, certain buildings and, eventually, all public places (agoraphobia), which crippled my teenage years. I never spoke about the abuse, still don't speak of it, but I got help with agoraphobia in my twenties. I have suffered from depression all of my life and believe it is because I held so many secrets buried inside me. I was full of shame and carried my mother's guilt. Today, I do not deal in secrets; I've taken off the masks and live a life of truth. It feels good, but nothing can erase the past; it is part of me and I am stronger because of it. Writing about it has been really good, and I have only begun to tap into the darkness of my life and let it out.

ÁINE MOYNIHAN

Áine Moynihan was born in County Wexford and now lives in County Kerry. Her first collection, *Canals of Memory*, was published by Doghouse in 2008. It was shortlisted for the Strong Award for Best First Collection at the DLR International Poetry Now Festival in 2009. Her work was included in *Best Irish Poetry in English 2010*, edited by Matthew Sweeney (Southword Editions). In 2015, Moynihan directed a bilingual production of a play called *Eclipsed* (*Faoi Scáth*) by Patricia Burke Brogan, about the Magdalen laundries in Ireland. She is currently working on collections in both Irish and English, and on a bilingual play.

CÚITEAMH AN *CURIA*

Caith uait an clóca dearg;
dóigh an biretta;
cuir ort sacéadach.
Siúl amach sa chearnóg.
Bíodh misneach agat.
Siúl díreach chuig bean
atá agóideach, uchtnocht.
Sín tú féin ag a cosa.
Iarr maithiúnas uaithi.
Lig di, ansan, tú a threorú
ar ais chun an tí, atá folmhaithe
anois dá ghiúirléidí spiagacha.
Lig di
tú a oiliúint
i bhféith na humhlaíochta;
conas fónamh don phobal.

CARDINAL SINS

Cast off the red cloak.
Burn the biretta.
Put on sackcloth.
Walk into the square.
Find some woman there.
Be brave. Walk right up
To a topless protester.
Prostrate yourself before her
And beg forgiveness.
Then let her lead you
Back into the house
Stripped now of its gaudy splendor.
Learn from her
What it is to be humble
And what it is to serve.

MOYNIHAN: This poem, in English and Irish, was born out of anger at the pain inflicted on women by the oppression and hatred, rooted in fear, which the institutional Catholic church displays towards us by excluding us from ordained ministry and seeking to control our sexuality. A male, celibate, clergy has bred suspicion and fear of women. Its exclusion of women from the priesthood is, I believe, discriminatory, unjust, and clearly detrimental to the well-being of the Church. The sight of rows of red-hatted Cardinals in the televised footage leading up to the last Papal election angered me. "Cardinal Sins" was fueled by that anger.

NATASHA MURDOCK

Natasha Murdock attends Arizona State University. She has won numerous awards for her poetry and has been published in *Up and Under Magazine* and *So to Speak*.

A LOVE POEM

Sometimes I am afraid
of the dark and my own naked body
and my own naked body drunk in the dark.
Sometimes I am
afraid of being
afraid
that you'll grow
tired of my crying
because sometimes
even when I don't
know that I am remembering
I am remembering
what it felt like
to be held sweetly and raped.
Because something goes wrong,
something misfires
and instead of remembering
it happened
I remember it happening:
his hands covering my mouth;
the taste of my cunt on his hands;
his too-hard dick;
his trying, and trying, to make it fit;
him tucking me into bed;
the sheet grazing my chin like a life sentence;
and the secret is, I didn't stay,
I stumbled out

after him,
to ask if he was okay
to drive,
ignoring the blood dripping
down to the rocks underneath
my bare feet.
Even then, I didn't realize I was crying,
I didn't have a word for it:
and now,
I don't know what's happening,
I don't know what's wrong,
I just know that it's wrong, and that sometimes,
still,
it is dark
and I am afraid.

WHEN YOU WAKE UP, YOU'LL REMEMBER NOTHING

1. *Third Time's the Charm*

He held me
down like a bandit
would tie a woman cloaked in yellow
to train tracks.

My defense: the answer
No, but
it wasn't enough
once or twice,
and the third never
made it from my lips
to the palms
of his hands, but mine
were busy anyway,

the silent *No* occupying the tips
of my fingers
which were digging
from some unfound dying
ambition to fight.

2. *Asking for It*

Eight years old running, holding a spoon, showing
Nana! I'd finished all the batter she'd given me,
I was smiling for more,
when she told me *No more, it's bad for you,*
while scooping my kid-spitted spoon
into the bowl, scraping the edges to fill it.

3. *How Does That Feel?*

It almost tasted sweet. It almost felt like whisking.
In me, it mixed a longing that I didn't know.
I still don't know.

4. *You're Exaggerating*

I preferred to keep a watchful eye on the night,
so for weeks it was 24-hour news and infomercials.
The terror chart turned red
and then black, maybe purple. Slides
of terrorists, men with beards,
strangers, slid across my vision. And in between faces,
I learned that *OxiClean will clean anything,*
remove stains that even I couldn't dream of.
It became a lullaby, a prayer:
It'll clean anything.
It'll clean anything.
Anything.

5. *Scarlet, in the Bedroom, with the Candlestick*

There were fingers pressed in places I had never ventured. My armpit
ached from the grip. The heel of his hand pressed my shoulder
inward. There was no rhythm, but soon I knew, I was not the first.
He was gentle when I wasn't struggling. I stopped struggling. I was
as militant as a refrigerator. I stopped trying to breathe. His palms
tasted like carpet and my sweat. There was a candle lit, vanilla, like
me. We had played Clue an hour before. I lost.

6. *Statute of Limitations*

A Major League baseball only lives, on average, through seven pitches.
85% of the universe is Dark Matter.
Vanilla is the most powerful scent for attracting males.
I was wearing it that night.
The word *listen* is an anagram for *silent.*

7. *It's Okay, Nothing Happened*

I am confused when I'm lifted, like a loaf of bread,
onto my barely covered mattress. I hear myself
crying, though he speaks, a shushing
in his voice: *You didn't do anything.* I say nothing. I move nowhere.
His kiss lands on my forehead, so like a lover's, and he drapes me
with a white sheet. I am too old to bleed from this, but still I drip.

MURDOCK: I wrote these poems after an unintentional vow of silence that lasted
several years. That silence about being a victim of rape was only made worse by the
many reactions I was further victimized by — including from those very close to me.
I was blamed and belittled. The question "What were you thinking?" was repeated
often in my life. Though I had written many poems before, this subject remained
taboo, even by my own standards.

But then I hinted at it in a poem. I tried very hard to mask it, to veil it, to bury it in vague poetic devices, but someone noticed it. They heard me. That person did not belittle me. He did not ask what I was wearing when I was raped or whether or not I had been drinking. He didn't ask what I had done to stop it. He just circled the tiny moment on the page and said *This needs to be louder.* Someone had heard me, despite myself. And so I began writing more and more. Hoping not only to be heard, but to heal. It felt like I was tearing a part of myself out for good, and it felt incredible to hang it up for everyone to see.

RASHIDA MURPHY

Rashida Murphy is a writer and poet based in Perth, Western Australia, whose work has been published in anthologies and journals. As part of a PhD in Writing from Edith Cowan University in Perth, she completed a novel entitled *The Historian's Daughter* that centers on displacement and abandonment. In 2014, she received a grant that allowed her to travel to India to complete her research for the novel, and in 2015 it was shortlisted for the Dundee International Book Prize.

TWELVE

I envied you
your gold Favre-Leuba
when you were twelve.

I told you I
couldn't wait
to turn twelve.

I hope you
never turn twelve
you said.

Four years later
when I was twelve
you panicked.

Don't touch her
you said
don't touch her *there.*

It won't hurt
our mother said.
It's only a nick. It won't hurt.

You held me in your arms
and said
take my gold Favre-Leuba

But don't let them
cut you there.
It hurts. It's not right.

Today, betrayed by theories
on clitoridectomy,
I thank you.

MURPHY: This poem was written in response to a conversation I had with my sister, several years after we had grown up and gone our separate ways. I had no idea that my family/community in India practiced the archaic and barbaric system of clitoridectomy. We were college-educated, liberal, and prided ourselves on our open-mindedness. I was appalled when she told me that I was the only female member of our family who had not been "done." When I asked why I had been left alone, she smiled and reminded me of the conversation I retell in the poem, which I had completely forgotten. So, for the fact that I have an intact clitoris, I thank my sister, who was not so lucky herself.

The Favre-Leuba is a brand of wristwatch that dates back to 1737. It was considered highly desirable by young, well-to-do, girls growing up in India in the 1970s.

GLORIA G. MURRAY

Gloria g. Murray has published poetry, short stories, and one-act plays in many literary journals, and her poem "In My Mother's House" was featured by Ted Kooser, in his online *American Life in Poetry* (Column #32). In 2015, Murray won first prize in the Anna Davidson Rosenberg Award competition sponsored by *Poetica Magazine*. Her one-act play *Madame Tanya* was presented at the Northport, Long Island, one-act festival in April 2013, and *What Are Friends For?* was included in the *Art of the One-Act* anthology (New Issues Poetry & Prose, 2007). Her first book of poems, *In My Mother's House*, was created with a grant from the Ludwig Vogelstein Foundation.

ONCE

husband, once
you carried me
a cross on your back
wore me
a chain around your neck
took me
a sacrifice
under your tongue

once, you swore
you never loved me
once
as with all gods
I embraced you, anyway

MURRAY: I wrote this poem after my husband refused to get my car fixed and I was stuck at a gas station with little money and no way home. I went to a diner, having only enough for a cup of tea and a muffin, and sat there thinking about the different ways women are abused by lovers, fathers, husbands, who get satisfaction from putting women in an inferior, dependent, and often frightening position. It wasn't until my husband passed away eight years ago that I was able to acknowledge that, as a victim in an abusive marriage, I had also suffered from post-traumatic stress disorder (PTSD). Chronic and devastating behavior from a supposedly loving spouse can traumatize you as much as being a war survivor can. That kind of marriage is a battle in itself. I have to say that although I am, yes, more lonely, I no longer live in fear of another person's domination. Unfortunately, it was fate that intervened, instead of my own courage.

Poetry did indeed save my sanity and my hope. Most of the poems I had written previously were about the situation I was in. Now I am free to write about other things as well and feel the growth in my poems and in my life. I say to any woman who feels she is stuck in a bad relationship — if you have two legs, *run,* run for your life, claim it, and whichever way destiny evolves, always, always, keep hold of yourself.

Terri Muuss

Terri Muuss has published poetry in *Bolts of Silk, Red River Review, Whispers and Shouts: An Anthology of Women's Voices on Long Island,* and in other magazines and anthologies. Her book *Over Exposed* was released by JB Stillwater in 2013, and her one-woman show, *Anatomy of a Doll,* has been performed throughout the US and Canada since 1998. Muuss co-produced and hosted the monthly Manhattan poetry series *Poetry at the Pulse* for two years. As a licensed social worker, she specializes in the use of the arts as a healing mechanism for trauma survivors and teaches a course at Rutgers University to social workers entitled "Youth Development Through the Written Arts."

Blank Day

Scraped clean
by the sounds beneath
her, his body
hissing like water
into an empty space,
she was opened
against the will
of her heel
dug sharply into
the dip of
the gray mattress.

Before he was in
her as white as white
above white
her veins dark as
bruises, he carefully removed
his shoes, folded and draped
his shirt then
his pants over
the bedpost, marking
where he'd been.

FATHER'S SECRET DRAWER

smells of ashes and sweat
and is cut in two by a black
cloth liner. On top: a gold
pen, tie tacks, small bag
of dried cloves, a picture
of his mother and a lump
of chewed gum.

Beneath: the metal casings
of shotgun shells, four huge teeth
with roots, a segment
of my baby hair trapped
between pieces of
tape and an assortment of thick
thumbnail clippings. In my palm

they look like mini moons. My father
uses them to pick
bits of food from between his yellow
teeth. At night, his teeth gleam —
a mouth of stars above me,
his fingernails smooth
as glass — they stroke

my skin, white as pork.

MUUSS: To me, writing about trauma is anathema. Yet finding words to describe that for which words fail has been my life's work, both as author and survivor. The only reason I persist in this seemingly impossible endeavor is that I hope I can provide some semblance of a voice for those who have none.

When the painful memories of my incest/sexual abuse began running through my brain 17 years ago, I thought I was alone. I thought I was a freak. I thought I was going crazy. Years later, after performing my one-woman show for countless survivors, and hearing their stories, I know I am not alone. Unfortunately, there are millions of survivors just like me, who have suffered from the pain of childhood sexual abuse. Global violence against women, and the silence surrounding it, is rarely discussed; when that conversation *is* opened, it focuses on violence happening to *other* women, in *other* countries, not Americans. The fact is that violence against women happens everywhere: In poor homes, rich homes, middle-class homes. In black families, white families, Asian families, Latino families. In faraway countries and right next door. So many women, all of them feeling alone. I write for them.

JAN NAPIER

Jan Napier is a Western Australian poet. She has published two books of short stories, *Smiles to Go* and *All the Fun of the Fair*, and was the in-house book reviewer for online sci-fi/fantasy zine *Antipodean SF* from 2009 to 2012. Napier's poetry has been published Australia-wide in *Westerly, Famous Reporter, Australian Love Poems 2013, Regime, Unusual Work*, and in other journals and anthologies, and it has also appeared in New Zealand (*Poetry New Zealand* and *Valley Micropress*) and America (*The World According to Goldfish* and *Maintenant*, Issues 5 and 6). Her first book, *Thylacine*, was released by Regime Books in September 2015.

LIKE THE MOON

Intense   insistent   he tugs at me
the way a cavalry horse takes hold
of the bit before the charge.
Changes my rhythms.
Causes internal conflict.
There is an undercurrent of blood.
In the aftermath he sits on high
silent   cold   like the moon.
Promises nothing.
Unseen shackles rattle.
Upturned palms ask.
He cracks a can   picks up the remote.
Doesn't understand.

Even rejection is communication.

TO BE A WOMAN

To be a woman
burn a numb candle
erase every last word
quiver like cat-lapped milk
at his rowdy blow
spice beefsteak with humility
bind the tempest of your ankles
fling vision into a fish kettle
espouse praise and mimicry.
Scrub that doorstep heart.

NAPIER: "Like The Moon" is a retrospective piece. My partner at that time (a psychiatric nurse!) was aggressive and abusive. It was my first, and happily my only, experience of physical violence. That man cleverly isolated me by driving my friends away with his rudeness and negativity; he terrified me into compliance and treated me as a doormat. And I was young and frightened enough to let him. Even when he was in a good mood, if he didn't feel like responding to me verbally, he wouldn't. If I persisted, he would hit me. It took me a year to get rid of him. But I did. That's where this poem comes from.

I wrote "To be a Woman" to highlight the fact that, for so long, women were considered no more than chattels. This was actually a point of law: women were listed as household belongings like washboards and crockery. They were not supposed to experience independent thought, were viewed as inferior in intellect, and kept, as far as possible, physically and mentally subservient to the wishes and wants of their male masters. This was in line with the thinking that made cruelty to animals socially acceptable in earlier times, when it was believed that animals had no souls and therefore couldn't feel pain!

LESLIE B. NEUSTADT

Leslie B. Neustadt is a former Assistant Attorney General for the State of New York. She took early retirement after developing an incurable form of blood cancer. Her essays and poems have been published in a wide variety of magazines, journals, and anthologies. Neustadt published her first book of poetry, *Bearing Fruit: A Poetic Journey*, in the spring of 2014. The entire purchase price of each copy sold has been shared among various nonprofits, some of which aid children who have been abused. One of the organizations that have received these donations is ECPAT-USA (End Child Prostitution, Abuses and Trafficking), which is the leading anti-trafficking policy organization in the United States.

CARRY-ON BAGGAGE

I carry my battered
duffel bag everywhere.
I wouldn't recognize
myself without it.
Nothing epic inside,
no craters carved
by roadside bombs.
It wasn't genocide or famine
that ravaged my life,
just my father's
nighttime incursions.
Some days the weight feels
oppressive as fog;
a ghostly mirage
that obscures my vision.
On others, it is a phantom
limb that still aches.
When old memories flood me,
fault lines appear
as familiar as my face.
I shove them in my duffel bag
and zip it shut.

TESHUVAH

Account and repent.

My father sits ragged, palsied,
a mere shard of himself,
the world slipping out of his grasp.
He who raged can barely whisper.
Once he cast a giant shadow,
flooded me with his fury.
His river of epithets wore me down.
On sunny days, a ringmaster of delight,
he enveloped me in excess.
When I was a little girl, my mother sickened.
He took me as his concubine.
Like a slender white birch, I bent amidst his storms.
Sickened by blood cancer in my fifties,
my marrow muttered,
Only justice will bring you peace.
I kindled a burnt offering of my failings.
Like the priests of old, I donned
a *choshen mishpat,* a breastplate
of judgment, over my wounded heart.
I challenged this man, my father,
to answer for what he had done.
Account and repent.
Slice open your heart.
Let that be your legacy.

Silence his only reply.

UNSPEAKABLE

Words spew forth,
sour and unspeakable
as my father in the night.
Insistent rhythms rock my body —
syncopated madness.
A wolf at my bedroom door.
Silence howled in the blackened night.
Disembodied, disemboweled.
Fingers in my entrails,
seed seeped into my marrow,
pregnant with his shame.
Little deaths each time
he called me *cunt.*
Until I threatened suicide,
hung it around his neck.

NEUSTADT: I came to write poetic memoir late in my life, after I found a supportive peer writing group for women. The founder created sacred space where women could share their writing and be honored for their life experiences. I had kept the shameful secret of my incestuous relationship with my father to myself for decades, and sharing my experience with compassionate and accepting women was profoundly healing. While it is difficult to bare one's soul in public, I pray that women who have been abused will be encouraged to share their experiences and hope that those who have not experienced the ravages of incest will understand better its long term effects. All too often, we demonize the stranger who violates children. While we need to prevent and help the victims of such horrific acts, most children are abused by someone they know.

Martina Reisz Newberry

Martina Reisz Newberry's most recent book is *Learning by Rote*. She is also the author of *What We Can't Forgive; Late Night Radio; Perhaps You Could Breathe for Me; Hunger; After the Earthquake: Poems 1996–2006; Not Untrue & Not Unkind;* and *Running Like a Woman With Her Hair on Fire: Collected Poems*. In 1998, Newberry won *i.e. Magazine's* Editor's Choice Poetry Chapbook Prize for *An Apparent, Approachable Light*. She has been widely published in numerous literary magazines in the United States and abroad. She lives in Hollywood, California.

Red Cat

Red Cat is a somewhat sweet wine found in upstate New York.

It might have been September —
I know it was early fall.
I imagined myself ill
with a fever brought on by
winds racing below the old
canyons. The mark of your hand
was still outlined on my face.
I sat on the porch with a
mug of sweet wine prophesying
to the ugly olive tree
that I would use "light shimmer
#3" to cover the
marks later on, but, for now,
I would rejoice in their proof
of my inward flame, my burning
failures. The mountains I could
see were the Inland Empire's
minor mountains and their too-
familiar shadows. Evenings
like that were miracles.

The children gone to their grand-
parents, blind with love that did
not bite their tiny asses
or damn them to the landscape
of another fatherly
detonation. The sound of
his car driving off was the
relief of nitroglycerine
when the heart throws a tantrum.
Here came tumbleweeds and small
branches down the street. The red
mercury up, the dark be-
coming dark and, as if by
surgery, holes were cut in
the sky to let through the
crystalline light of stars.
And there was the miracle —
just there in the sky: Jesus
raising his middle finger
to all that was fearful and
painful and bleeding. I knew
then what every woman knows:

the beauty that is beaten
out of us is replaced by
a secret and an oh-so-
holy meridian re-
served for the weak, the depraved,
the bitchy and the absurd. The
wind hammered the olive tree,
his car returned. I sat still
on the porch in my yellow
robe. There was still sweet wine in
my mug and I drank deeply.

WHEN HE IS GONE

I told myself... first thing I'll do is buy rock and roll music; I'll play it loud and dance by myself in the big room at the back of the house. No, no... first thing will be no dinner. The day he leaves, I'll cook no dinner; I'll have 3 drinks of Irish whiskey on ice and I will not listen to the news on television. When he leaves, the house will stare at me, ask *What now?* I'll say, *nothing. Nothing now.* First thing I'll do is take a shower and not cry in it and not be afraid to come out. I'll cuddle the dog even if she does smell a little funny, for who will be there to say so — NO ONE, that's who. I'll feed her scraps from the table and let her bark, and I'll never shout "Shut the hell up, Clementine!" I'll leave clean laundry on the bed, unfolded, and sleep in the bed that same night. I'll remember what *my* favorite ice cream is and I'll buy cheap sweet wines to drink. I'll break the yolks on every egg I cook for the rest of my life. I won't buy make-up to cover bruises and I'll throw away every elastic bandage in the house. I'll bump my arm on an open cupboard door — hard enough to bruise — so I can say to my neighbor, "Oh, this bruise? I hit myself on a cupboard door," and it will be true. I'll cuss out loud 5 times in 5 minutes. I'll learn how not to flinch and how to frown. I'll leave my shoes in the kitchen and forget where I left the car keys. I'll let the cat in and out 24 times. I'll make a sandwich, take 2 bites and throw the rest away. I won't look at anyone else first to see if a thing is funny or sad, I'll laugh if I want and cry if I feel like it. What I lost was not beautiful. When he goes, the first thing I'll do is buy rock and roll music.

NEWBERRY: My own experience with domestic violence has convinced me that, because it happens in the dark, inside the house, behind locked doors, a footstep on the path to stopping it is to shine light on the subject and to show it for the heinous act it is. Many of my poems do exactly that. It has to end. The violence, the pain, the scarring, the humiliation — it has to stop. Perhaps poetry can help.

GAIL NEWMAN

Gail Newman, born in Germany and raised in Los Angeles, lives in San Francisco. She is a museum educator at the Contemporary Jewish Museum and a poet-teacher for California Poets in the Schools. She has edited two books of poems by children, *Dear Earth* (self-published through a grant from Teachers and Writers) and *C is for California* (WestWinds Press), and *Inside Out*, a book of lessons for high school teachers. She co-founded and edited *Room, A Women's Literary Journal*. Newman's poems have appeared in a number of anthologies, including *Ghosts of the Holocaust*. Her most recent book of poetry, *One World*, was published in 2011 by Moon Tide Press.

REFUGEE NARRATIVE

When my parents came to this country
of crime-free and clean neighborhoods,
sanitary streets and public toilets,
refrigerators stashed with provisions,
real sheets and fresh running water,
black-and-white television and the movies,
blond bedroom sets, plumped pillows, sofas,
social workers, freedom
to walk in the street
without interrogation or public
hangings, without sequestered
ghettos, rations, food shortages,
shootings, genocide,
they sent us out alone into the streets
without worry.

Here's what I remember:
walking home from school
with my best friend Bonnie, we pass
a car pulled over at the curb, door

ajar, a man inside, belly balanced on steering
wheel, holding something in his lap, big, fleshy,
holding himself, looking down at his feet, eyes
half-closed, looking, not at us, pants pooled around knees,

feet flat on raised black accelerator pedal,
radio on — yet he knew
we were there, he saw us
he knew
and Bonnie said *Run* so we did.

Then the world became flat
and still,
quiet as when a car
is moving toward you and you know

you are about to crash but you can't
do anything and life slows down
to pauses between seconds,
to minutes between lives,
the air singed blue ash,
alone in this vague country.

G. NEWMAN: My best friend from childhood recently contacted me through
Facebook. We had not spoken for over forty years. When we met again and exchanged
memories, I was astonished to learn that she had been with me the day I walked by
a car with an open door and saw a man masturbating. I never forgot that incident. I
always felt a schism between my immigrant parents' vision of this country and my own
experience. When I share the poem with other women, many of them reveal similar
experiences in their own lives.

Because I was born into a family of Holocaust survivors, I was aware early on of the
moral imperative of bearing witness to injustice and cruelty. Every day, the news brings
images so disturbing that a poem demands to be written.

RICHARD JEFFREY NEWMAN

Richard Jeffrey Newman is a poet, translator, essayist, and college professor. His work focuses on the impact of feminism in his life as a man and the influence of classical Persian poetry on the lives of Americans. His books include one collection of poetry, *The Silence of Men* (CavanKerry Press, 2006), and three books of translations from Persian poetry: *Selections from Saadi's Gulistan* (2004) and *Selections from Saadi's Bustan* (2006), both released by Global Scholarly Publications, and a book on Rumi, *A Bird in the Garden of Angels* (Mazda Publishers, 2007), which he co-translated with John Moyne.

FOR MY SON, A KIND OF PRAYER

> *... for they know*
> *Of some most haughty deed or thought*
> *That waits upon his future days. ...*
> — William Butler Yeats, "A Prayer for My Son"

Just before his mother
pushed him through herself
hard enough to split who she was
wide enough for him to enter the world
I touched the top of my son's head;
and after he was born,
the midwife — Vivian,
I think it was —
held my wife's umbilical cord
in a loop for me to cut, which I did,
freeing our new boy's body
to enter the name
we had waiting for him;
and then Vivian laid him
against the curve of his mother's belly,
giving him to the breast
he would for years
define his world by;

and once that first taste of love
was firmly lodged within him,
she bundled him tight,
placed him in my arms
and, while I sang his welcome
in a far corner of the room,
turned to assist the doctor
sewing up my wife's
birth-torn flesh.

I don't remember what song I chose,
and it's been a decade at least
since I've told anyone
about my son's first moments
as my son, but they've come to me here,
in this urologist's waiting room,
because I picked up from the coffee table
the copy of *The Nation*
another patient must have left behind,
and the first article my eyes fell on,
"Silence = Rape," by Jan Goodwin,
introduced me to Shashir,
six years old and gang-raped
in the Congo. When they found her,
she was starving;
and when they found her,
she could neither walk nor talk;
and so they stitched together
the parts of her the men had ruptured,
fed her, gave her clothing;
and that night she slept
for the first time since no one knew when
in a bed that was not
the bush the militia had left her to die in;
and maybe the tent walls
shaping the room she lived in

when Goodwin learned she existed
had come to mean for her
a kind of safety; and maybe
that safety was fertile ground,
where words for what those men had done to her
dropped like seeds
from the mouths of the ones who rescued her
and began to take root.

I have not been gang-raped,
but a man much older than I was
when I was twelve
forced his penis into my mouth,
seared the back of my throat
with what he poured out of himself
and sealed into silence
everything that took me
fifteen years of pushing
till who I was split wide enough
that who I am
could speak his first true words.

"Mr. Newman?" The nurse,
white, blond, about my age,
calls my name,
one of the few she has not butchered,
sitting as I am
among the men of Jackson Heights,
where names that would twist
the tongue of any English speaker
are common, but I'm not yet ready
to leave Goodwin's piece.
Maria was seventy
when the Interahamwe
tied her legs apart
like a goat before slaughter;

and the women Goodwin leaves nameless,
most of them killed later by infection,
their labia pierced and padlocked
when their rapists were finished —
the story belongs to them as well.

"Mr. Newman?"

I put the magazine down,
bear those women with me
as I rise towards the door I need to walk through
so I can place in this doctor's hand
the left testicle I found a bump on
three days ago. A few
of my fellow patients
glance up as I pass,
one of them smiling,
nodding his head,
as if to say, "Don't worry.
It'll all work out."

I smile back, grateful
for his small empathy,
noticing as I do
that the flag pin on his lapel
and the name of the newspaper
folded in his lap
place his origin in,
or at least his allegiance to,
a country now making headlines
for stories like Shashir's;
and I know such things
don't happen only
over there; and of course
not one man in this room
has ever done enough,

could ever do enough,
to stop them.

So I think perhaps
this is where we're supposed to be,
a kind of purgatory
pregnant with poetic justice.
The door shuts behind me.
The nurse grins "Please, follow me,"
over her shoulder,
and leads the way in silence
to the room where I will wait.
A four-color poster
of the male reproductive system
dominates the wall.
Its penis, I notice,
includes the foreskin;
the plastic model
sitting on the cabinet
does not — something
to ask the doctor about,
but when he arrives
my only thought
resembles a prayer.

He snaps on
latex gloves;
I let my pants
fall to my ankles,
my underwear
to just below my knees,
and I watch him handle
what in my wife's language
are called my *tokhm*, my "eggs."

"It's probably nothing,"
he nods sagely,
stepping back,
peeling the rubber
off his hands.
I pull my clothing up,
tuck in my shirt.
"Still," he continues —
I'm fumbling with my zipper —
"let's check it again
six months from now."
He smiles, offers his hand
for me to shake, then moves on
to the next man in the next room.
I head back out the way I came,
where my friend smiles and nods again,
lifting his hand in a farewell
I answer with my own nod and smile,
the reprieve I've just gotten
predisposing me
not to assume the worst of anyone.

Outside, the wind
rips the hood
away from my head;
snow-gusts slap
back and forth
across my face;
and I am reminded how quickly
beauty turns cold, how easily
death wears friendship's face.
I want to know
how a man who loves his children
does not see their faces
in the eyes of the girl
whose vagina he is opening

with a bottle or a bayonet;
I want to know why a woman's screams
beneath the fourth or fifth or eleventh man in line
do not recall for even one of them
the voice of a woman who loves him,
whom he has loved,
keeping his penis soft.

My son will never know Shashir,
but he will know men
who could've been,
who'd gladly be,
among the ones
who violated her;
and he'll know women,
and other men like me,
who carry violation
within them. A time will come,
because it comes to all of us,
when he'll be forced to choose
where his allegiance lies.

These words are for him
on the day of that decision.

R. NEWMAN: In the 1970s, when the men who violated me violated me, and then well into the 1980s, when I first started struggling to name that experience, a language adequate to the task of that naming simply did not exist. Largely, if not entirely because of the women's movement, we in the United States had only just begun to speak openly about sexual violence against women and girls. *No one* was talking about — and almost no one was willing to acknowledge — the fact that it was happening to boys and men, as well. Men who carried violation within them, like I did, were quite literally invisible. Or at least that's how I felt until I understood that the language women were using to name their experiences of rape and sexual assault — and to assign blame and responsibility where it belonged, with those who committed those acts — could also be applied to my experience and to the men who had assaulted and violated me.

That realization didn't just transform me from a victim into a survivor. It also changed the way I thought of myself as a writer. What was the purpose of writing, I asked myself, if it was not to speak this truth? The other thing this realization did for me was demonstrate, in undeniable terms, the connection between the men who violated me, my experience of that violation, my healing, my writing, and feminist politics — that is, the feminist analysis of gender that made sexual objectification and victimization visible as expressions of not only personal, but also political power.

"For My Son, a Kind of Prayer" is one of those poems that began life as one thing — or, more accurately, as two things — and ended up as a third something else. Ten years ago, when my son was still little, I decided I wanted to write about the experience of being present when he was born. This poem's first strophe was the result. I was, however, unable to connect those lines convincingly to anything larger that was not already a cliché about the nature of fatherhood. So I put them away. That same year, I had edited out of a different poem about violence against women the lines about Shashir and Jan Goodwin's article for *The Nation.* Last year, I put the two fragments together on a page, and "For My Son, a Kind of Prayer," in that magic way that poems sometimes do, began to take shape. The connection — political, social, cultural, and personal — between the sexual violence I survived as a child, that, according to reliable statistics, one in six boys in this country survives, and sexual violence against women, has always been clear to me, but it is a connection that gets far too little attention. This poem is my way of beginning to give that connection the attention it deserves.

ÁINE NÍ GHLINN

Áine Ní Ghlinn is an Irish-language poet and children's writer, with eighteen children's books and four collections of poetry for adults published. Three of her teenage novels have won *Oireachtas* awards, and her collection of poetry for young readers, *Brionglóidí* (*Dreams*), was shortlisted for the 2009 Children's Books Ireland awards. More recently, *Daideo* (*Granddad*) — a book of teenage fiction — won the 2014 Irish-language Book of the Year Award, and *Nílim ag Iarraidh Dul ar Scoil* (*I Don't Want to Go to School*), a story for very young readers, was also shortlisted for the same award. *Daideo* also won the 2014/2015 Childrens Books Ireland Honour Award for fiction.

AN CAILÍN A THÉADH ISTEACH SA BHÁISTEACH

Srúill deor ar phána na fuinneoige. Cuisle báistí ar dhíon an tí.
Rithim a aimsiú. Mar sin a thosaíodh sé. Braon a roghnú.
Braon ar leith. É a leanúint. É a oscailt. Éalú léi isteach.

Tharlaíodh sé gach uile Dhomhnach go dtéadh sí mar sin isteach
sa bháisteach. Gach uile Dhomhnach ag leathuair tar éis a deich
d'éalaíodh sí léi isteach i mbraon báistí.

Uaireanta bhíodh uirthi an bháisteach a aimsiú taobh istigh. Dá
cloigeann. Dá samhlaíocht. D'éirigh sin ní ba éasca de réir a
chéile. Mar a bheadh lasc á smeachadh.

Tar éis trí mhí ní airíodh sí aon phian. Trí mhí eile is thosaíodh
an bháisteach láithreach ag rince, ag cuisliú ina cloigeann a
luaithe is a airíodh sí a chraosanáil.

Trí mhí eile fós is níor ghá di ach a choiscéim a chloisint ar an
staighre. Taobh istigh de bhliain bhíodh sí istigh sa bhraon
báistí le plabadh an dorais is a máthair ag dul ar Aifreann.

An bheirt acu imithe leo anois ar shlí a bhfírinne féin ach fós
gach uile mhaidin Domhnaigh éalaíonn sí léi isteach sa bháisteach.
Lasc á smeachadh. Braon ar leith. Lasc imithe ó smacht.

Ó am go chéile téann sé sa mhuileann uirthi teacht amach arís.
Ach sin scéal eile…
Dán eile…

THE GIRL WHO WENT INTO THE RAIN[*]

A trickle of tears down the window pane. Rain pulsating on
the roof. Finding a rhythm. That's how it used to be. How it began.
Choose a drop. Just one drop. Follow it. Open. Escape inside.

Every Sunday she would go like that into the rain.
Every Sunday morning at half past ten
she would escape into a drop of rain.

Sometimes she'd have to find the rain inside.
Inside her head. Inside her imagination. That got easier
as time went on. Like the flick of a switch.

Three months on she could feel no pain. Three more
and the rain would start to dance, to pulsate in her head
the moment she felt the touch of his breath.

Three months on again she only had to hear his footstep on the
stairs. Within a year she was inside that drop of rain the moment
her mother slammed the door on her way to Sunday Mass.

Both gone now to their eternal reward. Yet every Sunday
morning she still escapes into the rain. The flick of a switch.
Just one drop. A switch gone out of control.

There are times when she can't find her way back out.
But that's another story…
That's another poem…

---

[*] Translated from the Irish (Gaelic) by Áine Moynihan, with Áine Ní Ghlinn.

TÚ FÉIN IS MÉ FÉIN

Thógamar teach féir — tú féin is mé féin — ag
bun an mhóinéir. Do thrí scór bliain dod chromadh
ach fós bhí na ballaí chomh hard liom féin.

Chnag tú ar chloch an dorais. Bhuail isteach.
'Mise Daidí, tusa Mam,' a dúirt go séimh, *'is mé
ag filleadh ort tar éis obair an lae.'* D'ólamar
tae as cupáin bheaga bhréige.

*'Téanam ort, a chroí. Tá sé in am luí. Bain
díot.'* Is bhain. Bhain tú piliúr as balla na
cistine. Do thrí scór bliain dom phlúchadh.

D'éiríomar. Ghlan le do chiarsúr mé. Phóg mo
chuid fola leis an gcréacht a leigheas is
d'fhilleamar — tú féin is mé féin — ar theach
mo mháthar, ar theach d'iníne.

Ach pé sracfhéachaint a thugaim thar mo ghuaille
feicim fós ó am go chéile an chréacht oscailte
a d'fhág tú i mballa na cistine.

YOURSELF AND MYSELF*

We built a grass house — yourself and myself —
down in the meadow. You — hunched under your
three score years. Me — no higher than the walls.

You knocked on our stone door. You came in.
"I'll be Daddy; you be the Mum," you said softly.
"And I'll be coming home from my day's work."
We drank tea out of little toy cups.

---

* Translated by Áine Ní Ghlinn from Irish (Gaelic) with Áine Moynihan.

"Come on, my love. It's time for bed. Strip off."
I stripped. You plucked a pillow from the kitchen
wall. Your three score years stifling me.

We got up. You cleaned me with your handkerchief.
Kissed my blood to heal the wound, and hand in hand,
we went home — yourself and myself — to my mother's,
your daughter's house.

But whatever glance I throw over my shoulder
I still can see — from time to time — the gaping wound
you left in the kitchen wall.

NÍ GHLINN: While working as a radio journalist in Ireland, I began to explore the theme of child sexual abuse with a view to making a series of radio programs. The series was rejected by Raidió Teilifís Éireann in the very early nineties (a few years before all the clerical sex abuse scandals came to light). As I read through the material I had collected, the images gradually turned into poems. These came together in a bi-lingual collection *Unshed Tears / Deora Nár Caoineadh*, published by Dedalus in 1996. "Tú Féin is Mé Féin" comes from this collection. "An Cailín a Théadh Isteach sa Bhaisteach" / "The Girl Who Went into the Rain" comes from a later collection, *Tostanna* (*Silences*), published by Coiscéim in 2006. This poem is about the experience of "splitting," in which the child mentally/emotionally/spiritually leaves the abusive situation and views it from a safe place outside the body. In this case, the safe place is inside a drop of rain on the window pane (for someone else, it might be a crack in the ceiling).

Having survived abuse as a child, I already had a deep understanding of the subject but felt that the poems benefitted from the remove of writing through the experience of others. Perhaps this remove is just another form of splitting and viewing the situation from outside the realm of the personal — the poems carry echoes of personal experience, but poems that were purely personal generally ended up in the *Wallowing in self-pity* bin!

ALLENE RASMUSSEN NICHOLS

Allene Rasmussen Nichols is a doctoral student in Humanities at the University of Texas at Dallas. Her research focuses on poetry, playwriting and the representation of gender and sexuality in contemporary art and literature. Her poems have appeared in a variety of journals and anthologies, including *Naugatuck River Review, New Plains Review, Conclave, Lunch Ticket, Ginger Piglet, protestpoems.org* and *Dance the Guns to Silence: One Hundred Poems for Ken Saro-Wiwa.* Her plays have been produced in California, Texas, Wisconsin, and New York.

CHORUS

They will say the sky is not for you,
that the blue in your eyes is a reflection
of the shattered china on the floor
or that the scarlet stains on the counter
are your shackles or that if you die
often enough, your children will be free.

You must come to know the lie, to name
your bruises and broken bones, to call
these walls a prison, to make your voice
like steel, not to break when struck,
but to reverberate until this house
falls down.

You must teach yourself that you were born
to risk it all, not the next time you fall,
but today, while your breath reeks of poetry
and the sky beckons, and the sun itself
proclaims the promise that your body
can be strong and that your words
can bear the holy seal of joy.

NICHOLS: I address the subject of violence against women in my poems because physical and sexual abuse as a child left me vulnerable to abuse as an adult woman. I have, after many years of counseling, broken free of the cycle and free of my abusers, and I have discovered how wonderful life can be. I would like other women to know that they are not alone and that there is a way out. I also want people to be aware of the toll that such abuse takes, not just on women, but on society.

KIM NORIEGA

Kim Noriega grew up in Cleveland, Ohio, where she loved apple trees in the spring, nut roll at Christmas, and the Lorain-Carnegie Bridge at dusk. She moved to Southern California in her late twenties, where she learned to love subtle seasons and long beach walks in February. Noriega teaches poetry to adults and teens in public libraries, and facilitates literacy programs for low-literate families. Her poem "Heaven, 1963" appeared in Ted Kooser's syndicated column *American Life in Poetry*, and her poem "Name Me" was a finalist for the 2009 Joy Harjo Poetry Prize. Her book of poetry, *Name Me*, was published by Fortunate Daughter Press.

NAME ME

> *The power of naming is twofold: naming defines the quality and value of that which is named — and it also denies reality and value to that which is never named, never uttered. That which has no name is rendered mute and invisible: powerless to claim its own existence . . . this has been the situation of women in our world.*
> — from *Convicted Survivor: The Imprisonment of Battered Women Who Kill* by Elizabeth Ann Dermody Leonard

Name me the girl
with the slate-blue eyes,
the girl who sits under the apple tree,
your apple-cheeked bride.

Name me your lover —

the mother of your eight-pound baby boy.

Name me *sugar lips.*
Name me *honey-girl.*
Name me *sweet-potato pie.*

Name me the woman
with the black-and-blue eye.

Name me white roses.
Name me *I swear baby.*

Name me crushed larynx.
Name me fractured mandible.
Name me *but I was high baby,*
it don't count when you're high.

Name me *whore.*
Name me *get in that fuckin' kitchen,*
bitch.

Name me dislocated shoulder.
Name me *what ya gonna do,*
have me arrested?
Name me *I dare you*
to try and leave me.

Name me the woman
with seven broken toes.

Name me the *cunt*
you tell not to make
a sound.

Name me *tramp, slut, ugly*
ball and chain.

Name me the woman you love

to get up against the wall
and fuck with your .38.

Name me the woman
who found the dog
lying in a pool of blood
outside our daughter's door.

Name me the one who dug
the dog's grave; posted *lost* signs
the next day with our kids.

Name me the mother of children
who will never be safe.
Name me sleepless.
Name me the *little missus*
who bought a nine millimeter.

Name me *shows no remorse,*
name me *guilty as charged.*

Name me not sorry.

Name me widow.
Name me the woman in cell C 15.

Name me free.

VIOLA D'AMORE

*A fretless instrument with six or seven strings and a second
set of "sympathetic strings" that are not played but are made
to vibrate by the first set.*
— from *Encarta Dictionary*

I. *Domestic Violins*

I did that on purpose —
gave this section a cheeky title —
to get your attention.

II. *Violets*

He tells you it's *all your fault.*
You don't argue, tell yourself:
you just don't want to get him riled.

But secretly,
you believe him.

Your equilibrium's failing,
you fall, often
run into things
with your face.

Women who don't
but who should
know better,
sneer as you walk by,

tell themselves they'd
leave his sorry ass;
hit him back; make him pay.

You dab cover-up
to the bloom around your left eye.

III. *Violence*

The story goes
that my grandmother
told her second husband:
If you ever hit me, never sleep.

Still, when her son
smashed *his* wife's
jaw with a single blow,
everyone (except my aunt Linda)
slept just fine.

After reconstructive surgery
and false teeth,
my aunt Linda never wore mascara
or lipstick again.

IV. *Violins*

I'll never forget
the first time I told someone:
The walls in my kitchen
have holes the shape of my husband's fist.

The woman nodded, patted my cheek, said:
Better the walls than you, honey,
better the walls.

V. *Viola*

I know he turns to you
just when you think
he's finally drifted off,
strokes your bruised face
so tenderly you think:
He could change —

until he moves his fingers
to your throat,
begins to squeeze,
whispers:
If I squeeze a little harder . . .

while little white stars
explode behind your eyelids.

VI. *Viola d'Amore*

Maybe you're reading this poem
in secret,
at your desk, on your lunch break,
after you've called him to *check in.*

Maybe you're thinking about this poem
at the market — thinking

about those *little white exploding stars,*
thinking of his fingers squeezing your throat —
while you're choosing a nice cut of meat
to roast for dinner tonight with tender
baby carrots and sweet Vidalia onions.

Maybe you're thinking
about the holes
the size of your husband's fist
in your bedroom walls
while you're loading
groceries into the trunk of your car.

Maybe you're waiting at a red light
two blocks from home,
wondering how *I* know
what he whispers in your ear,

If I squeeze a little harder,
just a little harder . . .

Wherever you are —

I want to tell you:
If you leave him, you'll be protected.

I want to tell you:
He'll never find you.

I want to reassure you:
He'd never dream
of hurting the people you love
to get to you.

I want to lie to you.

I want to end this poem
with a choir of angels
singing a cappella:

Alleluia,
we can all be free.

But there is an angel
peering over my shoulder
as I write this,

and she is not singing.

NORIEGA: Raising awareness of violence against women is a focus of my writing and a personal passion. As a woman, mother, wife, daughter, friend and survivor of domestic and sexual abuse, I feel the urgency of this work cannot be overstated. Violence against women is ubiquitous and insidious. It is pandemic. Raising my voice on behalf of women and girls who have no voice — naming their experience accurately as *abuse* or *torture* or *rape,* instead of calling it *his bad childhood* or *drunkenness* or worse, *love* — is a privilege. In the words of Emily Dickinson: *If I can stop one heart from breaking / I shall not live in vain.*

I am pleased to note that the organization Men Stopping Violence has used my poems in their men's workshops to "bring the voice of women" into the room.

ELIZABETH OAKES

Elizabeth Oakes is the author of *The Farmgirl Poems*, winner of the 2004 Pearl Poetry Prize; *The Luminescence of All Things Emily* (Wind Publications, 2009), a collection of poems about Dickinson; *Mercy in the New World*, "persona" poems in the voice of an actual American colonial woman; and *Leave Here Knowing*, which explores the intersection of the material and spiritual worlds. She is also the author of *Solace: Readings for Transforming Childhood Trauma*, an ebook available for Amazon Kindle. Oakes, who holds a PhD from Vanderbilt University, retired recently after teaching Shakespeare for twenty-one years at Western Kentucky University, and now lives and writes in Sedona, Arizona.

WHEN I REMEMBER LUCILLE CLIFTON

> *they ask me to remember*
> *but they want me to remember*
> *their memories*
> *and i keep on remembering*
> *mine.*
>
> — Lucille Clifton, "why some people be mad
> at me sometimes"

and now a part of me
is the molested child,
for I am remembering Lucille's life
as she is remembering mine
as we are each remembering
the times the moon and the sun
just let something happen
that we didn't understand
that we didn't talk about
that some of us didn't remember
until someone who was, in a way,
our mother did it for us
in a poem and then we wrote
it out and remembered it
and let it go

out into that sun and moon
that still looked down on
us
wondering what went
wrong in this universe
that a woman I never met
was in a way my mother
or maybe my sister
or maybe me

that we were one tribe now
the tribe of the ones who are silent
in varying measures
who sometimes forget for whole
lifetimes except for that dark question
mark that hangs over us
how we never trust the truth
of our own body
ever

for one to remember is
to become a memorial
for all of us, this holocaust
of childhood, of being someone's
child who has no sense of what
it is to protect, who wants a warm
body so much he will take ours
in ways that our mothers may never
know or admit they know, for
what can they do, what can they do

OAKES: Oppression is silent. Empowerment is finding one's voice and telling the truth. When we do this, we form a tribe, no matter what may seem to separate us. It is as if drums beat, unheard by the physical ear but clearly heard, nonetheless. I found my tribe in poems, in the ones I read and the ones I wrote. Several years ago this poem came, mentored by Lucille Clifton, although I had never met or contacted her. At the same time, numerous poems came in a rush, resounding from a place in me I had forgotten. They came from me, they came through me, and they came for me and for the tribe members collected in this book, and for those who will read it and find a safe place, a place where one speaks for all and all for one.

ANGELA ALAIMO O'DONNELL

Angela Alaimo O'Donnell has published three collections of poems, *Saint Sinatra* (2011), *Moving House* (2009), and *Waking My Mother* (2013); and two chapbooks, *MINE* (2007) and *Waiting for Ecstasy* (2009). Her work has appeared in many journals and has been nominated for the Pushcart Prize, the Best of the Web award, and the Arlin G. Meyer Prize in imaginative writing. Her memoir, *Mortal Blessings,* was published in 2014. O'Donnell teaches English and Creative Writing at Fordham University, and serves as Associate Director of Fordham's Curran Center for American Catholic Studies.

PAS DE DEUX: *THE LOVERS*

Alvin Ailey Dance Performance, February 14th

They move against the smooth edge of art,
space dividing heart from eager heart.

Her taut body, goaded by desire,
slides in slow obedience to fire,

metal to magnet, flesh of soft steel,
an empty vessel urgent to be full.

Two lovers pool in sweet solution.
One begins the pull of separation.

Her eyes decline. She will not be possessed.
His arms that had so tenderly caressed

close now in straight embrace, so devoted
only a saint would feign not to notice

how difficult it is to breathe and to hope,
how absolute the hand upon her throat.

O'DONNELL: On a snowy Valentine's Day in New York City about 8 years ago, I had the pleasure of watching an Alvin Ailey student performance of a contemporary dance piece, *The Lovers*. The two young dancers, a male and a female, were poised beyond their years and strikingly beautiful. I was entirely engaged from the moment they began their slow, evocative dance. It was as if they were conducting a silent conversation, entirely through gesture, and we, the audience, sat silent and spellbound, eavesdropping. The dance served as a narrative, as well. The lovers began in amity, playfully touching, superficially skimming the surface of each other's skin, and then they gradually grew closer, more intimate, as their relationship developed from one of friendship to one of erotic love. This bliss, however, did not last. Gradually, the physical demands the male dancer placed upon the female became overwhelming, invasive, and an affront (though I hasten to add that all of this was conveyed with the utmost delicacy). By the conclusion of the dance, it was evident that the lover who had initially attracted her had grown possessive, controlling, and repellent. The young woman found herself trapped, overpowered, and intimidated by his size, strength, and will.

As a poet and writer, much of my life is taken up with words — and the fact that these two artists were able to convey the depths of a complex relationship without uttering a single syllable struck me as a species of magic. I wanted to find a way to capture and convey the physicality of the dance and its understatement in language. So I chose to write the poem as a sonnet, a form grounded in the tradition of courtly love poetry — but to use the form to interrogate the conventions and the falsities of that tradition. I altered the form in a number of ways, the most significant of which is the use of rhyming couplets. In the first portion of the poem, the two lines of the couplets work together, in a harmonious way — but as the poem goes on, and as the lovers gradually become emotionally estranged, the two lines of each couplet begin pulling away from each other and exist in tension. The poem, then, is the linguistic equivalent of the dance, echoing and enacting the steps of the lovers and the trajectory of their relationship. Finally, the poem concludes with the threat of impending violence, just as the dance did — leaving the reader with a sense of desolation. What might this young girl's prospects be?

Given this theme — the intertwining of passion, possession, and violence towards women — it would seem that *Veils, Halos & Shackles* is the ideal home for a poem like "Pas de Deux." In some ways, it is a microcosm of the themes of the anthology: the ways in which women are drawn into relationships that may seem kind but are not; the ways in which men feel free to make demands on women, both physical and psychological, violating their rights as fellow human beings; and the ways in which many cultures in the world approve of this, both consciously and unconsciously, officially and unofficially, leaving women with no recourse when they find themselves victimized by men.

JENNIFER O'GRADY

Jennifer O'Grady's first book of poetry, *White*, won the Mid-List Press First Series Award for Poetry. Her poems have appeared in *Harper's, Poetry, The Yale Review, The Kenyon Review, Southwest Review, Poetry Daily, The Writer's Almanac* with Garrison Keillor, and many other places. O'Grady is also a prizewinning playwright and has received two Pushcart Prize nominations. She lives just outside New York City with her husband, son, and daughter.

SUSANNA AND THE ELDERS

After the painting by Artemisia Gentileschi, 1593–1652

1

She is making herself and not herself —
anguish dressed in baroque repose,

a motionlessness that is never still,
arranged, betraying nothing —

the restrained line of an eyebrow or lip,
the arc of a neck, the skillful reflection

of a sleeve of the moon-white gown
in the olive-green water

gradually assembled, balanced there
in this unexpected moment,

this small world holding its breath.

2

Composed, nearly life-sized,
Susanna is saturated with light

that seems to come from nowhere
but inside her, as if she is incandescent, filled

with the dawning knowledge of her own beauty
that is the true beauty of the body —

defiant, uninhibited —
her knees rising from the olive-green water,

the soft bulb of a breast,
the shaded flesh of an upper arm

reaching down to cover herself
with the moon-white cotton gown

coiled around her hips.
Over her shoulder the elders leer —

two bearded, balding men looking for action,
their skin the color of boiled milk.

Placed behind her, they are partial figures
poised forever at the limits of her body

framed by the grotto's dark arch,
her face raised like a torch.

And behind them the blue, denuded sky.

3

Here in a modest museum room
pooling with light, a couple stands

before a painting of a woman caught
in the moment before surrender, or not —

the lustrous paint of her torso
still intact, undamaged —

imagined by a woman who was raped
and this is all they know of her, this

(the images hurtling against her flesh
leaving first violet blossoms, then blood)

and her painting of a woman captured
in the moment before decision, before

selecting the death of the body
(the lines carefully, calmly arranged)

over the death of the soul,
her lips sealed like a stone.

They are watching it together
and the woman is speechless, rooted there,

and the man is walking away.

O'GRADY: I'm very interested in the transformative powers of art, as well as the ways in which art, like language, sometimes fails us, like a bridge we work very hard to build but which not everyone is willing to cross. The Italian Baroque painter Artemisia Gentileschi was raped as a young woman and disgraced during the subsequent trial of her rapist — she was blamed for the rape. In the Apocrypha, Susanna was secretly watched by two temple elders while she was bathing. They approached her, wanting to sleep with her, and when she refused, they falsely accused her of adultery and she was sentenced to be stoned (but was ultimately exonerated). Section 2 of my poem actually describes the calmer Tintoretto version of Susanna and not Gentileschi's, which is more emotional. Gentileschi painted Susanna before her own trial, and scholars believe her rendering of the classic story reflects the sexual harassment she received as a woman painter in a man's world. Viewing Gentileschi's painting with the awareness of how many women are still, today, blamed for crimes committed against them was the impetus for writing this poem.

KESTER OSAHENYE

Kester Osahenye is a journalist, writer, poet, essayist, music critic, and social-media evangelist. He was born on July 22, 1973, and lives in Glasgow. He was influenced by the writings of Wole Soyinka, Chinua Achebe, John Pepper Clark, and Linton Kwesi Johnson, and was also motivated by the works of Amiri Baraka, Toni Morrison, Maya Angelou, and Gwendolyn Brooks. His work has appeared in numerous journals and anthologies, including *Jubilat, Sou'wester, The Oxford American, Lumina, Bittersweet,* and *Essence*. Osahenye's first book of poetry, *Cacophony from the Valley*, is forthcoming from Heinemann Publishers, UK.

STRING OF PROMISCUITY

Like a cow meant for the slaughterhouse,
her hands tied, her legs held apart like a woman in labor,
she cried and bit the hands of two
broad-shouldered men who clutched
her sweaty hands the way the palm-wine tapper
held a cudgel.

They laid her before the goddess of chastity,
and in a swift wave, the priestess raised the evil knife.
She prepared her totems and concoctions
like a dutiful housewife preparing lunch;
then she walked up to the girl,
pulled her legs further apart, and cut through her clitoris.
Like the oozing of water from a tap,
blood stained the dusty ground.
The girl's shouts pierced,
she dragged her feet and scuffled,
and like a sacrificial lamb, she covered herself in blood.
The women danced to the symphony of her cries,
while the priestess laughed at her exploits,
She said "the string of promiscuity
has been removed forever."

OSAHENYE: This poem concerns "female circumcision," a retrogressive cultural practice in my native Niger Delta that has led to the deaths of many women. Its more accurate name is "female genital mutilation." Despite the campaigns to end this practice, it still continues among some members of my tribe.

SHAUNA OSBORN

Shauna Osborn is a Comanche/German *mestiza* artist, wordsmith, and community organizer. She was a 2015 Artist in Residence for that year's A Room of Her Own Foundation's Writing Retreat, and she has received the Luminaire Award from Alternating Current Press, a National Poetry Award from the New York Public Library, and the Native Writer Award from Taos Summer Writers' Conference. Osborn is working on a series of indigenous comic books based on Comanche folk tales, a memoir, and a book-length choreopoem.

UNBOUND

based upon a West Indian folktale

Female spirit,
bound to domestic
    kitchen smells
    white powdered soap
    screams of unhappy children,
keeps her secret well.

Night conceals
lack of sleep,
    man snores,
    thick quilt warmth,
    reality of lost dreams,
midnight-blue fixed darkness.

Shutters open single window.
    no cause for concern.
    worries left inside
    empty shell.
all that exists
is air.

With darkness comes freedom,
     tight constrictive skin gone,
     draped over chair
     until morning —
left arm dancing
with draft.

Brine-scoured hide — the
     punishment for husband's possession.
     she must stay
     down here,
no higher ascent
without him.

Wind exists
for the woman
     tight lipped,
     oppressed by life,
     bound by her skin.
Souls travel through atmosphere
far away from
mental death.

Modern-Day Lavinias

for the murdered women of Ciudad Juárez: ni una más.

Stubs still itch
where my hands used
to braid long black hair

Mis dientes sueño
de la lengua
que frotó ellos limpio[*]

Fragments
left to imitate
the whole
won't do

Aliviar la tensión
que se encuentra todavía
en mi cabeza,
en mi coño[†]

Take their seed
from between my thighs
& build a path
right to their busted motors,
their limp flasks

Asegurar mis hermanas
el cuerpo que ha encontrado
será el ultimo
ellos ruina y enterrar[‡]

---

[*] My teeth dream language that rubbed them clean

[†] Relieve the tension that is still in my head, in my pussy

[‡] Assure my sisters the body that you found will be the last they ruin and bury

OSBORN: "Modern-Day Lavinias" reflects my reading of Shakespeare's *Titus Andronicus*. In the play, Lavinia, the daughter of Titus, is raped and butchered. Since 1993, over 1,000 women have been murdered in the border town of Ciudad Juárez. The victims are primarily young women who come from impoverished backgrounds and have common physical attributes. Similarities across the still-open murder cases include the rape, torture and mutilation of the victims. Very few attackers have been brought to justice and controversy surrounds the few men who have been convicted.

"Unbound" was inspired by a folktale I first learned about from *Black Ice*, by Lorene Cary. In the tale, a woman leaves her husband asleep in their bed each night before taking her skin off and flying away. She is careful to return before he wakes, but one night he wakes to find her gone, and he sees the empty skin. Upset by her leaving, he rubs salt inside the skin. When she returns, she cannot wear her skin any longer.

I write about the particular truths that one finds in contemporary society, most often from a persona sexed and/or gendered female. Because of this, the reality of gender-based violence, rape, social expectations, and gender roles often feature prominently in my work. I draw attention to the injustices faced by my personas because I feel that the only way to create change is through education and awareness. The instances in my poems stem from the real experiences of women I know or from my own personal experience. I know horribly traumatic things happen to women in our lives more often than we find out. I know that they happen far too often.

As an activist, I do what I can to advocate for survivors and to help our communities progress past rape culture and gender-based violence. Writing about it is just one of the ways to draw attention to the problem.

CHRISTINA PACOSZ

Christina Pacosz is a native Detroiter whose writing has appeared in books, anthologies, literary magazines, and online journals for half a century. *Notes from the Red Zone* (originally published by Seal Press, 1983, reissued by Seven Kitchens Press, 2009) was the inaugural winner of the ReBound Series, and *How to Measure the Darkness* launched Seven Kitchens' Summer 2012 Limited Edition Chapbook Series. She lives in Kansas City, Missouri.

REVENGE IS A DISH

for Sophia Kostrzewska Pacosz (April 26, 1914–December 27, 1986)

For all the sorrow
you caused her
the sleepless nights
and catatonic days
the loss of trust
the fear of every man   *her husband my father but not yet*
especially those who rape women after a lady's sodality dance at her church
Our Lady Help of Christians
(now a mosque)
For all the shattering
for the blame of others   *she asked for it she liked it*
for the shock treatments
for everything she
couldn't do for her   *self*
children to protect them
for the loss of love   *self*
for the loss of love
I would take you out
you horrors   *your crime burns my life still*
destroying all
everything
before it even began

PACOSZ: My mother didn't tell me about her rape, actually a gang rape — though she stopped some of the men from raping her by insisting she had to be home, that her mother would miss her — until just a few years before her death. The knowledge of her terror and her rape made a lot that hadn't been understood crystal clear. Or so I thought. But the decades have also made it abundantly clear how her violation and suffering had entered into our family dialogue. When life became too much for her, she ended up incarcerated in mental hospitals, where she was given repeated shock treatments and used as a guinea pig by the Lafayette Clinic in Detroit, which was conducting some of the initial research on schizophrenia. I have written in more detail about what happened to my mother and what it meant to ALL of us, including her children, long after the awful crime.

Rape brings sorrow unto the grandchildren and possibly beyond.

HINA PANDYA

Hina Pandya has worked on international development in rural areas around the world and, more recently, has served in specialist centers in London, helping women who have been sexually assaulted or raped. Using these experiences as a guide, she has now changed the focus of her efforts, and is assisting women in need in a range of areas that extends from policy writing to journalism; she is also writing about these women's experiences in order to increase mainstream awareness and to encourage actual change.

THE GALLERY

I entered the gallery and was mesmerized.
The art on the walls was colorful, expressive; it jumped out at me.
The gouache on the paintings reached out and tickled my senses.
I was feeling vibrant from this art
I couldn't wait to describe it.
I grabbed my complimentary glass of red wine.
It tasted like vinegar, but I didn't care.
Instead, a rush of urgency made me want to run around drinking in
          painting after painting.
After all, this was my boy's stuff. My son, my heart, my soul and joy.
On the walls of the finest gallery in London.
My heart was so full.
His first painting, a huge lily pouring almost out of the canvas. I could
          smell it.
The second, a waterfall; I swear I could hear it.
The third. Third. I stopped dead.

Sarah was dressed in a short black velvet dress, taking in
her son's paintings.
She wore a scarf around her neck that made her look messy,
although she thought she looked chic.
With the glass of red wine in her hand, sloshing about,
she passed Alan's first two pieces and came across the third.
That painting took all the excitement from her veins; her legs

went cold and blood drained from her face.

For as she looked up she saw a painting as large as the wall itself:

A woman's face. Her face. Covered with red marks and a black eye.

This painting was not as colorful as the rest, and its darkness
     overwhelmed her.

You stand overwhelmed, shocked and saddened.

You wonder how on earth he could have seen this.

Why on earth would he draw this?

How does he even have this memory?

You remember and think back to when you looked like this.

It was after a night out.

He can't have been but four years old.

You recall that he woke up, hearing you come in, that he'd walked into your
     room, watching your tears as you looked into the mirror.

You are heartbroken. He carried this. You never spoke about it.

You never consoled him. You never knew it had hurt him.

You notice that many people stand beside you, behind you,

all with glasses of free wine in their hands.

Seemingly remarking about the "depth of emotion of this piece," "the lines,"
"the pain."

You feel surrounded.

Suddenly terrified.

At any point now, someone will recognize that it's you in this picture.

PANDYA: I have worked on women's and children's issues since my earliest childhood, when I saw the mistreatment of my grandmother and mother at patriarchal hands and felt abhorrence and a sense of injustice that screamed for their protection, despite their complicit silence in the name of cultural taboos.

Since that time, I have come across many women, from all walks of life, who have suffered oppression: sexually exploited, trafficked women of Eastern European and Western European states; Yemeni women who are forced to stay indoors their whole lives — who set themselves on fire out of a need to regain some control; and many survivors of domestic violence and rape in London's hospitals. All of this must be spoken about if society is to have a chance of redressing the balance and stopping this awful, ignorant neglect and abuse of a most valuable set of people. We must not remain unaware of these hidden victims.

PUSHPA NAIDU PAREKH

Pushpa Naidu Parekh is a Professor of English and past Director of the Honors Program at Spelman College in Atlanta, Georgia. She has also served as an editorial advisory board member of the *Journal of English Studies and Humanities* and has published three scholarly books as well as articles on British, American, postcolonial, and diaspora literature. Parekh's poetry, nonfiction, and short stories have appeared in creative-writing journals in the United States and India, among them *Abha, Exposé, Passage VI, South Asian Review, The Southern Tablet,* and *Where Dreams Begin,* and in the Canadian humanities periodical *The Trumpeter* (Journal of Ecosophy), which is in the forefront of the long-range deep-ecology movement.

VIEW FROM A NIQAB

These strands of light
and shadow
playful hidings
and sudden glimpses
withering and wavering
like old photographs
colors fading
and then the dark —
for a moment
no movement.
Then the trails
of light
and shadows
blending
breaking
binding
billowing

Sun filtered
through window shades
of my niqab

I am
stunned.

PAREKH: As the keynote speaker for the "POWER of Women Conference" at SUNY Cortland, October 6, 2007, I reflected on my engagement with women's concerns globally as a lifelong one that interweaves a passion for women's empowerment, education for all, and a fierce support for social justice as well as human rights. My creative writing, teaching, and scholarly engagements map my own complex and layered journeys as a woman of color, a cross-border immigrant/citizen, a woman with disability, and a postcolonial transnationalist. In all these journeys, I have been an advocate for minority rights, inclusive of racialized, gendered, impoverished, and disabled groups.

I believe much work remains to be done in ensuring the safety, humanity, and rights of women as full citizens of the world. Violence against women is a critical issue that needs to be addressed from multiple angles, beginning with awareness-building. As a poet, I believe its existence today is a commentary on the limits of progress, and I hope to give women's voices a dimensionality and complexity beyond victimhood and simple binaries.

MATT PASCA

Matt Pasca's poetry has appeared in over twenty journals, including *Paterson Literary Review, Georgetown Review, Oberon,* and *Pedestal Magazine,* and in ten print anthologies. His first book, *A Thousand Doors,* was nominated for a Pushcart Prize, and his poem "Receiving Line" won the 2012 Great Neck Poetry Prize. After earning degrees from Cornell and Stony Brook Universities, Pasca has taught literature and writing at Bay Shore High School on Long Island since 1997. A 2003 New York State Teacher of Excellence, Pasca also serves as advisor for the school's award-winning literary-art magazine *The Writers' Block.* He maintains a steady performance itinerary that includes readings, as well as speaking and running workshops at colleges, conferences, and continuing-education programs.

FOR THE TALIBAN

We in the modern world envy
you because we do not have time
to do what we want. You uncover
secrets no physicist could fathom:
skipping Earth's orbit while we
breathe through contractions
of change. You expand by shrinking
horizons of the mind — mushroom flash
turning liberty into sand.

You have all day to make
sure no one in Kabul plays
the trumpet, cards or chess, or
screens a film. At your leisure,
you can ensure all non-Muslims
are wearing their Yellow Stripe,
that your shrouded women (allowed to bake
bread the way our inmates produce
license plates) aren't getting uppity, aren't
pointing out that you are stuck
in an oven of myopia.

Even Mother Nature, for whom nothing
is stagnant, has fled Afghanistan; you
have cut millennia down at the knees, forged
a reign of anachronism, where death
by stoning is in vogue, and females —
once judges, teachers and authors of your
constitution — are barred from
pen and page.

You hand guns to starving
boys and survey the demolition
of a Buddha, high above the cliffs
of Bamiyan where it has stood
since the days of Muhammad, whose
Islam you drag through the dust.

O Taliban, your world may be
timeless, but not immortal;
the *hijabs* and *niqabs* which veil
the promise of your nation
will open soon enough.

HEAD OF THE BOMB SQUAD

Best in the biz
said the chief —
Lenny's black beret draped
over a grenade
paperweight, pistol
in his buckle, broken
nose sniffing the real deal
from a fake, holes
in his bones blown
by foster fire.

His long, scarred
fingers were swift to thwart
detonation, but no one
in Jersey built as many bombs
in a crude cellar below
twenty-four stairs he climbed
to his daughter's bedroom —
head racing with demons —
where he crammed her
full of explosives.

But if mercy is crucial,
something must be said
for my shrapnel-filled
father-in-law, dead
at fifty-three:

He passed on
some tools of the trade —
just enough tenacity
and wit to help her
defuse, over decades,
the rounds he left buzzing
in her warm, white body.

PASCA: I first wrote "Head of the Bomb Squad" as a journal entry addressed to my wife's dead father, a man I'd never get the chance to meet. I wanted to find a way to express my contempt for what he had done to his daughter but I also wanted to fill the empty hole that anger digs within. My wife worked as hard as anyone ever has to break the shackles of incest and the subsequent rape, drug and alcohol abuse, and promiscuity it led to, as it so often does. I wanted to be as strong as she was, to move past the demonizing that comes naturally in such situations — to find compassion in the darkness.

My reference to the abusive foster homes her father grew up in (line 10) speaks to this effort. Lines 5–6 refer to a miniature pistol he carried in his belt buckle (one of four weapons he consistently carried). Since meeting my wife in 2003, I have met hundreds of victims of sexual abuse, including some of my own students, and am invested in the process of lifting the cloud that surrounds incest, rape, and sexual assault. As a white American man, I work each day to foster a reality where others are given the same privileges afforded me merely because of my skin, class, and gender.

"For the Taliban" came to me while I was at school, enjoying an off period between classes. It was September 6, 2001, five days before the World Trade Center attack. Injustice occurs everywhere and at all times, but such an obvious retraction of human evolution had been gnawing at me for months.

NOLA PASSMORE

Nola Passmore holds qualifications in psychology, creative writing, and Christian ministry. She finds this mix invaluable in writing about social-justice issues. Her poetry, devotions, true-inspiration stories, magazine articles, academic papers, and short fiction have appeared in various magazines, journals, and anthologies in Australia, the United States, and the United Kingdom. She and her husband, Tim, run The Write Flourish, a freelance writing and editing business, from their home base in Toowoomba, Australia. Passmore is a firm believer that hope can be found in the darkest of places.

PETALS

Bruised petals
cannot bear their scars
for long.
Curling into a shroud,
they brace themselves
for the return journey
to ashes,
to dust.

Yet, in the crushing,
a fragrance
is released,
sweeter than a perfect bloom,
richer than the life before.

I gather fragments,
inhale their breath.

PASSMORE: I have several close female friends who have experienced various types of abuse, including domestic violence, child sexual abuse, and satanic-ritual abuse. In spending time with them and hearing their stories, I've seen the long-term effects firsthand. However, I've also seen how resilient people can be in the face of traumatic experiences. Each of these friends has found great solace in their faith, and they have been able to help others through difficult circumstances. As well as acknowledging the horror of abuse, I think it's important to let people know that there is hope. In the poem "Petals," I tried to show how something beautiful can still come from tragic circumstances. My wish is that this anthology will highlight the injustice of these abuses but will also provide hope to the hurting.

LINDA PASTAN

Linda Pastan grew up in New York City, graduated from Radcliffe College in 1954, and received an MA from Brandeis University. She has published 14 volumes of poetry, most recently *Traveling Light* (2012) and *Insomnia* (2015), both from W.W. Norton. Two of her books have been finalists for the National Book Award, and one was a finalist for The Los Angeles Times Book Prize. Pastan was Poet Laureate of Maryland from 1991 to 1995, and in 2003 she won the Ruth Lilly Poetry Prize for lifetime achievement.

ON VIOLENCE AGAINST WOMEN

when Adam took
that second bite
he said

you'll get what
you deserve
and spat out the pits

and led Eve
in lockstep
from the garden

and oh
the sweetness
of blame

continues
toxic
down the ages

PASTAN: I have always been interested in, even obsessed by, Adam and Eve and the Garden. Their story, particularly Eve's, has been the template for many of my poems. And I have become increasingly aware of violence against women, in both its subtle and extreme forms, all around the world. So, when I asked myself how and where this violence began, my imagination turned naturally to Eden — where so many things started.

JENNIFER PERRINE

Jennifer Perrine is the author of *No Confession, No Mass* (University of Nebraska Press, 2015), winner of the 2014 Prairie Schooner Book Prize in poetry; *In the Human Zoo* (University of Utah Press, 2011), recipient of the 2010 Agha Shahid Ali Poetry Prize; and *The Body Is No Machine* (New Issues, 2007), winner of the 2008 Devil's Kitchen Reading Award in poetry. Perrine teaches courses in creative writing and social justice and directs the Women's Studies and Gender Studies Program at Drake University in Des Moines, Iowa.

A THEORY OF VIOLENCE

after New Delhi, after Steubenville

Under the surface of this winter lake,
I can still hear him say *you're on thin ice
now*, my heel grabbed, dragged into the opaque
murk of moments — woman raped on a bus;

girl plunged into oblivion, taken
on a tour of coaches' homes, local bars,
backseats of cars, the sour godforsaken
expression on each classmate's face; the dark,

the common route home, faint footfalls behind.
How many times have I bloodied my fist
against this frozen expanse to remind
myself there *is* another side, hope-kissed,

full of breath? I howl. The water begs, *drown*,
its hand pressing tight, muffling every sound.

AFTER HE BREAKS HER ARM

there's little I can do — the small conveyance
from the porch where she sat, one busted tooth
in her hand, to the hospital where she says,

car accident, just me, please, no cops.
In the harbor of my house, she sleeps
in my bed, the angles of her body wrapped

in my oversized pajamas, one sleeve
cut off for the cast. I wake her with tea,
burnt toast, runny eggs, though she winces

when she chews, the black whorl on her jaw
now haloed in green. Until her right eye
opens, I read her books, whatever's handy,

whatever keeps her here. Once, to cheer her,
I paint her nails, each a different color,
the enamel smearing up to her knuckles

when the crying starts again. The eighth night,
when she tells me she misses him, I'm kneeling
in the bethel of the bathroom, bent over

the tub, raking a razor through the thick
lather on her legs, and when she says,
take me home, I nick her ankle just enough

to draw blood, one rusty drop that slides
to the surface of the water, shimmies
its tendrils into the murk, and is gone.

PERRINE: Many of my poems address violence against women because the poems seek to engage imagination as an empathetic act. I am often concerned with creating voices for characters who are overlooked or silenced in other texts. Often, these characters are women who have been written into history as mere footnotes, and in these poems, there is an overt attempt to, in Monique Wittig's words, "Make an effort to remember. Or, failing that, invent." While I do not claim to speak for other people, I do attempt to imagine (and thereby help readers imagine) what these characters might have said had they been given the space to speak or had their version of a story been considered important.

This consideration of empathy is also part of my focus on poetry as a possible way to represent and respond to trauma. In all of my books, I wrestle with human cruelties — and I'm particularly concerned with ways to write about "inhumanity" without depicting the perpetrators of violent acts as monsters. Rather, the poems seek to acknowledge the ways in which we are all complicit in human suffering and, in so doing, trouble this complicity, while also recognizing the need to treat ourselves and others with compassion. In this way, my writing probes questions about representing and responding to social injustice and challenges the notions of the spectator or innocent bystander in the context of the horrific.

Rochelle Potkar

Rochelle Potkar is a fiction writer and poet. Her short stories have appeared in *Far Enough East, Sein und Werden, Women Writers, Muse India, The Bangalore Review*, and numerous other journals. Her poem "Knotted Inside Me" was one of the eight short-listed for The RedLeaf Poetry India Award 2013. Potkar has read her poems at Kala Ghoda Arts Festival, Vikhroli Skin, and PEN@Prithvi (all in and around Mumbai), and narrated a true-life tale at Tall Tales in June 2013. Also in 2013, she completed an Advanced Fiction Seminar, via distance learning, through the University of Iowa's international writing program. Her book *The Arithmetic of Breasts and Other Stories* was published in 2014.

A Definition

You wouldn't know what you render each night
Like fish don't know water

Forcing your displeasure into the pleats
of your wife and other women
mistaking their whimpers for moans
their endurance for excited groans

Your *mardanagi*
Your manliness
Your manhood

Then when you are done, you sleep soft like a baby

In the morning you reach the police station
your workplace
where a woman is crying foul

Raped?
Rape?!
What's that?!

"Should I show you what real rape is?" you ask, bending
your knees, jutting your pelvis

"My women don't shriek like you.
Stay quiet. Stay graceful. Go fuck off home!"

This world has found new meanings, you think,
for things that happened every day and always without squeaks,
    without squeals.
The world's been getting ahead of herself, you think,
shattering the silence of every submission,
disturbing your *afterglow* completely.

FRIENDS IN RAPE

She is a friend
and you've known her for ages:
lovely, accommodating, comfortable
always smiling at your jokes

You love her so much
that sometimes when you are alone drinking or talking
you want to show her ...

You have held on for so long,
but she doesn't love you in *that way,* she admits.
Still, can't she give back some love when you really need it,
like oxygen to the drowning, like blood to the dying?
Should love not translate into a portable language from feelings to touch?

You don't ask her, again,
if love isn't also in the unsaid.
She will come along.
Maybe she is just shy or hesitant —
she wasn't brought up in a culture that permits her to demand it.

But doesn't she smile at each one of your jokes?
And why is she here with you alone?
You will take the first step now;
you will break that ice.

She will accommodate your brimming love, your itch
that sees no logic
in refusal.

If not her, then who?
Some damn prostitute!

You have always picked up the tabs on outings with her.
Can't she now?
Oh come! Stop these *nakhras!*
I am going crazy.

Come on. This one time. You will really like it.
We are friends!
I will be gentle.

Oh, come on you bitch!
I've had enough with you and your hesitations.
You don't think twice
before bleeding through those blurry lines.

POTKAR: Atrocities against children, women, and the vulnerable have always troubled me, and most of those around me, but the 2012 Delhi gang-rape rattled us to the core. It unhinged our souls.

"A Definition" was written against the many Indian policemen who refuse to file First Information Reports of rape victims, thereby causing the first breakdown in the humanistic machinery of justice. They tell the victim to go home. They mistreat her or deny the existence of any atrocity against her by belittling or accusing her. I wrote "Friends in Rape" because in many Indian rape cases, it is found that the perpetrator was a friend or a friend of friends, whom the victim might have known for years. It then becomes a question of trust: whom to trust, and when the point has been reached when a woman should wrap up her "freedom," turn away, and return to safety.

JENNIFER A. POWERS

Jennifer A. Powers earned a BA in English from the University of Connecticut and an MFA from Western Connecticut State University. She has short stories published or forthcoming in *The MacGuffin, Folio, Diverse Voices Quarterly, Grasslimb, Hawai'i Pacific Review,* and other literary magazines. In summer 2015, Powers completed a five-week solo cross-country drive. She lives in Connecticut.

THANK YOU

I want to thank you for your smile like a fishing lure, for the flowers with razor sharp thorns. I want to thank you for your honeyed poetry and promises, for the ring that didn't shine and for losing yours. I want to thank you for the bitterness and the way I can't believe in certain things, for the purple welts you left on my skin and the broken dishes and bent silverware. I want to thank you for the miscarriages and the blood and newfound freedom, for hardening the knot in my throat and slicing up morality like one of your expensive steaks. I want to thank you for the tears I couldn't swallow and for the tears that wouldn't flow, for biting my lips and erasing my words. I want to thank you for teaching me how to lie, for the prescription drugs and bottles of alcohol that littered my secret dwelling. I want to thank you for the sound of shattered glass and the way my skin smelled like cigarette ashes from your hands. I want to thank you for the ulcers and headaches and twitches and diseases, for speeding off in your car and leaving marks of burnt rubber like black mambas. I want to thank you for abandoning me, and for coming back to tell me I'm not good enough. I want to thank you for thinking I'd never amount to anything, and for loving everyone else instead. I want to thank you for the mask you wore and I want to thank you for mine, for the stitches and bandages without apologies. I want to thank you for the emergency room bills and the way I felt your razor sharp thorns wrap around my wrists, neck and feet, for the way your eyes overflowed with contempt and heat. I want to thank you for butchering my wisdom, for letting me wait alone at tables to eat, for portraying the rotten food and dirty rooms and stained bed sheets as clean, for punching the walls and leaving drips of blood on the floor, for the way the ground pressed into my bare knees while praying, for letting go of my hand and walking out, for coming back, for teaching me. Teaching me! I want to thank you for teaching me the brutality of you, for preparing me for other monstrosities, for cutting off my eyelids and baring your teeth, for the way I now can see and how I feel something like the ocean clean my wounded head and bleeding feet, for making me see. I want to thank you for my freedom. I want to thank you for making me arrive at me.

POWERS: I wrote this piece because I have experienced some difficult and tumultuous relationships. This is a fictional piece, although it's reminiscent of certain times in my life that I've left behind. I'm a new person.

BRUCE PRATT

Bruce Pratt is an award-winning short-story writer, poet, and playwright. He is the author of the novel *The Serpents of Blissfull* (Mountain State Press) and the poetry collection *Boreal* (Antrim House). An adjunct instructor of Creative Writing at the University of Maine, he also teaches in the Honors College and serves as faculty liaison to the Women's Basketball team. In his role as editor of the anthology *American Fiction*, Pratt was named the 2014 Gold Medal Winner by the Midwest Independent Publishers Association. He is past Director of The Northern Writes New Play Festival.

ACCORDING TO A SPOKESMAN

Raped, beaten, and thrown down an embankment,
left by her three male attackers for dead,
her injuries are not life threatening.

The name of the victim has been withheld.
A man notified police as she was being
raped, beaten, and thrown down an embankment,

that he had been in the car with the woman
when his friends planned to assault and kill her.
Her injuries are not life threatening,

and the caller is credited with saving the victim's life
by leading medical personnel to where she was
raped, beaten, and thrown down an embankment.

The caller identified two of the suspects.
Another was found hiding under a bench.
Her injuries are not life threatening.

She should recover fully from her ordeal,
according to a hospital spokesman, because though
raped, beaten, and thrown down an embankment
her injuries are not life threatening.

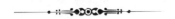

PRATT: "According to a Spokesman" was born in my reaction to an article in the *Hartford Courant* that detailed the ordeal described in the poem. While the events alone are horrifying — the victim suffered multiple sexual assaults, was beaten, and was then thrown down an embankment and left for dead — the article quoted a "hospital spokesman" as saying that her injuries were not "life threatening." Even if unintended, there is a callous lack of empathy and compassion in that statement that galls me to this day. There is a distinct difference, and it is more than semantic, between life-ending and life-threatening injuries. Trauma of the soul, and its attendant fear, can be as permanent as any visible scar or disfigurement, and to suggest that survival alone indicates that one's life is no longer threatened by such horrors as this woman faced is to miss the point entirely.

MARGARET RANDALL

Margaret Randall is a poet, essayist, oral historian, photographer, and social activist. From 1962 to 1969, she and Mexican poet Sergio Mondragón co-edited *El Corno Emplumado / The Plumed Horn*, a bilingual literary quarterly. Her most recent books include *Che On My Mind* (a feminist poet's reminiscence of Che Guevara), *More Than Things* (essays), *About Little Charlie Lindbergh* (poems), and *Haydée Santamaría, Cuban Revolutionary: She Led By Transgression* (a biography), which was published by Duke University Press in 2015. Coming in 2016 are her bilingual anthology of eight decades of Cuban poetry, *Only the Road / Sólo el camino*, also from Duke, and her latest poetry collection, *She Becomes Time* (from Wings).

I WAS ALONE THAT NIGHT

When I was a child the desert bloomed
right down to Highland High
our white-kids school
on the eastern edge of town.
Fierce winds whipped sand
to the backs of our calves,
sharp stings against young skin.

Cholla and prickly pear, stout barrel cacti —
their sudden flowers
met us long before those mountains
rose in blue distance,
watermelon light each afternoon.

Highland for the families who arrived
from somewhere else
and settled in the heights.
Albuquerque High for the tough kids:
New Mexican, Mexican American,
Black sons and daughters
of the Atchison Topeka & Santa Fe

or off-reservation Indians come to town
in search of work.
"Chicano," "African" and "Native American"
weren't words we had back then.
Only "Assimilation," and "The American Dream"
achieved unevenly.

Some girls said Albuquerque High boys
kissed better
and when the captain of the downtown football team
asked me out I trembled *yes*
beneath anxious folds
of Dotted Swiss.

When the running back's hand tore at my blouse
and his other hand charged between my legs,
I cried for him to stop,
to the couple in front for help.
Their moans sounded light-years away.
He laughed and pried deeper, at ease
with male right.

Through the triangle of window
a splash of stars
seemed distant and pale.
I took remembered advice
and brought my knee up
fast and sharp to his groin.

He let go and I pushed the door,
leapt free and ran
down a rocky road
till I hit pavement
and kept on running.

So I was alone that night
flying toward city lights

panting and crying
slowing to walk
then running again
until my house appeared.

Years later, I could use
the word *rape*
for what the high school football star
did to me that night
and knew by then he didn't follow
because it wasn't me he wanted,

only conquest there on that car seat
in the presence of buddies,
only the ancient ritual
of male entitlement:
another notch
on the stock of his teenage gun.

WEAPON AND SIGNATURE

When I was young, an occasional murder
upped the sales of our hometown paper
two or three days running.
Newspapers were important then
and violent death
an equal-opportunity visitor
claiming men and women,
poor and unprotected.

Sixty years later Internet sound bites
replace those papers,
TV conquers radio.
Scan the story, file the news
and move on.

Corporate control determines
how much we know
and for how long.

Murder, alive and healthy, makes its way
from the five-year-old
wielding his father's loaded gun
through post office or high school rampage
to the killing fields of war
and back.
The greater the human interest
the longer the public gasp.

Just south of these purple canyons
and clean skies
six hundred murdered women
on their way to school or work
haunt the streets of Juárez.

In every Mexican City, down to Guatemala
and north to Canada
dead women cry out
for someone to speak their names
without "prostitute"
or "sweatshop worker"
attached.

On Albuquerque's west mesa
the bones of eleven females
and one unborn child
rise through the leveled sands of development.
Every day they dig
costs corporate millions.
More of us accused in death
of living the dangerous life.

As long as they make sure we know
it's our oldest profession,
our fault,
like when they raped us
because our skirts were "too short"
or our dress "provocative."

Organized crime, drug cartel — power's sadism
changes its name
from country to country,
disappearing women
until they are found
in garbage dumps
or shallow desert graves.

Our sisters continue to die,
their names silenced in a time
when the erasure of women
is weapon and signature:
harbinger of what's to come.

RANDALL: I often address the issue of violence against women in my work, both the poetry and the prose. I live my consciousness of this issue, so it naturally appears in what I write.

DAVID RAY

David Ray is Emeritus Professor of English at the University of Missouri-Kansas City, where he also edited *New Letters*. His most recent volume of poems is *Hemingway: A Desperate Life*, and his other collections include *After Tagore: Poems Inspired by Rabindranath Tagore*, *The Death of Sardanapalus*, *When*, and *Music of Time: Selected & New Poems*, which offers selections from fifteen previous volumes. Ray's most personal and enduring collection, *Sam's Book*, has been re-released by Wesleyan University Press. His memoir, *The Endless Search*, was published by Soft Skull Press in 2003. He lives and writes in Tucson.

RED DRESSES OF RAJASTHAN

> *It is the tradition for husbands and mothers-in-laws to punish by burning a bride who does not bring enough dowry or who is disobedient.*
> — *The Times of India* (Delhi)

One sees red dresses in Rajasthan,
same style as those often worn
in the harem — silks adorned

with tiny mirrors that glitter
with each move of the dancers,
emitting light like stars.

But the elaborate marriage
can bankrupt a bride's father
and she can be made captive

to a mother-in-law like those
in fairy tales, and that witch
might later demand more dowry

at the threat of burning the bride,
tossing a match onto a kitchen
spill of cooking oil, an assault

sure to kill or disfigure beauty
the young bride has brought
along with the gold demanded

by ritual, tradition, obligation
so profound and burdensome
that parents fear bankruptcy

if they have one daughter too
many, and infanticide of girls
is not at all unusual. Knowing

of these ancient rituals, I dream
of women begging for rescue,
and how I would save every dancer,

those beautiful brides of Rajasthan
who should never be chained
to a kitchen or plow or a man,

and never be bartered or sold.

THE ROADMENDERS

> *"Through bankrupt countries where they mend the roads."*
> — W. H. Auden

Grandmothers mend the roads, lifting
their great pans high, heavy with sand
or gravel. They stoop in the dried-up
riverbed to dig the fill, squatting to chop
some stone as if it were a garden cabbage.
Young girls mend the roads here,
sun drying them up like vines, and their fruit
goes withered in fumes from lumbering buses
whose Punjabi drivers curse

to be caught in such lowlands
and hell, such potholes for wheels.
Such a ditch and these winding
trails should not even exist,
dug out by hands because the flood
has broken the heart of a bridge,
refuted its excellent logic,
fractured its place in the landscape.
For the gods want the roads
worked on, the supernumerary,
crooked, leprous, accursed roads,
want penance for the lives
of these women, the lives they spent
elsewhere, dancing, carousing with the mad emperor,
strolling in the green and cool gardens.
For such reasons, because of the gods
and their convictions against good bridges
and bad women, the formerly bad women
mend the roads, stooping in the sun,
lifting heavy mattocks and those pans
upon their heads. And if they complete
one road they can begin another —
the one stretching off into the distance,
twisting like a lazy serpent in the sun.
And at night, let them braid
the long black hair of their daughters.

TWO SISTERS

In Memoriam, Bessie Delany (1891–1995)

"Yoga, cod liver oil and garlic" were the secrets
divulged to the reporter by two African-American sisters.
One was a hundred and six, the other a mere hundred and four
at the time. They explained that they got off
to a good start — due to a protective dad. He would not

let them go so far as upstairs without a chaperone, ever —
not since they were toddlers. From their birth,
he told them never to look at, much less speak to,
a white man and he told them about those second
families, Thomas Jefferson's, for instance,

how the spitting images of scornful half-
sisters and half-brothers had been left out in the cold.
Nor would Daddy Delany allow his girls to accept
any form of loan or gift — lest they incur an obligation,
a debt too often paid with loss of pride or beauty of body.

And therefore they put themselves through school
by scrubbing floors, cooking, selling greens they gathered
in buckets, and they owed no man and looked not in his eyes.
And when they finished this grim report of policy, they laughed
and said they'd both be dead for sure — and long ago —

if they had married men, who'd have nagged them to their graves.
"And fast," said one, while the younger added one health tip more —
"And buttermilk," she said, "that's good too."

D. RAY: My writings about heroic African-Americans and members of other ethnic cultures include issues of fairness and justice, ecology, politics, history, and traditions. These works are scattered throughout my books, and in numerous magazines and anthologies. In writing about New Zealand, Australia, and India, I address the same themes on an international level, for the Maoris of New Zealand, the Aborigines of Australia, the Harijans ("Untouchables") of India, and others of stigmatized castes who suffer great indignities and violence. The focus of all my forays into these themes is that hope and healing are overcoming racism and injustice.

Note on "Red Dresses of Rajasthan": According to *The Times of India* in New Delhi, hundreds of women are murdered each year due to the tradition of "bride burning" by families of the groom after they have exhausted their extortion of obligatory dowries of gold, jewels, money, etc., a gift that sometimes leaves families of brides bankrupt. The burden of such sacrifices is a major cause of the abortion of females. The murders of brides are usually treated as accidental kitchen fires, and the groom is free to seek another victim. No doubt the grief is transient when marriages are arranged for greed, rather than love. Many brides dread marriage to a stranger almost as much as a widow must have dreaded being forced onto the cremation platform of her husband in the ancient tradition of suttee. Practice, especially in rural life, is one thing, and public pretension is another, for both bride-burning and suttee are officially illegal.

"The Roadmenders" was inspired by witnessing women of all ages working on streets and roads in India, under primitive conditions. After a hard day's work, in extreme heat and for very little pay, they return home to face domestic labor, their work seemingly eternal.

"Two Sisters," which is in my book *Demons in the Diner,* is one of many poems I've dedicated to African-Americans, for so many were heroic, historic, and iconic individuals. The Delany sisters were survivors, making their way in the world on their own terms.

JUDY RAY

Judy Ray was born in England and lived in Uganda for years before moving to the United States. Her books include *To Fly Without Wings* (Helicon Nine Editions), *Fishing in Green Waters, Pebble Rings, Pigeons in the Chandeliers,* and *The Jaipur Sketchbook.* Her most recent collection, *From Place to Place: Personal Essays* (Whirlybird Press, 2015), explores such subjects as the process of becoming a US citizen, untimely death, helping to solve a murder, and travel to places where she has lived for a few months or years. Ray now lives in Tucson, and has spent several years as a volunteer teaching English as a Second Language to adults in the community.

WOMEN PLANTING CORN

A painting of the Bishop Hill Colony, Illinois,
by Olof Krans, 1838–1916

Against brown hills in buttock curve
and clouds ranged like Mt. Rushmore heads,
a line of women slants across the frame,

poised with sticks in hand. Waiting
for a signal from the rising sun?
For a starting gun? But this is no race.

In long earth-tone skirts, bonnets like clouds,
aprons looped to make pockets, twenty-four women
make a team machine of coordination.

At each end of the line, a man in grey
with tall black hat stands like a wheel
of this human planting machine.

The two men stretch a string, mark the field.
The women poke with sticks, drop seeds,
cover and tamp — slow dance of the season.

They understand community. They understand
survival. Five months from Sweden on the ocean,
a few weeks coasting rivers and lakes,

the long walk across plains, and always work —
cave houses first, then building and clearing,
planting and caring, digging in with zeal.

Perhaps these twenty-four women knew Erik Jansson,
the murdered leader. Perhaps their fathers
or husbands or brothers sit now with the council

making new rules. Celibacy? Separation of children?
The words hiss around. Do these dutiful women,
in so perfect a unison, dream of disobeying

the council, of a bountiful harvest?
Do they dream of taking a rest, or a lover?
Do they dream of holding the measuring

string for a team of men to follow —
to poke, plant, cover and tamp? Try
to imagine another version of utopia:

twenty-four men poised like a row of windmills
hanging out laundry, while two women supervise
the basket-loads, the pegs, the shaking out.

J. RAY: The searing themes of this anthology are not obvious in my poem included
here. The painting by Olof Krans that I reflect on is in a "primitive" style, emphasizing
simplicity of line and form. But the strictness of rules and demands of labor in the odd
nineteenth-century community, the Bishop Hill Colony of Illinois, are represented by
the uniformity of people shown by the artist, and this particular painting shows women
as work machines. Despite the colony being founded by Swedish immigrants on the
premise of religious freedom, there was not equality. The leader, Erik Jansson — and,
after his death by murder, a council of seven men — dictated the rules of the society,
with no voice from the women, even concerning their children.

HEIDI ANDREA RESTREPO RHODES

Heidi Andrea Restrepo Rhodes is a Queer, Feminist, Latina/Colombian-American poet/ writer, scholar, artist, and political activist. Her performance work, creative writing, and photography have been seen or are forthcoming in places such as San Francisco's SomArts, Galería de la Raza, the SICK Collective, *Mixed Up! A Mixed Race Queer and Feminist Zine*, Brown and Proud Press, Harvard's *Queer*, *The Progressive*, *Codex*, *Wilde*, and the *Blue Lyra Review*. Her scholarship and advocacy have been focused on human rights in Colombia and oral histories of Queer and Trans people of color in the United States. Rhodes currently lives in Brooklyn.

MISSIONARY

colonization sits sticky,
residue, viscid, layering my aorta,
pulsing through my blood,
from my hypothalamus to my labial nerve,
deep beyond years beyond the days i've breathed beyond centuries
beyond the rapes of my grandmothers' grandmothers' grandmothers

colonization sits sticky,
with *palos* that holy hands took to beat,
with *postes* that crushed children
so cathedrals could be built
so that souls could be saved
in a world where already
the language of god was in the soil and the sound of jungle birds
and the harvesting of corn and plantain
priests staked their claim
planted crosses like dead trees
feigning the promise of eternal life
impaling the blood of the earth
centuries into a future they could not foretell.

and they told my grandfathers
how to fuck their women
for the glory of god
and what once were
potent dancing flowers
fierce with skilled weapons in their skirts
became in their eyes
machines to make more slaves,
slave-factories
before factories were factories

and oh how my grandmothers bled
and fought
and died
and refused to die
(for i am here)

and i drip,   wet,
this residue between my legs,
five hundred years of history
i carry between my legs
and in my bones —
these stories, carved against my will,
with the pointed tip of a *tagua* rosary

RHODES: Hegemonic discourse pathologizes "Queer." Our heteronormative, neo-colonial, hyper-Christian, racist, capitalist nation understands "Queer" as pathological and aims to neutralize it, to make it docile. To live Queer is often to embody that which does not make sense to the world, which does not fit, which refuses to be molded by social mandates to assimilate, to "unstrange" one's self (in Spanish, we are often called "la gente rara," which literally means "the rare people" but translates more suitably to "strange or weird people"). As a queer person of color, the weight of these requisites is multifold. For me, the violence of racism as it intersects with homophobia and heterosexism in this world digs into my muscles, deep, like barbed needles that agonize my might, constantly, every day.

This poem is a séance for me. An exorcism of a kind. Politically, it calls forth pieces of historical and bodily memory that are mine and never only mine. It calls forth the spirits of those I came from, who died and survived in infinite ways at the hands of colonization. It calls forth my own demons, of sexualized violence that haunt my skin, my body, my imagination. It subverts the burden and isolation of this madness, and fortifies healing by contextualizing it in centuries of social, political, spiritual, and historical trauma. It de-individualizes the presence of violation in the body, to reflect that how we move in the world, how we respond to different kinds of violence, does not have to do with us alone, but with a complex world, rife with violations founded in the racism, sexism, nationalism, and homophobias of empire and expansion.

On my mother's side of the family, I come from Colombian *mestizos,* as well as Sephardic Jews who left Spain centuries ago to escape persecution. I come from Indigenous and Afro-Colombian people, whose histories in my family have been forgotten, but whose presence remains in quiet ways. I also come from white, privileged places, and grew up with many of the privileges that often come with residency in these United States. The privileges gained through diaspora have also meant loss via generational forgetting. This poem, entitled "missionary," addresses the intersections between the racialized violences of the Spanish colonizers through Colombia's history; the intimacies of that history with the Catholic Church and the process of missionizing; the use of sexualized violence as central to the domination and enslavement of subaltern communities and their religious conversion; the institutionalization of legislation and policy which sought the "purification" of the racial constitution of the new nation; and the "unqueering" of the act of sex through rendering sex in the "missionary position"— for the purpose of reproduction — the only holy and acceptable sex act: another form of conversion. These are histories I believe we collectively and individually carry in our bodies, whether or not we are conscious of it. It is an unfortunate success of the colonial project that we are relentlessly subject to it, which requires our unremitting fight against it.

This poem is an act of memory in diaspora. It re-members me. Brown, Queer, and committed to counterhistories through the word, I remain a symbol of heresy and treason. We live and breathe and love and fight, and our survival remains insurrectionary.

SUSAN EDWARDS RICHMOND

Susan Edwards Richmond is the author of four poetry collections: *Increase, Purgatory Chasm, Birding in Winter*, and *Boto*. Her poems have appeared in the journals *Appalachia, Green Mountains Review, The Iowa Review*, and *Poetry East*, among others, and have been collected in several anthologies. She is a poetry editor for *Sanctuary: Journal of the Massachusetts Audubon Society*, is on the board of the Robert Creeley Foundation, and has taught at Clark University and at the Shirley Medium Correctional Facility. Richmond lives in Massachusetts with her husband and two daughters.

ADULTERER

Somalia, October 27, 2008

Each stone is silent. The first one
that hits the corner of her mouth
says nothing. Nor does the one
that bites her ear; the one that cuts
her cheek. Equally nothing.

The crowd that gathers, though,
is not silent. They are shouting
but not with a sound that begs
words. It is the roar of a hot wind
through a tunnel, a fire

across a dry, crackling plain.
Everything in sight is hungry,
a ravenous beast. Something
insatiable has gnashed its teeth
and risen up out of the desert.

There is no uncle, no brother
now, no kind-faced man
from the repair shop, no fruit merchant
who once gave a skinny girl,
a wraith, a plump mango to eat.

No one offered a mango.
Not the first time her father's friend
pushed himself into her, nor the second,
when a stranger from another town
wound his fingers in her hair.

There was pain, yes, and humiliation
and grief, and by the third time,
the man had no face, and there were
no words, everything sucked inward
to the numb unguarded cave.

Her mistake. She thought
there were supposed to be words,
she thought she could still draw them up,
words like a dipper of water,
quenching, from a deep well,

from a father to what passed above.
But there was nothing at the bottom
of the well but a vast reservoir
of silence, the pelting silence
embodied in each stone

that strikes her forehead, each
eye, her throat,
one for each of her 13 years,
and more. Each one more
silent than the one before.

CROSSING

He never told her to worship his body,
but she knew the first time
he closed the door

what he was asking.
"Love Jesus as a man," the priest said.
And she had not seen the difference.

Her mouth is open
to receive the sacrament.
His hands are coarser than the Lord's.
She would not have believed her savior
could be this needy, could bawl
into her young breast with sorrow.

Later, she will learn the choice
is never "yes" or "no"
but whether to go into the room.
Later, much later, with the taste
burning in her mouth, she will know
this was never the body of Christ.

But now she looks at the sharp,
narrow bone of his hip, and
for a moment believes,
"I am better than he is.
Jesus is weak." And because of it
she loves him more.

RICHMOND: I was drawn to the subject matter in both of these poems by the violence implicit in the depiction of girls and women as temptresses or seductresses men are somehow powerless to resist — a view that allows perpetrators of unspeakably savage acts to be excused and even glorified. The image of morally weak and broken men using — and often punishing — women for their own crimes is so powerful and repellent to me that I was moved to imagine myself in the place of these victims. These stories were both fresh from newspaper headlines, and such headlines repeat and reverberate in daily permutations in countries around the world, including our own.

ELIZABETH J. ROLL

Elizabeth J. Roll writes poetry in an attempt to illuminate those universal issues in the human condition (both overt and hidden) that impede as well as enhance life. She focuses particularly on the condition of women and children in society. As a clinical psychologist, she works cross-culturally with children and adults, confronting issues of development and growth as well as loss and decline. Her work as a visual artist in print-making and ceramic-tile design cross-fertilizes her poetry and emphasizes the healing power of all art. Her most profound learning, along with the privilege of working with patients, has been to be a mother and a grandmother.

RITES OF PASSAGE

beside his father
before G-d
he stands on the bimah
to become a man

his face smooth
yarmulka on curly head
fringed woolen tallis
across his shoulders
he peers cautiously
at the crowd
his voice crackles
as he chants
his palms sweat
proud men at his side
re-experience their own
initiation fear triumph

his training complete
his performance done

he is publically accepted
into the tabernacle
with celebration gifts
to ensure future success

beside her mother
before the mirror
she stands in surprise
she has become a woman

her blood-stained fate
is a secret
her face flushes
no one must know
she is prohibited
from the tabernacle
each new moon
left in her cyclical
solitude of shame

she learns to hide
within her body
her future course determined
without gifts ceremony
communal blessing
she can now wed
procreate in pain

her mother's face saddens
realizing her daughter
is no longer a child
remembering
her own cramped life

ROLL: Violence and oppression are two themes that I have struggled with all my life. Having been brought up in a Jewish family that lost many in the Holocaust, I was attuned at an early age to my responsibility to stand up against evil and the oppression of all people. I also was abundantly aware of the oppression of women in society, in the family, and in religion. I recognized my second-class citizenship as a girl and then as a woman; was infuriated by it; and did not want to pass this on to future generations.

I chose to become a psychologist because I was intrigued by and concerned about human behavior and wanted to understand external and internal oppression, as well as violence. I wanted to attempt to remediate suffering. Now, a senior, I feel it is my obligation to train the younger generation. Poetry is one of the vehicles that I choose to use in that pursuit.

In "Rites of Passage," I am expressing the story of many Jewish girls, especially in the more orthodox traditions, where patriarchy reigns. It is a specific example from one monotheistic religion that is also found in many other religious and cultural traditions. The poem represents the inter-generational trauma passed on from mother to daughter. The need to "hide within her body" prohibits the young girl from entering into womanhood with the confidence, power, and desire that is appropriate and that would favorably shape her future.

DAVID ROMTVEDT

In 2015, David Romtvedt, along with his wife and daughter, had the opportunity to visit Delhi where they taught and performed music at the American International School and at a city-run orphanage. His recent books include *Some Church* (Milkweed Editions, 2005), *Buffalotarrak: An Anthology of the Basques of Buffalo, Wyoming* (University of Nevada Center for Basque Studies Press, 2011), and a novel, *Zelestina Urza in Outer Space* (University of Nevada Center for Basque Studies, 2015). In the fall of 2013, Romtvedt taught the first Basque language course offered at the University of Wyoming.

DILEMMAS OF THE ANGELS: INTENTION

The angel loves Sundays — coffee and the paper —
but it's hard today. A man says he cannot
support a woman's right to abortion
even if she becomes pregnant after being raped.
Such pregnancies, he explains, are
intended by God.

She puts down her coffee, turns away,
and looks out the window into the silence
of the winter morning — the yard filled with leaves
fallen from the hundred year old cottonwood tree,
and the two squirrels darting around the trunk as if life
required no thinking.

Maybe the man's right — all killing is murder
no matter the horror of life's creation. Still, it eats
at her — if the Lord intended the pregnancy, he
intended the rape.

She feels his invisible caress and distant gaze,
hands pulling her gown aside, sometimes roughly.
He must know there can be no product
from their union.

That same Sunday morning, a woman gets up
before her husband and teenaged daughters.
She's waited all week for this pleasure —
coffee and the paper. But she's out of milk
so quick goes to the store, a corner grocery
like in a movie, run by an old couple
who know her name and the girls' names,
even her husband's. When she forgets
the money, they say, "Don't worry,
you can pay next time."

That's when it happens — the rape. The angel
would intervene, wrestle the rapist away,
but she knows it would do no good.

When the Lord got Mary pregnant
he never knew her. He wanted
a miracle and made the only
kind he could.

The squirrels are still running around the tree,
brains swirling in the emptiness of their heads.
The coffee's as cold as the winter wind
blowing the leaves against the window.
The angel would claw the skin off her bones
but she has no bones, no parts
anyone can touch.

She shivers, then unbuttons her robe.
Let the Lord watch and imagine
what he intends.

ROMTVEDT: This poem is from a series in which the angels grapple with problems usually reserved for human beings. The poem began when I read of an elected official in the United States who said that he opposed all abortion because everything that happens is intended by the Lord. I was stunned and, like the angel, wondered how every human act could possibly be attributed to the Lord's intention. If this were really the case, intention would be meaningless. Of course, since the angel is now trapped in the world of human sorrow, she, like the rest of us, lives simultaneously in the experience of rape and of silly squirrels, delicious coffee, and kind local businesspeople. Is there any unity to the Lord's various intentions? What about the things that remind us that the rapist is not the totality of life, even if we may sometimes feel overwhelmed by human brutality? In this case, I should say male brutality. What I like best in the poem is the angel's nonchalance — "Ok, my Lord, have a look and then go ahead and explain yourself."

GABRIEL ROSENSTOCK

Gabriel Rosenstock is a poet, novelist, playwright, and author/translator of over 160 books, mostly in Irish (Gaelic). He taught haiku at the Schule für Dichtung (Poetry Academy) in Vienna and at Hyderabad Lit Fest, India, and he also writes for children. His work has appeared in *Best European Fiction 2012* (Dalkey Archive Press) and other anthologies, and his recent books include Irish-language versions of K. Satchidanandan, Ko Un, Hemant Divate, and Dileep Jhaveri.

BILLIE HOLIDAY (GAELIC)

D'fháiscis pian
as sárbhinneas
binneas
as sárphian
nuair a éigníodh thú in aois
do dheich mbliana dhuit
b'in an chéad tairne
i gcéasadh do chine is do bhanúlachta
is d'ealaíne
go dtí sa deireadh
gur scanraigh do ghuth féin tú,
a ainnir i sról.

BILLIE HOLIDAY (TRANSLATION*)

You wrung pain
from the height of sweetness
sweetness
from the height of pain
when you were raped at the tender
age of ten
it was the first nail
in the crucifixion of your race, your womanhood
and your art
until at last
your own voice frightened you,
lady in satin.

ROSENSTOCK: There is something unspeakable about the life of the singer known as "Lady in Satin" and something unspeakable about the subjects of her songs, such as "Strange Fruit," a song I have translated into Irish (Gaelic). It's about unspeakable things we must write. I wrote the poem "Billie Holiday" after watching a video about her life and times. In a sense, rape is the story of the world, the history of our civilization, the illusion of our "mastery" over others and the universe. Witness not just violence to women but also the violence that has been done to languages and cultures.

---

*　Translated from the Irish (Gaelic) by Paddy Bushe.

SUMANA ROY

Sumana Roy's poems, essays, and short fiction have been published in *Granta, Guernica, Prairie Schooner, Caravan, Cha, Himal Southasian,* and other places. She writes from Siliguri, a small town in sub-Himalayan Bengal, India.

RAPE OF SUNLIGHT

You trapped sunlight like a tree.
Every autumn you wanted to take a new lover —
pet, clothes, toy.
You thought adulthood a disease.
Your torn shoes made our lives a museum of journeys.

I remind myself that you were only nine.
I remind myself that you'd asked me Ma Kali's age
and how you always said you were older than her.

In Brindaban, you said you wanted to be a widow.
You liked white. Its taste, you said, was what
you wanted to be: a tube of toothpaste in our mouths.

When your brother threw up in the car,
you cupped your palms.
Vomit was precious, you said.
One day you'd be vomit too, you promised.

Your catalogue of ambitions grew like nails.
You counted backwards to your birthday every morning,
restless to be ten.
"I'll change my name to 'Decade,'" you said.
"Decade" is prettier than "Dopati," your name, you argued.

Your grandmother had named you after the flower,
but you wanted to be Time, not sweet-smelling.
Time has more chlorophyll than all the trees in the world.

When they brought you to us that Friday morning,
blood sticking to your legs like a creeper,
your brother pointed to the sunlight lake inside your frock.
"Tomorrow I'll be the sun," you'd told him, planning for fancy-dress fun.

There were bottles inside you, and male snot.
A syringe in your hair. A button in your palm.

I do not remember the rest. Your father still seals our broken
windowpanes with posters of "Save the Girl Child."
Your grandmother stares at sunshine's death certificate.

ROY: This poem was born out of a particular incident — the rape of a five-year-old
girl in Delhi in the summer of 2013. Among other things, a candle and a 200 ml bottle
of hair oil were found inside her.

VIMMI SADARANGANI

Vimmi Sadarangani received her PhD in Translation Studies in 2010 and is an Asso-
ciate Professor of Sindhi at Tolani College of Arts and Science in Gujarat, India. She
has participated in various national and international literary events and has pub-
lished three collections of poems, four books of children's literature, and six books on
Sindhi-language learning. Professor Sadarangani is a member of the National Council
for Promotion of Sindhi Language, Delhi, and a former member of the Sindhi Advisory
Board, Sahitya Akademi, in New Delhi. Since 2011, she has also served as the regional
organizer of "100 Thousand Poets for Change."

TETHERED[*]   ڪنهن گانءِ وانگر

You and I   تون ۽ مان
never walked together.   ڪڏهن ڪڏ ڪون هلياسين

                                                       رستي تي هلندي
You walked ahead leading   تون اڳيان اڳيان
like some cowherd   جن ڪو ڏنار

                                                       ۽ پٺيان
and tied with a rope   نوڙيءَ سان ٻَڌل
                                                       ڪنهن گانءِ وانگر مان.
I followed.

SADARANGANI: Indian society is considered to be patriarchal by nature. In this
world, a parallel can be drawn between "woman" and "cow." Both are considered to
be docile, domesticated, and nurturing. But in our male-centric domain, a woman is
expected to be not only calm, docile, and multi-tasking, but is also expected to follow
silently in the footsteps of her man/husband.

---

[*] Translated from the Sindhi by Gopika Jadeja.

SMITA SAHAY

Smita Sahay is a writer, poet, and editor based in Mumbai. Her short stories, poetry, and book reviews have appeared in *Ripples, Asia Writes, Pedestal Magazine, Celebrating India, Muse India, Cha Journal, Women's Web, Kitaab,* and others. A computer engineer by education, in another lifetime she worked for Accenture as an SAP consultant. She is associate editor of *Veils, Halos & Shackles* and is working on her first book of fiction. Sahay has read her poetry at "100 Thousand Poets for Change" in Mumbai and Pune, and at the Prakriti Poetry Festival in Chennai. She received an MBA from the Indian School of Business (class of 2015).

THE CORONATION OF SHILAVATI

With your *man's head*
                    which held the unyielding concept of dharma
on your woman's body
                    which held the seed of Prasenjit
you knew a woman couldn't be king
                    any more than a man get pregnant.

Then why

as milk flowed down your widowed self,
then honey, then treacle, then water,
— as you sat drenched on the throne —
did you raise your head for the Raj-abhisheka, the coronation?

And why

when Mandavya ignored your head
raised in hope
and traced
instead the tilak's red approval above your navel

were you surprised?

You looked around:

the glowing curves
of the silken parasol, the shining bows, the conch-shell trumpets
were not for you, but for your son
who was growing in you, a curled fetus.

Shilavati
at that moment,
did you not wish for another dharma, wish
to break free of that hook
piercing the roof of your mouth,
that command you ruled,
not as a king, but only as a regent?

Had you raised your head,
wiped the mark off your navel,
and told Mandavya that his thumb had been off the mark, Shilavati,
that moment of quiet surprise would have burst
forth into questions, demanding
answers, leading us into a different world.

FOR NAMELESS, FACELESS WOMEN

for 16 December 2013, Delhi

Dear Society,

The stories you tell of Manu and Ram
and Rishi Gautam, and the way you tell them,
have robbed, humiliated and caged women
in adjectives, temptations, apologies.

Slaps. Rapes. Acid-splashes.
They retell the stories you tell.

Then why are you out there protesting
                    today, marching with candles?

Power lies neither with the lawmakers nor the enforcers.
It lies in stories — the power to alter DNA.
Your bards have produced mutants — generations of, millennia of, them.

Hangings. Castrations. Life terms.
They cannot clear a race's DNA.

Don't you see,

                 you have to change your stories?

Don't you see,

                 you have to change the way you tell your stories?

Your Poet

SAHAY: Oppression of women is one of the most unfortunate truths we live with, regardless of all discussions of, and steps towards, women's empowerment. Oppression in any form is gross injustice, albeit of a kind that cannot be addressed by laws but only by a change in the culture and beliefs we pass on through the first stories we tell our children — fairy tales, mythology, fables, or folk tales. I want us to stand back and take a look at these stories and the many ways our civilization cages a woman and strips her of her basic rights, from the right to an education to the right to dress as she chooses. It is the result of seemingly innocuous everyday practices that rape, dowry demands, female infanticide, female foeticide, and a general inequality is prevalent, even among the educated, so-called "progressive" portions of society. Unless we realize the horror of all that we perpetrate, and all that we take for granted, and until we decide to bring up our sons and daughters equally, oppression will continue. Through my work, I urge humans — men and women — to be humane, to stop treating a part of the population unequally, to stop looking at women as bodies only or as embodiments of family honor, and to look at them simply as human beings.

The Coronation of Shilavati: The Pregnant King, by Dr. Devdutt Pattnaik, is a tale of a prince who cannot become king unless he has a male offspring, and his mother, the capable, intelligent, dharmic Queen Shilavati, who can only rule as her son's proxy. And who has heard of a woman who was a king?

PERVIN SAKET

Pervin Saket writes fiction, poetry, and screenplays. She is the author of the novel *Urmila* (Jaico, 2015) and a collection of poems, *A Tinge of Turmeric* (Writers' Workshop, 2009). Her short fiction has appeared in *Journeys* (Sampad, UK); *Breaking the Bow* (Zubaan, India); the *Asian Writer* collection (Dahlia, UK); *Aliens* (Prime Books, USA); *Earthen Lamp Journal; Khabar; Love Across Borders — An Anthology by Indian and Pakistani Writers*; and elsewhere. Her poems have been published in *The Binnacle* (University of Maine, USA) and in *Kritya*. Saket was shortlisted for the Random House India Writers Bloc Award 2013 and conducts creativity workshops at the British Council Library.

THE LEFT OF THE HORIZON

My fingers grope an empty sky
I do not believe that
These binds will free my wrists
A day when the sun will melt these chains and
A night when darkness can be peace
I know I can hope for
Words, spoken and written
But in this world of binaries,
I am the other, the lesser, the left
I cannot even imagine that
The scales shall be evenly balanced
Torn, tired, tested,
Our children will emerge from wombs and
Naively
Weave dreams of a day when
The world will understand its daughters.

(Now read the poem in reverse order, starting with the last line.)

HANDS

Her father's hands are nothing
Like her mother's.
They linger tentatively
And sweep in a stupor of rigid moans.
Where her fingers contract, his spread
Taking in all of her skin at once
Before she can squirm or struggle, he has
Traced his path and then rubbed it gently
As if to wipe off the trail of crumbs.
It is a soft touch, she thinks as her heart
Turns cold.
Once she clenched her mouth so tight
That her jaw slipped and cut her lip
And he was particularly tender
When wiping the drops where it tore.
So she doesn't clench her mouth any more.

HANDS

Her husband's hands are nothing
Like her mother's.
She wonders how they can
Be so heavy and yet so quick.
Even the goose pimples erupt a minute
After he has kneaded and throbbed.
And in the darkness she pats them down,
Singing silent pleas to the sore, fuming flesh,
As if to appease armed red ants.
It is my husband, she thinks as her heart
Turns stone.
Once she clenched her thighs so tight
That later she had to shred the sheet
As the dull brown pond wouldn't vanish
And the neighbors had whispered before.
So she doesn't clench her thighs any more.

SAKET: "The Left of the Horizon" started as a question: What would it take to bring about equality in our world? The answer that resonated most was — a change of perspective. Hence, I began the experiment of writing a poem that changed with a change in perspective. I wanted the same lines, which were once shackling, to also speak of freedom. Words of despair would now speak of hope, and what was once bleak would now be celebratory — all this, without changing anything except the order in which the poem would be read. Apart from the themes that the words carry, I worked towards a structure that would emphasize that change is not as overwhelming as it seems — sometimes a fresh perspective is all it takes.

"Hands" was conceived as a response to the sexual abuse that women and men often tolerate silently. I wanted to emphasize the repetitive pattern of such abuse, and instead of using several verses, I preferred to follow a "mirror" structure. I believe that form plays an important role in how we perceive a text. The arrangement of words and lines is particularly powerful in poetry. I was also conscious about using the present tense, since it helps convey that such incidents are constant, ongoing, and irrefutably prevalent in our time.

ANU SANGWAN

Anu Sangwan is a talk-show host on ETV Rajasthan. She is co-founder of Prem Mandir Sansthan, an NGO working for the education of underprivileged children and the empowerment of women. Dr. Sangwan is an active member of Rays-Asha ki ek kiran, working for HIV+ kids and also for the cause of organ and tissue donation. She serves on the panel of the Rajasthan Police Academy as a resource person for gender-issues training. She has also published *Steps*, a collection of short stories about women, and is presently working on her second book of poetry. Sangwan has been awarded the Rajasthan Gaurav 2013 and the Women Icon Award 2014.

I See You, My Daughter

I see you, my daughter,
Lying on the roadside, near the garbage heap,
Covered in your mother's blood,
Your barely formed head covered with sparse hair, wet.
Your eyes are clenched and your chin touches your barely moving chest.
Your fists, too, are clenched, your arms crossed upon your unformed breasts.
Your knees are drawn up tightly across your tiny caved in stomach,
The placenta torn and sneaking through them like a withered snake.
Your thin legs are crossed at the tiny delicate ankles, your pink toes
Speckled with blood . . . I see you, my daughter.

I see you, my daughter,
Lying on the roadside, near the garbage heap,
Covered in your own blood,
Your sticky mottled hair lying bedraggled across your bare shoulders.
Your eyes are clenched and your chin touches your barely moving chest.
Your fists, too, are clenched, your arms crossed upon your once
          beautiful breasts
Now speckled with burn marks.
Your knees are drawn up tightly across your curved stomach,

Your womanhood torn and dry like a withered snake.
Your long bare legs are crossed at the ankles, your red painted toes
Spattered with blood... I see you, my daughter.

A journey of a million smiles... a million blessings... so many tiny
Dancing steps... so many birthday gifts... a zillion words... so many
          classes
And teachers... beautiful dreams... a journey of a million tears...
From your mother's blood to your own... from death to death...

I see you, my daughter.

SANGWAN: I wrote this poem, "I See You My Daughter," in the aftermath of the Delhi gang-rape in December 2012 and the continuous news reports of girl children being abandoned by parents, in garbage heaps or on the roadside.

ELLIN SAROT

Ellin Sarot's poems have appeared in *The Paterson Literary Review, The Deronda Review, String Poet, Women's Studies: An inter-disciplinary journal,* the anthologies *Women Write Resistance: Poets Resist Gender Violence* and *Les Femmes Folles: The Women 2013,* and online in "100 Thousand Poets for Change." In 2014 the Writers' Room of Boston awarded Sarot the first Gish Jen Fellowship for Emerging Writers, and she currently serves on "the Room's" board. One of her poems won the New England Poetry Club's Firman Houghton Award for 2015.

ENGRAPHIA

The mother's pain at birth told over and over
to the child becomes the child's pain,
the child's pain, then that child's child's pain,
heritable. Beatings regular (or irregular)
induce a habit, the pain of being beaten persisting,
one beating begetting another, another beating
another. It may be called congenital,
an engram: the cry, then silence,
then the poem.

SILENCE

Writing is hard when what you want to say makes you afraid
to remember what made you afraid, afraid of what you knew
was terrible, afraid that if you told something terrible would happen,
which was what you were told would happen when it happened,
afraid you would be punished for what happened, which certainly was
        your fault,
you were told, because what happened would never have happened had it
        not been for you,
and had never happened before. Writing is hard inside silence,
words go round and round and fall away, out of sight, out of mind,
as for years you went round and round inside silence, sentenced to this.

Writing is hard when what you want to say breaks you open
again, anger breaks open, makes you afraid, even now he's dead, that what
        you want to say
will break the wall between you and them, the ones you love who could not
for the life of them suspect what you know happened, would not believe
you, certainly would not believe it of him, and anyway
if it did happen, well, it was oh so long ago, why bring it up now,
        though a voice
you've always heard saying get away from this, take yourself away,
which you did, now warns you about that frail young neighbor,
        who barely leaves her house,
sometimes can't think, won't hear this or that, snail in a shell, oh so brittle,
you wonder, looking at her, did it happen again, to her,
and if it did, do you need to speak, for her, death
breaking you free, if only to say something, if only you could find the words.

SAROT: *Webster's* defines an engram as a "memory trace," and according to *Stedman's Medical Dictionary* (2002), engraphia is the formation of an engram. In neuropsychology, engraphia occurs when "an experience intentionally forgotten but not fully repressed... result(s) in the development of a neurotic conflict." In my own words, it is the process of inscription of a memory of trauma into a person's psychic body, where its force, consciously or subconsciously, affects behavior that often is repeated from generation to generation.

The poem "Engraphia" came to me through the word and its definition, which recalled Kafka's story "In the Penal Colony," in which a criminal is put into a machine of torture that over and over writes his punishment into his flesh, until the offender dies by inscription. Rape and incest, the subjects of "Silence," are traumatic events that leave insidious, unerasable memory traces that stain the lives of those abused and those around them — and maybe, in another way, one hopes, the lives of the abusers.

Violences of all kinds against women and girls appear to be unending, but a compilation of the record in poems from around the planet, which this anthology offers, works toward ending them.

K. SATCHIDANANDAN

K. Satchidanandan is an Indian poet writing in Malayalam, and he is also a bilingual critic and translator. He has 21 collections of poetry in the original Malayalam and an equal number in translation, in all the major Indian languages and also in English, Irish, French, Italian, German, and Arabic. Satchidanandan has also translated 16 collections of world poetry into Malayalam. He has taken part in more than a dozen major book fairs and literature festivals, including those in Jaipur, Delhi, Damascus, Abu Dhabi, London, Paris, Frankfurt, Leipzig, Rotterdam, and New York, and has received 27 awards, including the Indian National Academy Award for Poetry. He was the executive head of the Indian Literary Academy for a decade.

THAT STONE

I too pick up a stone
"Murderers!"
I raise it to my lips,
"Kill them!"
I raise it above my head.

"Let the man who has not sinned
pelt the first stone!"
Who is this bearded man?

The stone comes down
and falls on my own head;
my blood mingles with
the sacred blood from the cross,
"Kill me too!" I, the sinner,
stand naked with the murderers.

SATCHIDANANDAN: I wrote "That Stone" as a response to the gang-rape and murder of a paramedical student in Delhi. There were many demonstrations of protest and many people in the city, including men, took part in these. Many men also blamed women in general for such situations — for dressing seductively, traveling alone at night, and so on. I felt that this rape-murder was a call for introspection for all men who misbehave, or have at any time misbehaved, with women. The whole context reminded me of the episode about Mary Magdalene in the Bible, where Jesus tells the men preparing to throw stones at Mary that those among them who have not committed any sin should throw the first stone, and no one from the crowd came forward. "The Stone" is one of my many poems that deal with the suffering of women and join their demand for freedom and justice, though here this empathy works obliquely.

JANE SATTERFIELD

Jane Satterfield is the author of the poetry collections *Her Familiars* (Elixir, 2013), *Assignation at Vanishing Point* (Elixir Press Book Award, 2003), and *Shepherdess with an Automatic* (Towson University Prize for literature), as well as *Daughters of Empire: A Memoir of a Year in Britain and Beyond* (Demeter, 2009). Satterfield's awards include a National Endowment for the Arts fellowship in poetry, the William Faulkner Society's Gold Medal for the Essay, the *Mslexia* women's poetry prize, and the 49ᵗʰ Parallel Award for poetry. She is the literary editor for the *Journal of the Motherhood Initiative* and teaches at Loyola University Maryland.

HER FAMILIARS

> *Hopkins was particularly fond of getting people to confess to having signed a pact with the devil, but charges also included bewitching people or livestock to death, causing illness and lameness, and entertaining spirits or familiars, which usually turned out to be household pets.*
>
> —Nigel Cawthorne, *Witch Hunt: The History of Persecution*

Just past her birthday (thirteenth)
my daughter's engrossed
in the antics of the Pretty Committee
who, swish bags in tow,
shop for *amazing* LBDs.
So while I'm lamenting
the mere fact it exists —

this primer for learning
popularity skills & the proper
product lines — why not take a tip
from today's radio guest
who assures me the "mommy makeover"
is a blessing for women
not yet past their prime? —

that a little time under the knife
perks up the buttocks & pulls in
a gut, erases the damage
done by all that devotion
to your little dears. Just the ticket

to recharge my spirit & sex life.
Ever notice how age or oddness
offends? Same with widowhood or
willingness to buck the trends. Just look at
the woodcut, frontispiece to
The Discovery of Witches,
London, circa 1647, where one-legged
Elizabeth Clarke, whose
mother (maybe witchy
with words or wise with a cure?),
a heretic, hung before her. After three days
without food or sleep, Clarke finally confessed

the names of her five familiars: *Holt,*
Newes, Sack-and-Sugar, Jamara,
& Vinegar Tom — cats, rabbit,
spaniel & greyhound. And consider
Faith Mills of Fressingham
whose three pet birds
wrought havoc by breaking
a cart & inducing (by magic!)
a cow to jump over a sty.
An affection for animals, it seems,
in the eyes of the powerful,
was as good as witchcraft,
a grievous (*read:* hanging) crime. Thank God

the girls in the Pretty Committee
all find the right dress &
strappy stilettos; thank God

they twitter & text to stay
in step with the times. The pressures
of fashion are many; the plot,

as my daughter says, will improve: soon
one of the gang will be on the outs.
From gossip, innuendo, & grievance
anyone can construct a water-tight case.
How came you to be acquainted?
was the favored question
of Hopkins, the self-appointed
Witch-Finder General, bearer of
needles & bodkins, Puritan
cloak & cape, the best accessories
of his time. The feeble, the poor, &
otherwise unpopular didn't
stand a chance. From fees
charged to the estates of the accused
he made a not unpretty profit.

HOPE

After the painting "Hope I" (1903) by Gustav Klimt

All afternoon the painter's addressing
the riddle of flesh
in an angle of light.

Fiddly work to get it right,
now that love stands Atlas-backed
under astonishing weight.

Hope in their native tongue's this *expectancy* —
where they've lain, what lies in wait.

So much for masks, the gilded screen,
the carpet of flowers —
the instant of eros
where laundress = goddess —
a subject
made & unmade.

Harm hovers, a circle
of crones on the horizon.
Still, her glance is unabashed
& still aroused. Meeting his.
That practiced, penetrating gaze:
strokes terrible & true.

— Mistress of heaven, dust, debris…
If she's naked now,
what will she take off next?

SATTERFIELD: "Hope" is one of a series of Klimt's paintings of an expectant model. Klimt was known to have exploited his models sexually, as well as economically, and more than one critic has stated that the juxtaposition of maternal beauty and spectral imagery in the paintings conveys a terror of female eroticism.

As the daughter of an Air Force veteran and longtime reservist, I grew up with a heightened awareness of our nation's military forces. The work of keeping peace, and of providing national security, noble as it is, can have unintended violent effects. So when I began to study and write poetry seriously in college, it was no surprise that I was especially drawn to work that explored themes of violence and oppression as a means of fostering awareness and offering consolation. I remember being struck deeply by Seamus Heaney's "Punishment" and Adrienne Rich's "Rape."

Despite differing contexts, both poets reveal tacit cultural assumptions about gender; they expose the unsettling link between individual bodies and the body politic. These themes enter my own poems, sometimes directly and sometimes indirectly. Whether I'm writing about the prevalence of sexual trafficking and a mother's fears for her daughter, sixteenth-century witch trials and contemporary high school cliques, or male artists' exploitation of models, I seek to raise awareness of moral trespass and cultural complicity. My own experience of gender violence — of boundaries crossed once consent is withdrawn — is something many of my own students have struggled with, in person and in print. In writing about violence and suffering, we also seek to heal, to honor the resilience of the human spirit.

Ada Jill Schneider

Ada Jill Schneider is the author of several volumes of poetry, including *This Once-Only World* (PearTree Press, 2015) and *Behind the Pictures I Hang* (Spinner Publications, 2007). She has reviewed poetry books for *Midstream* magazine, and directs "The Pleasure of Poetry," a program she founded, at the Somerset Public Library in Massachusetts. Her poems appear in many anthologies, including *Sestinas in the Twenty-First Century* (University Press of New England), *Love After 70* (Wising Up Press), and *Letters to the World* (Red Hen Press). Schneider has an MFA from Vermont College.

A Ten-Pound Bag

First you scrub them, then you gouge out
their evil eyes and rotten spots. Slip a sharp
knife under their skin and peel away
what you've been unable to scrape
from your frayed burlap brain.
Cut into bite-sized pieces of fear.
Add water. Bring to a furious boil
by remembering the man in the dark hallway
who exposed himself when you were twelve.
With a fork, stab and mash the sticky leer
off his face. Smash for your mother's sake, too,
the times she endured her uncle's touch,
the one who paid her steamship fare to America.
Add pepper for the day your father left,
salt for his guilty phone calls that soured
birthdays and holidays. Whisk your frenzied rage
until every last lump submits to butter
and you feel so light, you're not even hungry.

SCHNEIDER: Here I was, in my sixties, still terrified of discovering some man lurking in a dark corner. And there was my mom, in her eighties, still stinging from the shame of being molested in her youth and the frustration of being helpless to protest. I wanted to pulverize and expunge these memories once and for all. I did so in the kitchen, the one room in the house of which I am master.

LAYLA SCHUBERT

Layla Schubert worked with Lucia Perillo, Rodney Jones, Allison Joseph, and others at
Southern Illinois University Carbondale, and completed a BFA in Creative Writing in
1997. She later earned a PhD in Medieval Literature and an MLS in Library Science
in Oregon. Recently, Schubert and her husband, Erik, received an honorable mention
in the Glimmer Train New Writers competition for a co-authored short story; her
poem "Dry Socket" was published in Issue 15 of *Diverse Voices Quarterly*; and two of
her poems appeared in *Heart* (heartjournal.org). She was also awarded an internship
at Tin House Books.

NINE VOLTS

for Billie Boyce & Alexandria Ison. And all of the others.

Someone else's nightmare stares,
nameless. Accusing. Unavenged,
from grainy black-and-white tabloid sheets.
What is a picture worth when it shows
a woman bound to a post, two gaping holes
where breasts should rest, soft and full,
and chunks of thigh gone to where discarded flesh goes?
She hangs, framed by headlines — head up, shoulders back,
not the defeated and resting corpse she should have been.

Sometimes it's a shame what we can live through when there's nowhere
        to run.

I read on. The man who inscribed Pol Pot's ideology onto living bone
is born again and likens himself to St. Paul . . .

A girl, I stuck my tongue to nine-volt batteries.
Held my breath. Counted to ten, twenty, thirty.
Hurt myself; no one could hurt me.
From razor scars to tattoos, words enter skin, embed.

At thirteen, one of the girls who stood in the alley
dangling a cig from a burgundy-lined lip,
big bust and black-rimmed eyes
drawing blatant leers from mulleted boys,
was found in an alley by garbage men,
clad in red socks and cigarette burns.

When I asked why we didn't hang a picture
of her in the gym with the other dead kids,
Mrs. Cadigan. Math teacher. Student council advisor,
said that we didn't hang pictures of dead kids like her.
Mr. Cadigan, the D.A., said her naked, fetal coil,
face-shielding arm frozen, seven-inch hole in her skull,
might be accidental. After all...

And after twenty-four years her day may come
because of the others like her,
says a friend with a jailhouse tattoo
reading "In memory of Billie"
because she, too, is no good.
Billie's only one of a long line
of photos fighting to free themselves
from the pages of forensic texts,
mortis-stiffened limbs refusing
to conform to dumping grounds.

Begging for decency.

The battery. Again.

Once upon a time in California,
a trucker turned in a tit to the lost and found.
Its owner was found in a culvert with two other corpses.

Nine volts of raw memory and this from a history book:
when the world was at one of its wars,
an American artillery unit took prisoners,
with them a nursing mother — tossed onto a straw-filled cart.

When the commander remembered, it was too late for mercy.
He cringed at the mess his boys had left
and fired one shot.

A libation for pity.

There are two terminals. The female contact is negative.

I met Alexandria Ison on the number 8 bus.
We chatted about her rat before she jumped out on Burnside.
I didn't know then that she went by Tomorrow.
I didn't learn that until I read it in *Rolling Stone.*
I remembered her because she brought her rat on the bus
and people parted from her like the Red Sea.
I love my pets, too, and I don't want
to end up like her, rotting and strangled,
with four others dumped in the woods. One more missing.
I want Tomorrow.

Transistor. Current. Oscillating. Between live and dead.

We are all composed of corpses.
Do you remember when Yosemite swallowed
Silvina Pelosso and Joie Armstrong and Carole and Juli Sund?
After a meal of apples, rice, or plump chicken breasts,
we each become the dust of My Lai, the soil of S21,
the bone-cradling dirt in the ditch at Fin Cop.
I am nine volts closer to this.
Deep in the desert a girl fought back.
It was 1984. She was drenched in acid
to still her wagging tongue
and dumped into the scorching sand.
She lived, and she walked. Blind.
Her flesh running from her bones with every step,
one foot in front of the other for hours.
Can you imagine being the one who found her?
Standing in that blazing sunset border,

realizing that the figure approaching,
the naked body mounted by a skull and collar bones,
was not a goddess coming to bring divine justice to all of us
but a mortal who you would have to drive to the hospital,
fourth degree burns needing decades of surgeries:
artificial eyelids, corpse-scavenged corneas,
curled into a ball for months with her new nose embedded into
her chest to heal. At fifteen, receiving
a new windpipe to raise her voice and sing

I can.

But I am safe here with my battery.
Powering the transistor.
Pulling ugly stories from the air.

SCHUBERT: I am no stranger to violence in its most pernicious forms, having grown up with my blighted, alcoholic mother fighting off memories of incestuous rape and memories of my father occasionally hitting her when she stood up for herself. An acquaintance of mine, Billie Boyce, was raped and murdered when I was in seventh grade. Her killing and the aftermath of victim-shaming in her school and community left a lasting impression on me of the futility of seeking justice if you were "that kind" of girl.

I began working in the sex industry when I was eighteen, to earn extra money for college. From that vantage point, I saw many things that I cannot unsee, all the while augmenting my culture's despicable treatment of women who dared to claim ownership of their own sexualities. In November 1998, I survived a sexual assault that led to delayed-onset PTSD. Around that time, I read articles on S21 and My Lai, and Alexandria Ison was murdered in Portland shortly after I briefly met her. I also read about the attempted murder of Cheryl Bess and assorted atrocities against women throughout history. This catalogue of events led to my writing "Nine Volts." Writing this poem was painful — so painful that I put off editing it for over a decade. However, this anthology gave me the impetus to finally give it the attention it deserved.

CATHERINE SERCOMBE

Catherine Sercombe is a published author, education-business partner/manager/tutor, wife, and mother of three, who recently graduated from Tabor Adelaide with an Associate degree in Creative Writing. She writes poetry (traditional, modern, and Australian bush poetry), short stories, creative nonfiction, songs, scripts (skits, puppet plays, comedy, drama, musicals), devotions, and bible studies, always with the goal of enlightening and enriching the experience of her readers and audience. Her songs, drama sketches, and poems have been performed in schools, churches, Indigenous communities, and public events in Queensland, Northern Territory, and Western Australia. A native of Queensland, Australia, Sercombe is a member of Quirky Quills Writers, Omega Writers Inc., and Christian Writers Downunder.

SPECIAL CLEARANCE / EXPOSED

"It needs a special clearance. I think you can walk."
Boss slowly scans the length of my legs,
already

     Exposed

by the too-short-for-sport regulation bank uniform,
first week's pay consumed before earned.
His practiced gaze strips pantyhose.
"Your lovely legs look up to the task," he slithers.

     I shiver,
clutch
the check,   escape
through the door.

Feet follow the footpath in Fortitude Valley,
downtown low ground CBD wannabe,
seventies, eighties,
backstreet brothel city.

Push each foot, forward in turn,
chase the other,

                    race

the other,
half a building, half a block.

Sounds of the city:
commerce and companies,
congas and timpani,
tom-toms and snares,
trucks belch, cars rev,
brakes squeal, tires skid,

                    something
                    is
                    wrong...

"Hey Pretty Chicky, wanna come for a ride?
Me and me mates'll give you a good time."

                    adrenaline
                    accelerates
                    I slip skid burn curb turn
                    the corner don't slow
                    don't stop don't
                    imagine

                    what

Red convertible mimics me,
like a tow, clings to me,

                    grabs me,
                    drags me,

black-patent pumps convert
from polished leather to lead.

"Aww don't be shy, Chicky."
"You work at the big bank, Honey?"
"Yeah, with all that lovely money?"
"We'll 'ave a piece o' that!"
"Or a piece of

             you!"

Metronome heartbeat:
pulse allegrissimo
pace agitato
footsteps presto,
cat calls   follow me,
caterwaul,   growl,
wolf whistles   pierce me,
             penetrate,
             snarl,

footsteps faster,
turn the corner,
glass door,   I go
inside.

Blast of dry conditioned air
licks at, laps up my

             cold

sweat.
Head teller scans me,

             "How
             can I

help you, Miss?"

             push
the check   through the gap
             in
             the glass cage

"Special clearance   ?"
swallow
breathe
just
breathe

"Are you okay, Miss?"

grayed... edges...
black... mists...
fain... ting...
fall... ing...
bla... ck...
ou... t...
o...
WHY?

"It was a joke,"   Boss says
"A jest,   initiation,
nothing sinister.
Don't get your
knickers in a knot,   Babe!"
He sleazes
a lip-smile.   I
want to   spit.
      I
want to   weep
      and
      scream

"Sexual harassment!"

      but
      no one
      listens.

Damn
them
to
hell!

Next special clearance,
Boss books a taxi.

Exposed...
vulnerable...

I shiver...

something
is
wrong.

SERCOMBE: This poem was written with two messages: reading the whole poem reveals the trauma and vulnerability of a young woman in a working world where men hold the power; reading just the indented words speaks of rape — the ultimate abuse of that power.

I began my working life as a fifteen-year-old junior bank officer in Australia, in the 1970s, and this poem reflects my experience. As a junior, you were at the bottom of the power structure. As a female, you were lower still. Although issues of gender discrimination and sexual harassment are more readily addressed in the workplace today in most western societies, the vulnerability of the weak in the hands of the powerful continues to darken and stain society in too many places worldwide. Rape is not only a sexual crime; it is an abuse of strength and power, which strips its victims of their dignity, autonomy and self-worth. Those who use their strength and power to manipulate and abuse others, in any form, rape the collective soul of our humanity. All the while that occurs, something is wrong.

RAVI SHANKAR

Ravi Shankar is founding editor of *Drunken Boat* and author/editor of eight books and chapbooks of poetry, including *Deepening Groove*, winner of the 2010 National Poetry Review Prize, and W.W. Norton's *Language for a New Century: Contemporary Poetry from Asia, the Middle East & Beyond* (co-edited with Tina Chang and Nathalie Handal). He has been featured in *The New York Times*, been a commentator on NPR and the BBC, and been awarded a Pushcart Prize. His most recent book, *What Else Could It Be: Collaborations and Ekphrastics* (Carolina Wren Press), was published in 2015. Shankar teaches at Central Connecticut State University and in the first international MFA program at City University of Hong Kong.

BREASTFEEDING AT THE BLUE MOSQUE

Hidden from a queue to bag shoes a woman nurses a child
under a wool scarf in the shadow two fluted minarets cast
pitched towards incessant sun, a necessity somehow an insult
to *sharia* law, no matter what sustenance a lemonwedge
of breast, God's own, yields, puckering a tiny mouth
until bright eyes glaze to doll loll. Fairly alien to ponder
raw biology of milk conveyed by ducts lined with capillaries,
made from pouring stuff of stars: nourishment that manifests
minerals for bone from pulsing light.
                            Too close to the slickheat pushing out
between the legs of nearly every woman not your wife
but her as well? How could it be that her very being derives
solely from her relation to you, that she could have no value
in the calculus but to function as temptation, or its dome-
blue corollary, disappointment? No cover covers up
those integers holding the place of zeroes, Iznik tiles or after-
life virgins. Ostrich eggs on chandeliers don't dissuade spiders.
If the fear of the Lord is not the beginning of our wisdom,
then *La ilah ha il Allah* is a breast in a mouth, else nothing is.

SHANKAR: In 2010, I was asked to be a visiting faculty member at Eastern Med-
iterranean University in Cyprus, a country that I did not know much about at the
time. Preparing for an idealized vision of a seaside paradise, I quickly discovered some
rudimentary facts — for instance, that while the southern portion of the island is
mostly Greek and part of the EU, the university is situated in northern Cyprus, which
is considered occupied by every country but Turkey, and there were certain places where
women had to cover their heads and where certain liberties I took for granted were
forbidden. Fascinated by Turkish culture, my family and I (including my newborn
daughter) traveled to Istanbul where we marveled at the mosques, ate *beyaz peynir*,
and drank thick, dark coffee. But at one of our stops, the famed Blue Mosque in
Sultanahmet, my daughter got hungry and cried to be suckled. What ensued and the
nearly cartoonish lengths that we had to go to so she could be fed — and the greater
irony that this taboo against the body, against femininity, was transpiring in a house
of worship — was what engendered this poem.

The poet and critic Lisa Russ Spaar featured "Breastfeeding at the Blue Mosque" in the
Chronicle of Higher Education's "Arts and Academe" blog, where she wrote:

> Milk may arguably be our first language and the mouth our primal mind.
> Women have been breast-feeding their own and others' infants presumably
> since the dawn of humankind, and while this act of sustenance and nurturing
> should seem the most natural of activities ("mammal" < L. mamma, breast),
> controversies abound across time, place, and culture regarding who, when,
> where, and why women should breast-feed, particularly in public spaces....
> The richly ululating texture of the Arabic in this Muslim proclamation of
> faith — "There is no deity except God" — is evocative of the sounds of
> suckling and meant to remind us that we all, men and women, are equally
> children of the universe, deserving of respect, dignity, the right to praise,
> to nurture and protect, and to be protected and nurtured, especially in our
> most holy places.

I don't think I could put it any better! But as an interesting coda to this poem, when
it was published, one of the first comments was from someone who called himself
Imam1950, who wrote, "this is hate spech, not a peom. Ravi Shankar is well known
for hate speech. It is strange that the Chronile gaves space for such hate peoms/articles.
[*sic*]" That comment made it clear to me that efforts to deify the human body and
sanctify the maternal impulse — the very principle of caring and sustenance that life
itself derives from — are still under attack. And when I read recent stories like that of
the woman accused of adultery in the Syrian city of Hama who was stoned to death
by ISIS militants, aided by her own bearded father — or when I read statistics like the

latest from the US Census Bureau showing that women make 75% of the wages that their male counterparts do — I realize how much further we have to go as a society to achieve equality and compassionate understanding.

Mukta Sharangpani

Mukta Sharangpani holds a PhD in Anthropology from Stanford University and has taught at Stanford, University of California Davis, Santa Clara University, and De Anza Community College, where she is currently an adjunct faculty member in the Department of Social Sciences, and at FLAME University in India. She is interested in issues of gender imparity and their manifestation as gendered violence, especially rape and domestic violence. A strong proponent of theater for social change, she has written and performed several pieces based on sexual abuse, trafficking, and marital violence. Sharangpani has served as president of Maitri, a nonprofit supporting victims of domestic violence and other abuses in the Bay Area of California, and as Commissioner on the Domestic Violence Council for Santa Clara County.

Saptapadi

(The seven steps in a Hindu marriage ritual)

1. Redblueblack
2. The color of my marriage
3. Welts on bare skin
4. Blood and fear
5. And at the back of my tongue
6. The coppery taste of
7. Your lovemaking

Sharangpani: My overarching research interests can best be described as an inquiry into the relationship between culture and gender-based violence. I am interested in examining how cultural notions about sexuality, community, nation, tradition, and modernity influence gendered identity. I remain particularly committed to the idea of a feminism that transcends borders, for I believe that what we observe as very local, often violent, incidents have deep and complex connections to transnational events, policies, and processes. "Saptapadi" deals with the issue of marital violence. It aims to serve as a reminder that while violence is generally assumed to be stranger-inflicted (as in Nirbhaya's case), many women experience violence at the very hands of those they trust or rely on most — their families. Violence within the home is a manifestation of a long and complex history of negating, denying, and policing women's voices. Any inquiry of violence against women must take into account the overt and underlying way in which women are rendered invisible, irrelevant, and immaterial through what are seen as legitimate and celebrated social institutions such as marriage, motherhood, and family.

K SHARIFA

K Sharifa was born in Gulbarga, in Karnataka, India, and works as a senior auditor in Bangalore. A poet, literary critic, and feminist writer, she has been active in women's and human-rights movements. Sharifa has published more than seventeen books and has received several awards for her works, which include *Nurenala antaranga* (*Nuren's Heart*, Kannada Sahitya Parishad, 1997), *Mumtajala mahalu* (*Mumtaj's Mansion*, Navakarnataka Publications, 2001), and, most recently, *Burkha paradise* (*The Paradise of Veils*, 2009) and *Santa fakeerala joligeya rotti* (*The Roti in a Lady Saint's Bag*, 2013), both from CVG Publications, Bangalore.

BE A WOMAN, ONCE, O LORD!*

It is rancid kitchens for us.
It is slimy postnatal rooms for us.
No chance for throwing tantrums.
O Lord, shouldn't you once visit
The sunless cells that are our lot?

My son
Who went to the town
Died in an encounter;
My husband
Who went to war
Came back as bloody rags;
And my daughter,
In unbearable shame,
Hanged herself after being raped.
To know the depths of my pain,
O Lord, shouldn't you be born a woman once?

If I step out to earn a meager meal
Unseen hands push me behind curtains
And training their guns on me;
I shudder at the slightest sound,

---

* Translated from the Kannada by Kamalakar Bhat.

Go pale, become breathless, miss a heartbeat;
I am totally lost.
How shall I live, O lord?

The man who has the world's contract in his hands
Has declared a war at the borders.
To know my indescribable pain,
To know what it is,
O Lord, shouldn't you become a woman once?

SHARIFA: I wrote "Be a Woman, Once, O Lord!" not only for Muslim women but also for women the world over who believed in humanity and were anxious. It was a time when Iraq, Iran and Afghanistan were experiencing the terrible effects of war. It was a time when women and children of Islamic countries were shaken by the fear of war. It was at a time of such global war-weariness that this poem came to be written.

A woman, whatever her nation or her religion may be, is opposed to war. She never wants a war to take place. Hers is the constructive, rather than the destructive, culture. I have been disturbed by the woman of this world who is rendered helpless after losing her near and dear ones to war. The inspiration for this poem is the woman with her child on her back, gun in hand, struggling to survive in this world. The fact that her anxieties are totally ignored, amid the many problems and challenges being faced by the Islamic world, is the reason I wrote this poem. I pray in this poem for the Lord to be born a woman once, so He can experience the pains and problems of women that can't be voiced in public.

STEVEN SHER

Steven Sher, a native of Brooklyn, now lives in Jerusalem. Since 1977, he has taught at many American universities and has also led writing workshops in Israel and the United States. Sher is the author of 14 books, including, most recently, two new poetry collections: *Grazing on Stars: Selected Poems* (Presa Press, 2012) and *The House of Washing Hands* (Pecan Grove Press, 2014).

MY DAUGHTER AT THREE ASKS IF GOD IS A HE

At three, she asked, *Is God a he?* —
and the tremors spawned in innocence
shook heaven to its core.
At four, my daughter thought
if you grab the penis
of a boy, pull it

down around his feet
so he can step from it like pants,
you will find his labia.

Paint a mustache on a girl
dressed like a doll, and she,
voilà, becomes a man.

At five, my daughter thought
that even God — no male of males,
no greybeard savior —

cannot decide what sex to be
or how to spare
the heart its pain.

SHER: My daughter was born in an Oregon university town where our family was active in a Jewish community whose members ranged from the observant to the nontraditional. While there were strong women models at both ends of the spectrum, religious services (even most of the nontraditional ones) were led by men. Spiritually precocious, my daughter at age three asked my wife and me at synagogue one day: "Is God a he?" The poem set in motion, I tried to imagine what an inquisitive young girl might make of God's gender, as well as her take on whether God favored boys. Thirty years later, my daughter, strong in her faith, is raising her three children in Jerusalem.

Enid Shomer

Enid Shomer is the author of seven books of poetry and fiction, including *The Twelve Rooms of the Nile*, which NPR named one of the six best historical novels of 2012. Her poems have appeared in such leading magazines as *Poetry, The Atlantic, Paris Review, Boulevard, JAMA: The Journal of the American Medical Association, Parnassus,* and *The New Criterion,* and in more than sixty anthologies and textbooks. In 2013, Shomer received the Lifetime Achievement Award in Writing from the Florida Humanities Council. She has been the subject of two feature interviews on NPR, one on *All Things Considered* and one on *Weekend Edition Sunday.*

Theater of Dreams

> *Let objects stand for people. Talk only to possessions, not those who possess you.*
> — Instructions for a Jungian exercise

The dream begins in her childhood, deep
in the basement of the house. Now we each take a role.
It's the objects that speak in this drama from sleep:

one person plays the cement floor, another the heap
of clutter that stands for her father — mostly old tools.
The dream begins in her childhood, deep

in her father's arms. She remembers the shrugged-off hope
in his shoulders, his body stiff as his levels and rules.
It's the objects that speak. In this drama from sleep

the floor says *I'm turning to marble* when she weeps.
The thrown shoe, the shouting, the strap hung on a nail —
the dream begins in her childhood. *Deep*

enough now, says the floor, *I'm shining with grief.*
She hugs herself, sensing her bones like braille.
It's the objects that speak in this drama. *From sleep*

you spin a thousand selves, says the clutter, *to keep
the promises he broke.* Now unwind the spool
of dreams. Begin in childhood, deep
in the objects that speak in this drama. From sleep.

SHOMER: "Theater of Dreams" was the result of my interest in theater games (for psychotherapy) and the villanelle coming together. I wanted to write a strict villanelle, but one which broke new ground (unlike what occurs in most villanelles, the lines in this poem wrap around). I was very excited by this poem, especially as it was the first villanelle I ever wrote. The subject of the poem — the relationship between a cruel father and his daughter — speaks for itself, I think, though because it is worked out as a psychodrama, with objects standing in for people, there are, I hope, many moments of provocation in the poem provided by the metaphors. In terms of this anthology, I would say that the oppression of women begins at home, and we see that in this poem.

M. E. SILVERMAN

M. E. Silverman is editor and founder of *Blue Lyra Review* and review editor of *Museum of Americana*. He is also on the board of *32 Poems*. His chapbook *The Breath before Birds Fly* was released by ELJ Press in 2013, and his poems have appeared in over 75 journals and anthologies, among them *Crab Orchard Review*, *32 Poems*, *Chicago Quarterly Review*, *Hawai'i Pacific Review*, *The Southern Poetry Anthology*, *The Los Angeles Review*, the *Mizmor L'David Anthology: Volume 1: The Shoah*, *Many Mountains Moving*, and the *Because I Said So Anthology*. Silverman recently completed editing *Bloomsbury's Anthology of Contemporary Jewish American Poetry* with Deborah Ager.

LOSING MY RELIGION

> *"Oh life, it's bigger / It's bigger than you / . . . that's me in the corner."*
> — R.E.M.

When the sanctuary fills
for Simchat Torah, my first love
sits below the podium, separated
from me by two rows.

The Rabbi sings, sways and shifts
from foot to foot
with the Torah above his head.
He walks the seven circuits around the room.

I watch the rabbi's daughter
recite prayers and wave
a white and blue flag.
She sits by her husband,

a blond Hemingway type,
full of sun and travel,
at ease with stories,
and built like a bull.

Everyone is ready for the merging
of endings to beginnings
but I can't help but notice
her discomfort:

the back of her neck shines
a berry-pit bruise
and, beneath sunglasses,
a dark-moon eye.

The room revels
in laughter, people kiss
strangers, give candy to the kids.

We welcome the new book.
Into the ark, we close the old one.
We sing. We clap.
A room full of joy.

Gently, she cups her left hand
to whisper into this guy's ear.
He laughs a little too loud.
The sermon quotes Einstein,

how our very existence is not lines
but curves like a ceremony
that starts at one point
and ends elsewhere,

like the realization that a room
full of praying people
can keep secrets.

Lord, maybe today
I will have the strength to call the cops?

Rain Chaser

with lines from Toni Morrison

Forget that *all water has a perfect memory*
and is forever trying to get back
to where it was.

Give me this moment
without his violent storms,
in a motel where I now sleep alone.

Let me listen to distant moans
and lovely laughter, to the way weather
moves, how raindrops slant,

sound like marbles spilling on a floor,
seeping into every dry spot,
remembering where it used to be.

A westerly gale swirls
and in the harbor, nervous boats bounce.
The river floods these places.

Signs and tree limbs knock
against spaces they don't want to go.
The wind shoves them down.

I know these forces,
these shifting skies.
I'm drawn to thunder.

I pick up the phone.
Dial our number.
Rain descends

on this soaked roof,
runs down spouts and windows,
upon sills and the backs of bricks,

fills a barricaded pool, pushes
beneath this foundation
where a water particle is more likely to go

to where it has gone before,
where water dreams in cyanotype
and everything drowns out of focus.

SILVERMAN: "Losing my religion" is an old southern expression for being at the end of one's rope — the moment when graciousness gives way to rage. Listening to the song lyrics, if one missed that key detail, s/he might think that the song was clearly a comment on the Judeo-Christian tradition. I hope my poem is both.

MYRA SKLAREW

Myra Sklarew writes fiction and poetry, as well as nonfiction essays on science and medicine. Her recent publications include *Harmless* (poetry); *The Journey of Child Development: Selected Papers of Joseph Noshpitz,* co-edited with Bruce Sklarew; *If You Want to Live Forever* (poetry); *Crossing Boundaries: Trauma and Memory* (Purdue University Press); and poems and essays in *Prism, The Light in Ordinary Things* (Volume One of the Fearless Poetry Series); *Amistad Journal; The Posen Library of Jewish Culture and Civilization* (Yale); and the *Catalyst* (National Institutes of Health). *A Survivor Named Trauma: Holocaust and the Construction of Memory* is forthcoming from SUNY Press. Sklarew is Professor Emerita, American University, and former president of Yaddo Artists' Community.

VIOLATION

> *I thought sorrow would drown me,*
> *but then my sorrow learned to swim.*
> — Tranquilino Castaneda

Even the mourning dove stands guard
over its dying mate at the traffic circle;
no matter the crush of oncoming cars.

Even the male frog refuses to abandon
its young, making a home in its vocal pouch
for its tadpoles until they hatch.

What does it mean for a man
to use what perpetuates life
to destroy life? To inflict a wound

so deep into the body of a woman?
Does he try to erase the mother
who bore him? Or obliterate himself?

It is not love he brings to this meal.

SKLAREW: I have thought for a long time about what it means to violate a woman, to use that means to express rage and aggression. Many have written on the subject. But to destroy that most sacred process, the progenerative function that renews and ensures the continuance of life, seems to me a form of suicide, a wish for the obliteration of the perpetrator. The epigraph to this poem was spoken by Tranquilino Castaneda on public radio. He was one whose wife and children were raped and killed and whose last remaining small son was taken by one of the military and raised, never knowing who his real family was until he grew up.

The massacre happened in a Guatemalan town, Dos Erres, during the civil war there in the1980s. Over 600 villages were destroyed; over 180,000 people were killed or "disappeared." The government denied this, but eventually, in this particular town, bodies were found. The one surviving son of Tranquilino Castaneda was Oscar Ramirez, who learned only at age 31, through DNA testing, that Tranquilino, then 70, was his real father. He was 3 when taken from his original family and had no memory of them. One can read/hear the transcript on *This American Life*.

However, Tranquilino's story is not what initiated the poem; my eternal work on Lithuania, Holocaust and memory, and my belief in the natural world as our teacher, are what did. But I happened to hear a portion of this radio program and it seemed appropriate to the poem.

AMY SMALL-MCKINNEY

Amy Small-McKinney is the author of a collection of poems, *Life is Perfect* (BookArts Press, 2014), and two chapbooks of poetry, *Body of Surrender* (2004) and *Clear Moon, Frost* (2009), both from Finishing Line Press. Her poems have appeared in numerous journals, including *American Poetry Review, The Cortland Review, The Pedestal Magazine,* and *Blue Fifth Review,* and are forthcoming in *Tiferet Journal.* Several of her poems written during her cancer treatment are to be published by Les Femmes Folles Books, in their forthcoming anthology *Bared.* During her tenure as 2011 Montgomery County Poet Laureate, she founded a program using creative writing for healing.

VOICES

Provincetown, USA

What I love most is morning.
My line cast for stripers,
their obedient mouths.
The girl was pretty, tall, lean enough.
In the graveyard, the headstones
shut their eyes, she could not hear
their sympathy. I heard her *No,*
but who can stop
in the throes of opening?
I do not wake every morning
and thank God I am a man.
That was another life.

Rwanda, Africa

Lake Kivu plaits through the Rift valley.
I was the Hutus' favorite daughter,
Pauline Nyiramasuhuko. My mouth
a volcano, a danger to anything
that breathed. My nation insisted

I become their nation, scissors opened
and closed. I sent my son, Shalom,
to young Rose with the Tutsi name —
A Plea to God — to where she hid, the fields
where she fought back.
I called to the Tutsis, exhausted as rain:
Here is your food. Here is your shelter.
All of their death took only an hour;
a red-chested cuckoo asked why.
I told him: My eyes are split open.
I am not sorry.

Merewala, Pakistan

Sometimes, I still hear her in the shallow water
of the Indus. She was never my true child,
my snow-white crane, entreating me, *Feed me, Faz Mai.*
The sustenance that might have called her home
was only rain, this child who floated out of me
into a blister of nothing.
And my cousin Naseem, like me, forced to spread
herself into our country of dread, into the fields
where white bulbs of cotton were dying.

Massachusetts, USA

I blamed myself, my body, how dutifully
I inhaled an era. I did not blame him,
refused to remember the Portuguese stones of loss,
the nearby sea smacking its futile fish,
or later, how it slipped into the waters
of the Holiday Inn — my thumbnail, my lily.
Naseem Mai, then, I wanted to be you, wanted pesticide
to flow through my body like fresh milk.
Now I am milk. Now, another son has eyes so blue.

Bombay, India

This will never end, my wandering
out of my Bombay backyard where peafowl
sashay to the males' courtly *help help*
of recognition. I miss them more
than mother or father, their sendoff basket
of fruit. When the males release their plumage,
they call *ahhh ahhh*. The peahen mutters
Hell-o Hell-o.
I cannot tell you what you want to hear,
cannot remember the travelers' eyes, faces, words,
any kindnesses as I drifted out of my skin,
as my mouth became the rapist's chick, wingless, blind.
This will never end.

SMALL-MCKINNEY: I remember a period of time when I read news article after news article about rapes in places I have never visited and rarely thought about. This poem, "Voices," came to me suddenly and without warning. I began to write and each section emerged as a dart on a map of the world, each narrated by the voice of a perpetrator or a victim. Obviously, I cannot speak for others, but somehow their stories entered me and became, in part, my story. Borders were disassembled; the poem flowed between far off lands and home. Now, years later, this poem could be written again, just with different names, different borders, and that makes me profoundly sad.

LUCIE SMOKER

Lucie Smoker is proudly no longer a victim of domestic violence. Her top-selling suspense novel, *Distortion* (Buzz Books USA, 2012), features a young artist recovering from a highly abusive first relationship. Smoker's work has been featured in *Salon, Your Teen, Outside in Literary & Travel Magazine, Art Focus Oklahoma,* and *The Blood-Red Pencil,* among many others. Her award-winning six-word memoir appeared in *The Best Advice in Six Words* (St. Martin's, 2015).

IN A SHARD OF THE BEDROOM MIRROR

You
can't stand to look
at me. All bloodied up, I accept
responsibility because you need me to
listen better. You are sensitive and I'm just
strong, but during the hitting that flips
around. You grow powerful while
I shrink. And you hate that
my weakness drives
you to smash
me.

SMOKER: I wanted to explore the moment right after abuse. Immersed in shock, insane excuses reveal the dysfunction on both sides of the relationship.

KIRTLAND SNYDER

Kirtland Snyder has published three chapbooks of poetry — *Winter Light* (prologue by poet Cid Corman), *Soldiers of Fortune* (a collaboration with the American painter Leon Golub), and *Big, Broken-Hearted Arias* — all from Innerer Klang Press. In 2007, Snyder won the Stanley Kunitz Award for Excellence in Poetry and was nominated for a Pushcart Prize in poetry. His Holocaust poetry is among the works of American and British poets examined in Susan Gubar's book *Poetry After Auschwitz* (Indiana University Press, 2003). He has also published poetry, fiction, and nonfiction in many literary magazines, anthologies, and newspapers.

INTIMACY

If you're lucky in life you will learn to love a woman,
you will learn to keep moving inward on the long journey
to the heart, your most audacious enterprise,
like trying to find the source of the Nile with the Nile
your only map, a living watercourse through a dark
continent whose deepest wellspring you will name Victoria.

Will has nothing to do with it, and will has been till now
your deepest resource, your iron discipline, your dogged
determination to possess the earth and its creatures
to do with as you will, to lord it over the creation, to make
for the sake of breaking, to name for the sake of maiming —
burning your brand into living flesh and fiber.

You are a man, which means you have manned yourself for
what you imagine is an onslaught, a meet, a tourney, a joust;
justice is what's meted out at the end of a lance, you think,
whose blood sops the dust has lost, whose ship shells
the continent wins, the other man dead is an end, his women
and children captive, the spoils which crown your victory.

Your life as you live it is a thing external, a show of force
of body parts: arms stuck out from torso brandishing fists,
legs stanced on canvas balancing blows, head contending
forward, eyes squinting below a jutting overhang of brow;
take out your shaggy cock and you're Zinjanthropus
on the broad veldt, about to cave in the head of your foe.

Think of that cock, how lacking in subtlety it is, how unashamedly
it lifts its head at the slightest provocation — what balls it has!
It's like a battering ram banging down the gates of the fortress.
What heft it has when it's hard; no wonder you're inclined to feel
invincible when you sally forth with it leading you like a knight in the lists,
why shouldn't she open her legs to receive such a vanquisher?

How do you make the inward journey when your cock is pointing
every way but inward, when all your consciousness concentrates
in a spurt that travels so short a distance from your body, then collapses?
Everything you are, you think, is riding on that vector.
Everything you are, you think, is riding on that blue-veined husky.
Everything you are, you think, is riding on that member.

The longer it is, the better; thicker, too, is better; it should be comely.
A lot of cum is better than a little cum, come what may.
Mapplethorpe shot it to look like a cannon, with big cannon balls.
Mapplethorpe shot it to look like a blood sausage, like a black pudding.
Mellors gave it a name and a thick Northumberland accent.
Schiele painted it orange and swollen, grasped, in the mirror.

Now think of the vulva, how interior it is, even its exterior is interior.
It enfolds multiform chambers and antechambers.
Life originates and incubates there, has continuance there.
Each woman in her turn turns inward to go to this inner life that is hers,
drops her bucket down into the deep element and draws it up again,
enacts a rhythm that is tidal in its give and take.

What rhythm, O man of stiff comportment, do you enact but that of
thrust and parry? Even with your uniform off you are martial, your cock

fending off closeness like a drawn sword. Thrust it at a woman
and Osric can be heard to shout, "A hit! A palpable hit!"
There is a kind of rigor mortis even in your most effluent moves
as if death were fist-fucking you, with you affecting nonchalance.

Composed of vitriol and violence, your affections are a masque, a kind of
half-time entertainment. Crowd-pleasers, they gleam like Astroturf,
with unreality. They form a ground for misadventure. A killing field.
This is how you feel most fully: the head-on confrontation, unnuanced,
brute strength pitted against brute strength, playing by the rules,
an absolutely stripped down goal masculating a world devoid of women.

Where is the "tenderness toward existence" called for by Kinnell?
Why do even your most profound encounters with nature end in a kill?
What does a dead doe draped across the hood of your car do for you?
You lied about the wolf's depredations when the wolf was willing
to befriend you, to justify your slaughter of the wolf.
You lied about the Indian nations, calling them savage that sanctified life.

Your rape of the Sabine women was just one in a continuum of rapes.
You beat and otherwise abuse the women you say you love and when they
finally throw you out you come back and — *fuck the restraining order* — you
stalk them like deer in the forest and kill them in front of their kids and
then you kill the kids and maybe you kill yourself but more likely not —
giving yourself up to the authorities to pour out your heart for pity.

If sentimentality is "a failure of feeling," what else
can be said to be your ruling passion? Of course you make
a show of feeling — your loyalty to the team, the flag, the boss —
but this is merely a recitation of truisms guaranteeing masculinity.
To feel, you must first be willing to fling aside conventional wisdom,
to be fallible, vulnerable, split open to the pineal gland, remade, unlike.

To feel you must go to the woman who is so unlike and be willing to be so.
You must go to her with a willingness to be made in the likeness of woman.
You must go to her forgoing your greater physical strength, with all your
    weapons laid

aside, with your cock limp, with your hands at your sides or in
supplication, palms turned upward, small flames starting up from them,
putting yourself in her hands like a lump of clay scooped from a riverbed.

A man goes to a woman not with feelings but with ideas, with stratagems.
He goes to her tactically, to enact a plan whose outcome is a win for him.
His seduction is calculated, quantified, plotted on the x and y axes.
It begins in the brain and remains in the brain as it travels.
It is an intellection running down the brainstem, down the spine,
charging the penis to stand at attention and penetrate enemy lines.

Perhaps he wants her to wear a little something for the occasion.
Perhaps he wants to cinch her up tight in a leather harness.
Perhaps he wants her on all fours in front of a mirror.
Perhaps he wants her hands tied with a stocking behind her back.
Perhaps he wants her on her knees with his cock stuffed in her mouth.
Perhaps he wants to see ankles lashed to the bedpost, wet split beaver.

There is such a terrible violence in a man which hates the woman, which
hates her essentialness, her separateness, her wholeness, her womb;
it is the same violence that wants to *blow the tits off the world,*
that wants her to submit, to acknowledge greater man.
This is the terror man has as his patrimony, his hegemony, his acrimony,
terror which doesn't stand on ceremony.

SNYDER: The ironically titled poem, "Intimacy," was born of my acute awareness
of the latent violence in men toward women, and of my desire to expose this violence
and the terrible damage it leaves in its wake. Any man who is paying attention — to
his feelings and actions, and to history — has to admit this. Our greater physical
strength is the first in an arsenal of weapons men have used to subjugate women from
time immemorial. One thinks of rape as a martial and a political instrument wielded
to send a message of conquest — of men over other men. The Russian army raping
German women as it overran Germany is just one of myriad historical examples of
such a message. Eldridge Cleaver advocating the rape of white women as a means of
righting the wrongs of racism comes to mind as well. Using the law to deprive women

of the right to vote, to become educated, to work for equal pay, to exercise control over their bodies — in short, using the law to deprive them of the opportunity to become the equals of men — has been, and continues to be, high on the male agenda. "Intimacy" attempts not only to shine a light on this agenda, but to offer an antidote to it. The poem aspires to a kind of awakening of a new sensibility in men, by which their relations with women may come closer to true intimacy.

Sreekumar K

Sreekumar K, born in Punalur — a town in Kerala, south India — has worked as an English teacher in several schools. At present, he is employed as a facilitator at L'Ecole Chempaka International, Thiruvananthapuram. He is also a columnist, translator, and script writer, as well as a partner in Fifth Element Films, which released *The Painted House,* the story of a writer, that won international recognition. Sreekumar writes in English and Malayalam.

News Review

for a girl who was murdered many times by the media.

Looking over the prospective corpse
Headlines vied with each other
Pools of blood on the roadside
Blackened into ink on newsprint

Those who had done it
Told those who hadn't yet
That everything will be done,
Though nothing could be undone now
They were also politely told
To make no noise about it

Her mouth covered in linen
Thin linen
She had to sign a paper which said
She didn't want anything done
For her, or in her name.

In a soft tender voice
Her heartbeat told her breath
Not to leave now
Her eyes told the sight
Not to vanish now

Out in the street
Water from the water cannon
Tastes of salt
Not from the sea far away
But from an ocean within

SREEKUMAR K: Though atrocities against women are not really news these days, the incident at Delhi was shocking. Some friends asked me why I had not responded to that terrible event in any way. This poem is my answer to that question.

HANS JORG STAHLSCHMIDT

Hans Jorg Stahlschmidt is a German-American writer who has lived in Berkeley, California, since 1982. He is a clinical psychologist specializing in couples therapy, and he also works as a building contractor. Stahlschmidt's poems and stories have appeared in many journals and anthologies in both the USA and Germany, among them *Madison Review, Atlanta Review, Manoa, Texas Poetry Review, Cumberland Poetry Review*, and the *Anthology of Magazine Verse and Yearbook of American Poetry*. He has received a number of poetry prizes and awards.

AWAKENING

In the moment he came he was like all other men,
his holiness vanished, his face lost in distant desire,

sticky semen was thickening inside her. He had placed
his warm hand like a golden cup over her eyes, had spoken

of oneness; now he arranged his orange robes, concealing
his penis in the long flowing fabric the way children hide

behind dusty curtains playing hide and seek. He covered
her bare breasts and dark triangle with a damp sheet and

closed the door gently behind him as she screamed. Now
she knew why the temple curtain in Jerusalem tore and dark

thunder shook the walls, why Mirabai rode away high on
an elephant's back. She stayed in the waters for hours, knowing

that the river had to flow through her; imagining the pure
cold waters from Mount Kailas, she opened her thighs to

the current until she was sure he was washed away. When
her skin began turning blue she waded back to shore

walked and walked until her whole body became flesh
again, red earthy flesh no man could ever betray.

STAHLSCHMIDT: The poem's subjects are a blend of real persons and imagination. I spent a year in India in the 1970s, visiting several gurus and staying in an ashram for nine months. I witnessed the power and seduction these men exerted and saw, firsthand, that women were often used for personal gratification under the cloak of spirituality and religion. Later, in my work as a psychologist I treated followers of gurus and masters who had been sexually abused by their idols. I felt that women were especially vulnerable to the abuse of power in these groups due to the historical role women played in society at large and particularly in religious movements, their place in the group's hierarchy, as well as the dedication and hope women felt in regard to their personal growth. I also love Mirabai's ecstatic poetry and was interested in her plight in 16th-Century India as a woman following her own life path in conflict with traditions and norms.

JAN STECKEL

Jan Steckel's full-length poetry book *The Horizontal Poet* (Zeitgeist Press, 2011) won a Lambda Literary Award for LGBT writing. Her chapbooks *Mixing Tracks* (Gertrude Press, 2009) and *The Underwater Hospital* (Zeitgeist Press, 2006) also won awards. Her fiction, creative nonfiction, and poetry have appeared in *Yale Medicine, Scholastic Magazine, Bellevue Literary Review, American Journal of Nursing, Red Rock Review,* and many other journals. Steckel's writing has been nominated three times for a Pushcart Prize.

YOU COULD BE A PRETTY GIRL

If only you got your nose fixed,
and did something with your hair,
my mother said to me,
you would be a pretty girl.

If you cut your hair above your shoulders,
got rid of all those split ends,
then someone could actually see your face.
You have such a nice smile, when you choose to use it.
Your skin isn't that bad, you know.
If you could just stop touching your face all the time...
If you wore something besides jeans and sneakers...
If you weren't so *serious,*
such a terrible grind,
then even though you're built like an ironing board,
you wouldn't scare all the boys away.

If only I could look in your face
without seeing my own,
you could be a very pretty girl.

PREVENTIVE DENTISTRY

On my world, women's mouths are also their vaginas.
Because they have to give birth through their mouths,
all their teeth are prophylactically removed.

The Knocking Out of Teeth used to be done
at the age of first menses as a coming-of-age rite.

Girls were grouped in age cohorts for their instruction
on how not to cry out when the blows came,
how to stanch the blood afterward
and pack their mouths with cotton.

In our modern age, this barbarism has disappeared
from all but the most isolated reaches of the planet.

Now girls have their teeth extracted under anaesthesia,
once their jaws have stopped growing.

They are fitted with dentures, taught by their mothers
how to cement the false teeth in, how to clean them,
and when it is and isn't appropriate to remove them.

Once in a while a pervert molests a dentate girl.
Such men are judged mentally ill,
as they risk the integrity of their penises
by inserting them into such a dangerous place.

The victim's dentist has to subject the girl
to an oral exam so invasive
it feels like a second rape.

The feminists of your world object to our customs,
but their attempts to censure us are insensitive
and the worst kind of cultural imperialism.

You don't hear us railing in the United Planets
about all the obscene things
you let your women put into their mouths.

STECKEL: "Pretty Girl" is actually composed of things my mother said to me over the years, which made me wonder what had been said to *her* over the years. I must emphasize that I love my mother very much, and she loves me very much, too. She has said many more kind things to me than negative ones. Women are taught, though, to hate their own bodies, to be ashamed of aspects of their personalities, and we pass this self-loathing on to our daughters without meaning to. The sexism that sets us up to be victims isn't just something men do to women. It's also something that women do to women.

"Preventative Dentistry" upsets a lot of people. My husband can't stand to hear it. I meant it as a metaphor for clitoridectomy and infibulation (female genital mutilation) as practiced in sub-Saharan Africa and the Middle East.

MARGO TAFT STEVER

Margo Taft Stever's chapbook *The Lunatic Ball* was published by Kattywompus Press in 2015. Her earlier books include *The Hudson Line* (Main Street Rag, 2012), *Frozen Spring* (2002), which received the Mid-List Press First Series Award for Poetry, and *Reading the Night Sky*, which won the 1996 Riverstone Poetry Chapbook Competition. Her poems, essays, and reviews have appeared in magazines and anthologies, including *The Webster Review, New England Review, Minnesota Review, West Branch, Seattle Review*, and *No More Masks*. Stever is founder of The Hudson Valley Writers' Center and founding editor of Slapering Hol Press. She has read her poetry at numerous locations, including the Geraldine R. Dodge Poetry Festival.

NOTHING'S HOLDING UP NOTHING

El Salvador, 1982

Under the floorboards with the wood
rot, the insects, termites skittering to
and fro, the mother hides with her child,
her nipple in the infant's mouth,
but her milk won't let down.

She did nothing, but the officials
suspected, decided to make an example,
the child dragged out, beaten,
the bellies of flowers, blackened,
the bells, the bells,
the long toll of roots...

It is hard to believe anything
was ever alive under here, under
these boards, anything alive
for long under these boards.
Filaments break off and powder
as if they never were wood,
as if the hollows were roads

going somewhere, as if the mother's
breasts could fill with milk, as if
her child could breathe again.

SPLITTING WOOD

It was the thought of his entering
their infant's room that drove her.

She remembered his face the first time
she saw him. Now, half gone from whiskey,
eyes hooded like a hawk's,
he said he'd kill the children when he woke.

The neighbors heard it,
the screams. They heard.

His workman's hand,
his gnarled hand dangled down.
The knife lay by the bed.
She slipped from the covers
while he slept, placed her feet
on the floorboards just so.

The dogs barked outside, snapdragons,
flowered tongues, and all the wired
faces of the past strung up. The ax
hung on the porch, woodpile nearby,
each log plotted, uneasily entwined.
The children's tears were rain,
tears were watering the parched hills.

The wild moon foamed at the mouth.
The wild moon crept softly at her feet.

The arms that grabbed the ax
were not her own,
that hugged it to her heart
while he slept were not hers,
the cold blade sinking in his skin.
She grew up in the country splitting wood.
She knew just how much it took
to bring a limb down.

STEVER: My reason for writing these poems, and many others on the subject of women's oppression, stems from being a woman and from my resulting empathy and concern for the suffering that women and children are forced to endure. "Splitting Wood" is about an actual client that one of my brothers-in-law represented as her attorney. Although she was an abused woman, she was jailed for many years as a result of her ax-murder of her husband, even though she was protecting the lives of her children.

"Nothing's Holding up Nothing" is my recollection of the horrific situation in El Salvador during the 1980s, but similar stories have unfolded too, recently, in other places around the world.

KATERINA STOYKOVA-KLEMER

Katerina Stoykova-Klemer is the author of three collections of poetry, most recently *The Porcupine of Mind* (Broadstone Books, 2012). Her first poetry book, the bilingual *The Air Around the Butterfly* (Fakel Express, 2009), won the 2010 Pencho's Oak Award, given annually to recognize literary contributions to contemporary Bulgarian culture. Stoykova-Klemer hosts *Accents* — a radio show for literature, art, and culture on WRFL, 88.1 FM, Lexington, Kentucky. In January 2010, she launched Accents Publishing. She also co-wrote the independent feature film *Proud Citizen* and acted in the lead role.

DAD, DO YOU REMEMBER,

your fist flew
through my face
between my pigtails.

Do you remember your face

in the mirror over the sink
while you were teaching me
to wash blood

with cold water.

STOYKOVA-KLEMER: I wanted to submit to *Veils, Halos & Shackles* because I believe awareness goes a long way towards stopping violence against women, and I'd like to do my part. I've written a series of poems about growing up in a physically and emotionally abusive environment. For quite a few years, I couldn't really write about anything else.

DAVID ALLEN SULLIVAN

David Allen Sullivan's first collection, *Strong-Armed Angels,* was published by Hummingbird Press, and three of its poems were read by Garrison Keillor on *The Writer's Almanac. Every Seed of the Pomegranate,* a multi-voiced manuscript about the war in Iraq, was published by Tebot Bach in 2012. Sullivan's translation from the Arabic of Iraqi author Adnan Al-Sayegh, *Bombs Have Not Breakfasted Yet,* was published in 2013, and *Black Ice,* about his father's dementia and death, was released by Turning Point Press in 2015. Sullivan teaches at Cabrillo College, where he edits the *Porter Gulch Review* with his students. He was awarded a 2013–2014 Fulbright fellowship to teach in China.

ELECTRIC BODIES

Across the street from Walt Whitman's home
in Camden New Jersey
they've built a women's prison. Visitors who are barred from access
have developed a sign system
they use from his front porch,
and ethnographers come from far afield
to study the unique language,
their notebooks on their knees
or resting on the pitted cast-iron fence,
and he would have loved the discrepancies and sincere
attention to those in need, and he would have hated
the need for it at all,
the long fall from a mother's arms
into the barred cells that hold all our hearts.
And he would have stood with the women
who were being abused,
before they struck back in anger and fear and hopelessness,
and he would have held their heads in his hands
and rocked them afterwards,
and he would have said:

We are only the sparks of our disasters
rising over Camden's women's prison
to settle in the hearts of our friends
who sign — I'll be here when you get out —
and mean it.

SULLIVAN: In May 1873, Walt Whitman arrived in Camden to visit his elderly widowed mother and his siblings. He wound up living at 330 Mickle Street, where he produced many of his writings. In 1888, the block featured laborers, roofers, carpenters, railroad workers, a dentist and a physician, a baker, painters, clerks, sawyers, dressmakers, designers, a minister, machinists, an iron molder, a blacksmith, a publisher, salespeople, and milk dealers.

In February 1988, Camden County opened its new correctional facility. The front door of the Whitman House provides an unimpeded view of the jail's rear wall, across Mickle Boulevard. Family members come to sign to inmates from the street. Sociologists come to analyze the sign systems that have been developed. Whitman's passionate embrace of *all* Americans, as in his great poem "I Sing the Body Electric," inspired me to write this poem.

RJ T

RJ T is a woman, a doctor, a writer, a previously unpublished poet, and an avid Postcrosser. She lives in India and wishes to remain anonymous, due to the sensitive content of this poem.

THE BITTEREST AFTERTASTE

I often wonder,
How at 7 years of age
I didn't realize that I shouldn't have talked to you.

I knew of course, that I shouldn't talk to strangers;
But you were only politely inquiring
About the floor on which a Mr. someone lived,
And I was 7 and prancing about in my new skirt that day.

My mother had taught me
Not to open the safety grille of the house to strangers;

So that day,
When I walked alone to the shop across the street,
Feeling like a big girl, all of 7 years old,

All I did, as you followed me home,
After you had lifted up my skirt,
And your hand had found its way to my butt-crack,

All I did, was ring the doorbell to my house,
And then go inside and shut the safety grille
Before I answered your questions

Because my mother had taught me
Not to open the safety grille of the house to strangers
(And I was scared only of kidnappers,
Not of strange men who lifted up little girls' skirts).

You stood calmly on the other side of the grille,
And asked me where a Mr. someone lived in that building

(You never said anything about why just a minute ago
Your hand had been touching my butt;
And my 7-year-old brain,
Did not think to question you either).

I told you simply:
"Let me go and ask my Momma,"
And I only asked her about the Mr. someone's address, of course;
I told her nothing about your hand inside my skirt.

She told me to shut the door and send you away,
And that is exactly what I did.
That is exactly all I did.
Until today,
When I wrote this poem
And thought of what else happened that day.

How foreign they felt, your fingers,
Alien, unnatural, disagreeable

Not painful, yet so uncomfortable
Not hurting, yet unwanted
Momentary, yet an imprinted, unpleasant memory.

Your finger lodged against my butt-crack.

The thought twists my mouth into an ugly grimace,
And leaves my tongue with the bitterest aftertaste.

The adult in me knew something bad was happening that day,
The child in me knew I didn't like you at all,
But the polite, scared girl in me continued to pretend that nothing had
        happened.

The polite, scared girl in me
Still continues to pretend nothing ever happened that day.

But the woman in me knows she has to write down, in words,
How it felt.

RJ T: Having grown up in a bustling Indian city, I've had my fair share of "Eve-teasing" and groping in my teenage years. As I grew older, the incidents became less frequent, which points out that weaker sections of society, those unlikely to retaliate, are more frequently targeted for such crimes.

The incident described in this poem remains my most disturbing childhood experience. I understand that women and children are being taught to speak up and fight back when any crimes are committed against them, but I also know, from personal experience, how difficult it is to speak up and to raise a voice. Though some may well be capable of taking care of themselves, there will be many intended victims who won't be. It is the responsibility of the rest of society, of each one of us, to ensure that no child or teenager is subjected to any kind of violence and abuse. Heightened awareness, education, and stricter laws are the only ways to achieve this, especially in a country like India, where Eve-teasers, molesters, and rapists frequently go scot-free and no one even blinks an eye.

ANIQUE TAYLOR

Anique Taylor studied at the Sorbonne (Diplome) before returning to Connecticut to finish high school. Her poetry MFA is from Drew University. She has read at many venues, including St. Mark's Poetry Project, Dixon Place, Speakeasy, ABC No Rio, and Cedar Tavern. Her work has appeared in such magazines and journals as *Rattle*, *Adanna*, *Earth's Daughters*, *Cheap Review*, and *The National Poetry Magazine of the Lower East Side*, and her manuscript *Where Space Bends* was a finalist in both the *Minerva Rising* and the Blue Light Press 2014 chapbook contests. Taylor teaches a community poetry workshop, Bard LLI, and is organizer of a community spoken-word reading series.

AFTER THE DANCE

Theme from a Summer Place Musak
comes on as I push my shopping cart between
cereal and catsup in the Upstate Market
and I'm thirteen again on Main Street's night.
Theme from someone's window, violin lies
of my unmapped future, like cut flowers
tastefully arranged in a vase. Antique street
clock hands mark two a.m., the half mile of stores
closed shut like a secret. Kathy's key unlocks
us into a hall behind the music store. Up narrow
back stairs, garlic-chickened air, the map of flaking
green plaster, the stale smell of families falling.

Back from a gig with her brother's band
honey-sway-hip-bone-sweet-flesh-slow dance
and Joey, the drummer, sixteen, a possibility
between the dark of each note. Kathy & I tiptoe
invisible across the living room; her father
in beer-stained undershirt lurches
towards us from the kitchen. I stop. Grin,
foolish, a visitor from cocktail-party parents
who argue politics over a tide of martinis,

as Kathy grabs my arm, splitting open the skin
of some lost memory, yanks me into her bedroom,
throws her shoulder against the rattling door,
her breath heavy
even after the pounding
stops.

FLYING

The punch barrage catapults me backward,
I miss the brindled couch, round coffee
table with Lazy Susan where Mother sets out
sliced cheese, yellow hors d'oeuvre
napkins so martinis don't leave a ring,
trip past braided legs of black
clawfoot lion table, family snapshots under glass,
penguin ice bucket, Gordon's Dry Gin,
soar along picture window bank bordering cathedral
ceiling, birch leaves a thousand shades of green in moonlight,
past mother's turquoise butterfly chair
where, her scotch-on-the-rocks in roly-poly
glass, she argues cocktail-party politics,
coast past the baby grand, the loneliness
of Chopin in my fingers, by Matisse's Odalisque
trapped in her picture (who alone sees me),
glide by father's armchair, his large warm hands,
pray this time I'll swoop, bird-girl nymph,
wind lifting me into a different dream,
when, the hollow smack of brick
to backbone —
and I cannot
breathe

A. TAYLOR: I grew up in a time when what happened in families was private. Women were dependent on men to earn money. The Classifieds ads listed "Help Wanted Male" (junior executives) and 'Help Wanted Female' (secretaries). A woman's value was in how she looked. Women were supposed to be sweet and supportive. Things happened in houses, even in the "best" neighborhoods. One didn't talk about these things.

One day, the world began to shift. Questions were asked. We stopped setting our hair, wearing girdles, being silent. We began to create our own businesses, to become who we were meant to become. We began to talk and write about things that happened in these houses. We began to break through invisible shackles of marginalization and learned that we were not invisible, stupid, fat, ugly, no matter which neighborhood we came from. We discovered we were real and we mattered. I address this subject because it is my story.

MERVYN TAYLOR

Mervyn Taylor is a Trinidad-born poet who divides his time between Brooklyn, New York, and his island home. In New York, he has taught at Bronx Community College, The New School, the Young Adult Learning Academy, and in the New York City public school system. He has published five books of poetry, including *The Waving Gallery* from Shearsman Books (2014). Taylor's work has appeared most recently in *Black Renaissance Noire*, in the anthology *The American Voice in Poetry*, and in *Taos Journal of Poetry and Art*.

LOW

for Sara Kruzan, who killed her pimp

Did he shoot you up,
put you in a low room,
make it difficult for you
to stand, did he shove

you out on cold nights,
say come back with gold
or not at all, did he walk
the block and watch your

limbs move in the dark,
did he set you up in
low-lit places, bang on
walls till they shook

your eyes, your teeth,
your insides, did he
promise you nothing
more than x's to mark

where last you stood
dripping, smoldering,
the fire going out,
what was left

drifting at last
into a latitude where
his loaded gun became
yours, the hull of

a rescue vessel out
of raging water that
made the sound of
kittens in boxes

being drowned, the
gurgle of his voice
going under, the song
your soul was singing.

M. TAYLOR: I wrote this poem shortly after viewing a news item about the recent release of Sara Kruzan, a woman imprisoned for several years for the shooting death of her pimp, who had forced her, from an early age, into a life of prostitution. I thought about how unfair the law could be when it comes to matters involving the abuse of women, not only in America, but in countries around the world.

SHIRISHA THAMMINEEDI

Shirisha Thammineedi has been working as a lecturer for six years in Andhra Pradesh, India. She is deeply interested in feminism, women's writing, and blogging.

TO THE BRIGHT WORLD

To the bright world, you are the creator and the protector
The destroyer in you comes out in the dark
When you think it safe for the animal in you to prowl
A few minutes of your pleasure
Leaves dark trails on the long years of my life
You worship the ten forms of mother goddess
For protection from evil
I am no goddess, a mere woman
And you take the form of a demon
My mother realizes
Curses her fate
She is afraid of the divorcée tag
Silence becomes her sole companion
So the world survives
Your majesty rules
You go to your work
Twirling your moustache
Trampling on my dreams
With your heavy feet
Under those iron boots
A creature refuses to perish

THAMMINEEDI: I have heard of many instances of girls being raped by their fathers. I feel this is a heinous crime, so I penned down my feelings about this issue.

Naomi Thiers

Naomi Thiers has published two books of poetry, *Only the Raw Hands Are Heaven* (Washington Writers Publishing House, 1992) and *In Yolo County* (Finishing Line Press, 2013). Her poetry and fiction have appeared in numerous magazines, including *Virginia Quarterly Review, Colorado Review, Pacific Review, Antietam Review, Potomac Review, Iris, Belles Lettres,* and *Sojourners.* Her poetry has been nominated for a Pushcart Prize and featured in anthologies. Thiers has taught at several colleges and has led poetry workshops in schools and shelters for the homeless.

Little Sister

Someone lives through such a thing, like men home from cruel wars, she should wear a medal; recognize each other, recognize ourselves.
— Jeanne Schinto, *Children of Men*

I know her junior high school. I walk past it
when I take Mercelita to the clinic.
It's an ugly building: it reminds me
of the *guardia* barracks in Guazapa.
The bottom half is orange. The top half
is rough cement. The broken windows
have boards on them, and some have twisted bars,
but there's a patch of soft grass
between the school and 16th Street. If I turn
my head I can see them all facing front.
(I want to sit there too, even
with Mercelita banging on me,
even though I can't read: me
among all those black faces.)
Maybe I've seen her.

          The radio said
she's in the 9th grade. He spoke to her
through the chain-link fence.
I know that playground.

The boys play basketball, the girls walk in groups.
He called her away from her girlfriends and said
I've watched you. I know you.
I'm coming for you after school.

When I walk home from the market,
my head hurts, Mercelita gets heavy
and I know this is the way she walked
that day, past the little-kids playground,
by the stone steps of Sagrado Corazón,
where the young monks come out and stand
in long brown robes, watching the street,
down Park Road, where the apartment buildings
are close together and dirty. I continue
to 14th street, but she turned
into her building and he followed her
to the 3rd floor hallway that has no light bulbs.
He held the knife up to her face and said
I know how to use this. Then he cut up
her arithmetic book and he pushed the knife through
the book she was reading for English class.

He held her shoulders down on the stairs
and pushed away her skirt and her knees,
so quick that no one walked out,
with the knife touching her face.

A man from my country, the radio said.

I know that ceiling she had to look at,
how the cement swells in and out
against your face while he moves in you
and when he gets up, the cement comes down
and touches you.
                 I told only
my little sister, and she's dead.

I watch the girls in groups on the playground,
Mercelita pulling at my hair and screaming.
Which one is she? That red coat?
I could walk around and call to her through
the chain-link fence. I don't know her language.
But I know the room in the Guazapa barracks
is inside her now, and he crouches inside it, saying
I know how to use this.

And the knife comes down
through every book and every pleated skirt,
and every time she touches her own cheek:
a blade.

PRAYING WITH MY EYES OPEN

At ten years old, I asked my mother what
a word meant that I'd seen scrawled on a wall.
My mother stopped her iron
and answered all my questions with her eyes
clear, slightly tipped with sadness as the sun,
slanting through April trees outside the window,
lit up the light gold hairs along her arm,
thin remnant of her animal protection,
like mine.

The sun caught in the sky's throat that same spring.
I walked down to the swimming pool alone
and a boy stepped out from behind the trees,
his hand held like a gun concealed.
His free hand held me down and stripped
the fruit. He made me close
my eyes, and through the terror I saw
my mother's muscled arm, the warm gold hairs,
my last chance at protection, reach for me
and fall away.

For ten years
I didn't remember this, and when I did
my country whispered in my mouth:
Shut up, cunt, statistic.

Tonight my childhood's years away
but certain moments hang, light
trapped in resin.
I hold my newborn daughter in my arms,
her body red as blood-foam,
the retina, the knuckles, the domed ribs,
the waving chambers of her heart, the cells
she labored, blind inside me, to perfect.
I see her used, torn, as a man
uses a magazine.

I would hold my arms against the sun
for her, but in this land I have
few shields. Tonight,
I pray with my eyes open:
Be merciful.

THIERS: I don't generally set out to address particular subjects. But I try not to avoid subjects simply because someone calls them "political." Rape is a saw-toothed shadow that women must *always* keep one eye trained for as we walk down any urban street, an assault that sows fear in the breath (even if we just hear tales . . .), a violent shadow that shackles our steps. In recent years it's made headlines that sexual assault has literally killed young women in India and in my country. How can a poet walk down any street and write about what she sees: the feathery willow trees, the sky, the amusing or alienating urbanscape — all the usual poem topics, even her inner musings — but never write about the shadow, sensed, half-seen, on that same street?

WHITNEE THORP

Whitnee Thorp recently graduated from the Bluegrass Writers Studio at Eastern Kentucky University with an MFA in Creative Writing. She has taught English language, writing, culture, and history at two universities in Zhangjiajie, Hunan Province, China, and is currently an Associate Professor in Humanities at Oglala Lakota College, a tribal college on the Pine Ridge Reservation in South Dakota (one of the poorest reservations in the country). Thorp's writing has appeared in such journals as *Inscape, Splinter Generation, Emerge,* and *Poemmemoirstory.* She lives in the beautiful Black Hills of South Dakota.

SINS LIKE MINE

I know the sins
of being touched
by my father
those nights when
my stomach
was as tight as my braids
beating around
on white pillows.
Sundays he sat
next to me in church,
cross in his hands,
Bible in my lap,
singing the Lord's praises.
As I prayed to Him
I would stop swelling.
Mama thought
I was just going to be tall
and Indian-boned
like her Mama was.
Scriptures taught
my sister and me
daily lessons about hell
burning unwashed sins,

482   VEILS, HALOS & SHACKLES

but I couldn't
bring myself to confess
I had eyes
like mine
growing
inside.

THORP: I was moved to write this piece because I was raised in the South by two wonderful women. As someone who loves the South, I am not naive about the fact that oppression of women still occurs on a daily basis, especially in rural areas... even in America. For me, the point of this poem was to showcase the juxtaposition of abuse and religion in society and to reveal how abuse happens. Abuse, particularly sexual abuse, can be something that develops over time, and, especially for young people, it is hard to tell anyone about it — and even more difficult if the source of the abuse is someone they know or even love.

TARIN TOWERS

Tarin Towers has been living and writing in San Francisco's Mission District since 1995. She is the Pushcart Prize-winning author of a book of poetry, *Sorry, We're Close* (Manic D Press), as well as four chapbooks. Her work has appeared in many journals and anthologies, including *Eleven Eleven, Exquisite Corpse, A Gathering of the Tribes, The Fray, American Poetry: The Next Generation* (CMU Press), and the *Coffee House Poetry Anthology* (Bottom Dog Press). In 1999, Towers toured with Sister Spit, a lesbian-feminist spoken-word and performance-art collective based in San Francisco.

BECAUSE HE SAID I CAN'T I SAID

> *A voice says, "Cry out."*
> *And I said, "What shall I cry?"*
> — Isaiah 40:6

I said: I'm not ready
He said: Well I'm ready

Another He said: Not until I titty-fuck you
I said:

Another He said: I'm doing this because I love you
I said:

Another He said: Come, damn you, you know you love it
I said:

Another He said: Is it big enough
I said:

Another He said: Tell me how big I am
I said:

Another He said: Why did you break up with me
I said to myself: *My god it was a one-night stand this guy is crazy*
what should I —

Another He said: If I didn't love you so much I don't know what I'd do
       with you you crazy bitch
I said to myself: *He loves me*

He said: No. No more condoms
I said: *No no no no no no no no no*

He said: *Fine, goddammit, have it your way* and finally stopped, and fell
       asleep while I lay there
weeping until dawn

I said, on the phone, to his voicemail: I finally figured out that you
       raped me, Peter
He said, on the phone: I didn't listen to your voicemail
I said: I just need a little more time
I did not say: I'm calling the police

Because he was my boyfriend and *noonewouldbelievemeanyway*
Anyone I tried to tell about it asked me if I was high
Which is the same thing as saying
You asked for it
I said to myself:
I said to myself:
I said to myself:

What shall I cry?

TOWERS: I am a survivor of rape. For a while, after a relationship met a violent end,
I lost my way and became addicted to drugs and — worse — I, a lifelong poet, lost my
ability to write anything in my own voice. After years of hard work, I'm successfully
recovering from both my addictions and my rape. I've found my voice again, and I'm
clean.

What helped the most in getting me back on my path was finding spiritual community
and discovering that other women I knew, strong and intelligent and kind, had been
raped. I was not at fault for being duped, or for being an addict, or for my assault. I

could not get over the fact that I thought I "knew better" and yet still had trouble believing that the rape happened — and I had trouble believing that I had trouble believing my own story. Speaking one's truth in writing and in community is the hard work of helping regain one's sense of sovereignty and agency in the world.

Eileen Tull

Eileen Tull is a poet and performer currently based in Chicago. Her work has been presented throughout the United States, most notably in San Francisco, Chicago, and New York City, and her poems have been published in several online publications and international anthologies.

Everest, or How Do I Get Down?

I was my rapist's Everest.
It's because I was there.

Wrong place, wrong time.
Wrong street, wrong walk.

I was my rapist's friend.
It's because I was just that.

No moving forward
Out of the friend zone.

No kiss, no caress, no consent.
No . . . no, no, no.

I was my rapist's accident.
It's because I didn't say *No.*

He didn't realize my drunken mouth
couldn't open.

He didn't realize that no *No* was not *Yes.*
He didn't know I wouldn't remember.

I was my rapist's temptation
It's because I *wanted* it.

I wanted to put on a short skirt.
I wanted him to see it

I wanted him to pull it off.
I wanted him to make it hurt.

My rapist took Everest
Because it was there.

TULL: The state of my country shocks me. The protection of the rising rape culture shocks me. The prevalence of victim blaming shocks me. I did not write this poem, "Everest," from personal experience or a biographical perspective. I have never been sexually assaulted. I am lucky. I have not been sexually assaulted. Yet. This poem is a foreshadowing puzzle. Which rapist will be my rapist? Sexual assault seems so statistically inevitable, and that is a frightening reality for women to live with. The poem is also a reflection of post-assault, a victim attempting to piece together why her, why then, and how? I write about this subject because I need to. The dialogue needs to continue, to flow forward until, frankly, we live in a world with no rape. And that may never be, so I will keep on writing.

ANN TWEEDY

Ann Tweedy's first chapbook, *Beleaguered Oases*, was published by Creative Press in 2010, and her second chapbook, *White Out*, was published by Green Fuse Press in 2013. Her poetry has appeared in *Clackamas Literary Review*, *Rattle*, *damselfly press*, *literary mama*, and elsewhere. Her manuscripts have also been selected as finalists for the Blue Light Press Annual Chapbook Competition, the Robin Becker Chapbook Contest, and the New Sins Press Poetry Book Award, among others. Originally from Massachusetts, Tweedy was a long-time resident of the West Coast until 2011, when she moved to Minnesota to teach at Hamline University School of Law.

ENMESHED

a friend likely has MS, my strong young friend,
with a new positive outlook after years of anger,
living in her first house. *the drugs they give me*
mess with my head, she says. *i can't drive*
or go to court — other attorneys have to cover
my hearings. meanwhile, my 7-month-old
is crawling, standing holding onto things,
going forward into physical strength
while she goes backward, more quickly now than the rest of us.

sometimes, when i touch my baby's delicate hands, carry him
across the street, stroke his wisps of hair,
all i can think of are torturers
in other countries, the cruelty that surrounds
us, pressing in though we can't see it —
in Somalia, rapes at checkpoints,
the four-year-old shot down at the gate of his house,
the thirteen-year-old girl stoned to death
in a stadium of 40,000.
my tenderness to my baby is the opposite of violence
but part of that same continuum, so i try to take in
that there is only, for sure, this one moment — anyone
could do anything next.

i think of C. struggling with this new
illness, probably the one that she watched her mother suffer with
for most of her life. i want to blink her back to a few months ago,
before it set in, but opposites carry each other,
sick and well, violent and tender, heaven and hell.

A KIND OF PERSONAL STRENGTH

the locker room after yoga
feels safe, comfortable.
closing gestures — resting posture, namaste —
have slowed us. spin cyclists, up next,
are mostly pressed
at the classroom door when we stumble out.
latecomers end up in the locker room
with us. i'm half dressed when a woman
who used to be in yoga comes in, having switched
to spin because of her ankle.
my ears catch snatches of *i don't hike*

anymore with him. i go alone now.
i'll move in June when night school's over.
move out? the other says. *yes, i have to.*
he punched me twice because i wasn't hiking
fast enough, a mile and a half from the trailhead,
once in the face and once in the stomach.
i'm sorry, says the friend, her voice stilled by the news.
i'm sorry. again. *and he won't get help. i gave him*
six months to go to therapy and now it's up.

i try to focus on what i'm doing, hook
my bra, button my shirt, tie my shoes,
get to the sink to wash my face, summoning
the litany of familiar steps.
she comes to the sink
as i'm washing my face, and i move my bag over,

say "sorry." leaving, my first thought is
you're lucky — never to have faced anything
but the orange peeler hurled
at grandma in family mythology.
and i think of the woman — her firmness and bravery
to stand there in public and say *he did this*
and the grace of having a shocked friend
know it was wrong.

TWEEDY: I usually don't have specific goals in mind when I write poems, so I can't say that "Enmeshed" and "A Kind of Personal Strength" were motivated by the goal of ending violence against women. However, working to end violence against women and to increase social justice for oppressed groups generally are personal goals, so it makes sense to me that they are manifested in much of my poetry. "Enmeshed" was inspired by research I had done about conditions in Somalia when I represented a Somali woman in her political-asylum case. After reading about how commonplace horrific crimes are in Somalia, especially against vulnerable women and children, I became haunted by the stories I'd read and with my own random fortune in not having to fear such things.

The other poem, "A Kind of Personal Strength," grew out of a compelling story I had overheard in a locker room that stuck with me and pestered me until I wrote about it. In my mind, it connected with stories I'd heard about my grandparents' abusive and sometimes violent marriage and made me think about my luck in not experiencing that sort of abuse, either as a child watching my parents or in my own relationships as an adult.

SHERI VANDERMOLEN

Sheri Vandermolen has served for fifteen years as editor in chief of Time Being Books, an independent publishing company based in St. Louis, Missouri. She graduated Summa Cum Laude in 1990 from the University of Missouri, Columbia. In 2008 she relocated to Bangalore, India, where she explored for six years via camera and pen and witnessed the 2013 Maha Kumbh Mela. Her verse pieces have been published in various international literary journals, including *Ashvamegh, Camel Saloon, Contemporary Literary Review India, Earthen Lamp Journal, Foliate Oak, Muse India, Jersey Devil Press, Papercuts, Taj Mahal Review*, and *Verse-Virtual*.

GIRL CHILD

"Save the girl child,"
states the squatter's-rights placard
intrepidly hanging
amidst jewelry-store banners
and real-estate billboards
whose clichéd hollow gazes
take in the dizzy spin of NH7, below.

Bangalore's IT elite are not immune
to this holdover dilemma —
the familial demand
that each couple bring forth a baby boy
to fulfill ancestral duties
and shoulder the financial burdens
of the clan.

The Prenatal Diagnostics Techniques Act,
in place for two decades,
holds little sway, when black money
can buy, for anxious parents,
the immediate verdict
of a portable ultrasound machine,
illegally used, in the privacy of home,

to determine if a quick, but never easy, fix
is needed — a quiet termination
of their once-anticipated joy.

Save the girl child. Save us all.

LIGHTS OUT

for S., in her blooming strength

The five-amp shudders,
  shuts off power
to the only lit bulb in your house.
You swiftly snatch up your fidgeting toddler
and nestle him securely in your arms.
Thank heaven he's less unnerved
by monsters of the night
than you are.

Your widowed mother
feels her way to the other side of the room,
smoothly consoles your newborn,
just as she does during the daytime,
when you're out laboring for a wage.

She moved in with you
shortly after your husband
vanished into dalliance's shadows,
with claims that his new job,
installing wiring for corporate sites,
would keep him away —
in Hyderabad, Mysore, south Bangalore,
who knows where —
for reliably vague months to come.

Having devotedly handpicked him,
three years ago
(he belonged to a sound family,
seemed an ethical man
of your own Seventh Day Adventist faith),
she immerses herself in guilt's undulations,
knowing his prolonged absence
and the corrosive voluble gossip
surrounding his companioned whereabouts
have eroded your confidence,
effaced your resilient nature,
dimmed the pride that danced in your eyes
when you first became engaged.

He's been back in town some furtive time
but can't be obliged for explanations.
He calls at his convenience,
your little boy happy to babble to papa.
Occasionally, he stops by,
tosses his son onto his broad shoulders,
gives his baby daughter
a deceptive caress across the cheek,
and drops off a pittance of income
meant to buy a bag of rice, keep the lights on.

Instead, the main circuit of your home is shot —
another fuse blown —
and you're still wandering in the dark.

VANDERMOLEN: As a US citizen who was a long-term resident of Bangalore (a modern urban environment frequently referred to as the Silicon Valley of India), I found it striking that so many of the people we came to know personally — women and men of all ages, from business associates to day laborers — were forced to grapple, quite vehemently, with issues regarding their extended families' traditional values. They shared intimately faceted (and yet remarkably similar) stories of the intense pressures that had been placed upon them to marry before the age of thirty and produce children immediately, regardless of the emotional toll, and they were also quite candid about the emotional blackmail they felt vining about each decision-making process. The brutal rape and murder of Jyoti Singh Pandey sent jarring waves across the subcontinent, bringing women's rights to the media-lighted forefront; even so, blunter, darker considerations still surface from the depth of generations when topics related to gender equality arise behind closed doors.

"Girl Child" sprang from my viewing a small campaign placard situated, incongruously, amidst billboards appealing only to affluence's eager fingers (ads for real estate and Malabar gold); it spoke conspicuous volumes, despite its unassuming size. "Lights Out," on the other hand, emerged from a personal experience with a local friend of mine, who came from a well-meaning family but nevertheless fell into an abusive arranged marriage, where she was treated as chattel, nothing more. She ultimately left the man, with the support of her widowed mother — a bold move, given the resulting community derision. Tireless campaigners are making the first infusions of change for women like her, but it is an evolution that will be years in the making.

DIANALEE VELIE

Dianalee Velie lives and writes in Newbury, New Hampshire. She is a graduate of Sarah Lawrence College and has a Master of Arts in Writing from Manhattanville College, where she has served as faculty advisor of *Inkwell: A Literary Magazine.* Her poetry and short stories have appeared in numerous literary journals and many have been translated into Italian. Velie is the author of four books of poetry — *Glass House* (2004), *First Edition* (2005), *The Many Roads to Paradise* (2006), and *The Alchemy of Desire* (2013) — a book of short stories, *Soul Proprietorship: Women in Search of Their Souls* (2010), and a play, *Mama Says,* that was given a staged reading in New York City.

UNDER ONE HUNDRED WORDS

Cherry-chocolate colored bricks circle
a storm drain, then ascend into steps,
creating an amphitheater for the sunshine
spiraling around my students. Warming
their chilled musings into tornadoes of thought,
they devastate the landscape of innocent pages
with images of exams, chaos, cold beer,
sex and mothers: a birth of turbulent poems
in this twisting labyrinth, this corkscrew

called education. I stare at loosened
cement surrounding a few hot bricks,
so easy to pick up and throw,
like the brilliant poems
my students hurl at me in this arena,
where I teach outdoors, today.
Today, when the news has weighed
my heart with sorrowful stones,
the weight of ancient artifacts.

A napkin stained with lifeless red
berry juice cavorts in the wind
and I feel her blood spilling down
the conduit through my veins,
in a stadium in Mazer-e-Sharif,
northern Afghanistan. A nameless woman,
mother of seven, stoned to death
for committing adultery, while several
thousand spectators watched.

In under one hundred words,
the *New York Times*
unceremoniously reported,
"Afghan Death by Stoning,"
a nondescript column,
barely two-by-two-and-a-half inches,
journalistically perfect,
objective and brief.

I am glad I am here,
irradiated by light,
poet, mother, professor,
where only the sun poses
as an aggressive gladiator,
declaring his hard-line rule
after a long religious absence,
heralding in May, the month
for celebrating mothers. I ignore
the *Do Not Enter* sign on the campus mall,
chiding me not to write about her,
but if I ignore her, I trespass against her.
Swirling into a reflective vortex,
I float with her image, penetrating
the noetic blue ocean of sky,

and she hands me a Mother's Day gift,
the three hundred words of this poem,
and I bestow upon her
this posthumous pardon,
promising to immortalize
her name, a name
I don't even know.

VELIE: I was teaching a poetry class outdoors the week of Mother's Day at the State University of New York at Purchase. The day was perfect with the promise of summer. The students and I were sitting around a small sort of amphitheater and writing poems from my prompt, "spiraling." I always write when my students do, and I let the prompt take me where it wants to go. That morning, over coffee, I had just read the tiny article about the woman stoned in Afghanistan — a mere blip in all the news. The sharp contrast between our lives was striking and heartbreaking. "Under One Hundred Words" was the result.

NEELIMA VINOD

Neelima Vinod writes fiction and poetry. Her debut e-novella *Unsettled* has been published by Indireads, a South Asian publishing house.

ACID HURT

Do not surround me
I am frightened
I disappear in fear
Words come out of my mouth

In return
A ribbon of burn

Sears the skin,
I am skeleton
This is it
Me.

No soul
No wings
Just body
The pain.

Motorbikes disappear
You get bail
You have your face
The illusion of something inside.

But hollow man
You couldn't scale the snake within
The one that hissed at your kisses
And hated your eyes.

GOODNIGHT

Come here woman
Give me your pittance
Let me drink and make a din
With coconut trees around me to piss on
And night the color of dreams.

What? You won't give. Then here's a slap on one cheek!
Now show the other. Nicey does it.
There. Another. You bleed so easily and all those sobs
Mess up your housedress, the one that would be better *off.*

Get up will you? Wash yourself. A mess you are.
That's it, get me my umbrella, it rains outside and the approach road
Will flood. Liquor calls me. That's the spirit, wipe and clean, go and bathe,
Tidy the room, pick up the pieces, mend! I want it spic and span when
        I return
With the sea sway in my limbs and the dream-coated tongue.

Stop crying! Fools, the feminine. Weeping when promises lie in glass.
If only figures did not hold the moon, the lunatic swell of expectation,
If only you were mannequins... but isn't that what you are already?
Your breasts firm like rock, I stroke them and rise before I leave.

Goodnight wife, goodnight woman, goodnight girl, my slut, my slave.

VINOD: Regarding my poem "Acid Hurt": Acid attacks are surprisingly common in the subcontinent, and the primary targets are young women. I wrote this poem in one sitting and haven't made too many edits. A desperate narrative emerges from a single angry voice that cannot understand how corrosives that melt your face are so easily available and so recklessly thrown.

Concerning "Goodnight": This poem reflects the way alcoholism can spoil relationships and sour gender relations. When I wrote it, I could hear the man in the poem continuously chatter. The woman he was with said nothing, and that is what the whole poem is about — a woman's muting, her silence. Surely, in this case, the woman deserves better.

RINKOO WADHERA

Rinkoo Wadhera is a writer, painter, and dreamer who works when she is not writing and dreams of becoming the editor of her own poetry journal. Her poetry and feature articles have appeared, or are forthcoming, in *The Reading Hour, e-women of the subcontinent, Indian Ruminations, Prosopisia*, and *The Second Genesis — World Anthology of Poetry*.

THE DISAVOWAL OF PATCHWORK

Instructions:
use a fine needle. thread with
floche of your azure thoughts to
sew the tassels of tedium
and unease.

Memorize the *exact* pattern
of your sadness and darn
the outside edges of melancholy.
Sable satin seams the surplus
of sadness satisfactorily.

With a tambour hook, catch
the sighs from a lament and secure them on
your appliqué of ache.
To picket the path of memory, work with
a lattice band
from a tangled moment
that dangles in regret.
As it weaves a criss-
cross pattern, winding
through the abbreviated crochet of silence
pregnant with peeves, do not
pick on the knots of everyday speech.
It breaks the thread.

Disclaimer: None of the
techniques of patchwork will be able
to intertwine together
the ribbons into which you were
ripped by a single look.

WADHERA: My poem "The Disavowal of Patchwork" takes the age-old technique of mending as its vantage point. This practice was popular among women for repairing torn fabric. The fabric that I refer to in the poem is the moral fabric of the society and all that has held the world together, preventing anarchy. The lament of "Patchwork" is an apology for Nirbhaya and all women who have died like her, shamed by our fellow human beings, the humans who turned into monsters, perverse and merciless.

One consideration that propelled me to contribute this poem was that it hurts to see the many incidences of violence against women go unpunished and, many a time, unreported, in our country.

MARGOT WELCH

Margot Welch spent many years writing and working as staff psychologist, counselor, and educator in court, community, school, and university settings. Author of *Promising Futures: the Unexpected Rewards of Engaged Philanthropy* (2006), she now focuses on writing, music, and family. Her poetry, fiction, and nonfiction have appeared in *Sojourner*, the *Postcard Press*, *Persimmon Tree*, *About Place*, and the *Berkshire Eagle*. She lives in Cambridge, Massachusetts.

MILLIE

1954–1980

In my sleep
a phone rings

your voice is strong as ever
I know right away

you can't tell me
how you got my number

I can't ask
without putting us both in danger

you call to say   it's someone else
lying in the morgue   cleavered

murdered   someone else
wearing your brave bright face

it's not safe to talk
you want to tell me you'll be back

may have a different face
may not be able to say who you are

but I should expect to hear from you again
fighting for yourself   your kids

to stay alive
you want to say

it's just a disappearing act
keep listening

WELCH: At the Boston Juvenile Court Clinic in the late 1970s, I started a time-limited, small-group program for allegedly abusive and negligent mothers. These were women whose children had been taken away from them, who were encouraged to participate by a few probation officers as a way to show the judges how serious they were about wanting their children back. The group focused on attachment and separation, and the women entered frightened, ashamed, and desperate to get their kids back. The abuses these women were alleged to have committed re-enacted, more often than not, the hideous abuses they themselves had suffered. Wickedly, in the judicial system, it is easier to punish than to support — at who knows what cost? From our very first group meetings, the "Care & Protection" mothers discovered they had devastatingly intimate things in common. Over a period of three years, two of these women were murdered. Millie has never left me.

Nor — I discover again and again — has a shuddering, visceral memory of violation, even though, as far as I can recall, nothing amounting to violent trauma has ever happened to me. In library stacks, where the floor was metal grates, a man was masturbating below me, looking up my dress. There have often been night footsteps behind me, as I find and clutch my key and race to the front door. Two house-prowlers invaded my younger life and left their faces at my bedroom windows for years. A psychiatrist kissed me, putting his tongue into my mouth when I reached out to shake his hand, thinking this would be our last session. Now I suspect enduring re-collection is, perhaps, embedded deep in most girls and women.

Colleen Wells

Colleen Wells writes from Bloomington, Indiana. She volunteers for a homeless shelter and a state hospital and also loves crafting with recycled materials, especially the caps from beer bottles and broken jewelry. Her work has appeared in *ORION*, *The Georgetown Review*, and *The Potomac Review*, among other publications. Wells holds an MA in English from Butler University and an MFA in creative writing from Spalding University. Her book *Dinner with Doppelgangers – a True Story of Madness and Recovery* is forthcoming from Wordpool Press.

Morning Pills

My husband pushes me
into the truck.
I fight back
spitting Doritos in his face.

He calls 911.

Later I scream for him to leave
from beneath
my cocoon of
hospital sheets.

Begging the night nurse
to take pictures,
I point out
the mottled purple on my
thighs and arms.
Instead, she ushers me to bed.

In the morning
I take the handful of pills,
green, white, and yellow
that I'm given.

They disappear
inside me.
They disappear,
like my options.

C. WELLS: I have experienced various forms of cruelty since childhood, sometimes from those who should have had my best interest at heart. For me, one of the most positive ways to deal with trauma is to write about it. Through writing, the healing can begin.

JUDY WELLS

Judy Wells received her BA from Stanford and her PhD in Comparative Literature from UC Berkeley. She taught writing in Bay Area colleges before becoming an academic counselor for adults at St. Mary's College of California and a faculty member of St. Mary's graduate Liberal Studies program. She has published ten collections of poetry: *The Glass Ship* (2015), *I Dream of Circus Characters: A Berkeley Chronicle* (2010), *Little Lulu Talks with Vincent Van Gogh* (2007), *Call Home* (2005), *Everything Irish* (1999), *The Calling: Twentieth Century Women Artists* (1994), *The Part-time Teacher* (1991), *Jane, Jane* (1981), *Albuquerque Winter* (1980), and *I Have Berkeley* (1979).

THE PART-TIME TEACHER SOMETIMES FEARS FOR HER STUDENTS' LIVES

The part-time teacher sometimes has her students read their English IA papers in front of class. She has not read them yet. She asks for volunteers.

A beautiful woman stands before the class and reads a paper in which she states that her husband beat her, and not only beat her, but hid in their house, and stalked her like prey in the jungle. The class is very silent, and she reads how she was pushed through a window, and forgave her husband in the hospital as blood streamed down her arm. She said she could not feel a thing; she had made herself a piece of wood, like Celie in *The Color Purple,* when Mr. beat her. She had made herself a piece of wood.

And she was white and middle class and had a good job, she said, and a child. And he was white and middle class and had a good job. Their friends all loved them as the perfect couple, and he stalked her at night if his socks weren't in a row in his drawer.

She saw a shrink who placed an image in her head. She was not wood; she was a pitcher of milk pouring out her contents. And he asked her how long her liquid love, her rich flowing milk, could pour into her man — for her lifetime (which might be short), for a year, for a month? And she poured herself out till she was dry. It took a very short time. Then she left him.

The part-time teacher knows that some women write to save their lives. The part-time teacher knows that some women speak to save their lives, and their sisters' lives.

J. WELLS: I wrote "The Part-time Teacher Sometimes Fears for Her Students' Lives" when I was an instructor at a San Francisco Bay Area community college, teaching a night class filled with women who were re-entry students. We often have the stereotype that domestic violence happens only among the poor and marginalized, but no — it occurs at all levels of society. Although this college was in a working-class community, the woman who inspired my poem commuted there from a middle-class suburb. I was stunned by her honesty and courage to read her composition aloud to our class. This is one of the hidden roles of the English Composition teacher: We are often privy to dark secrets of our students and become compassionate listeners, counselors, and recorders of their troubled psyches. I felt that my student wrote and read her work both to heal herself and to help others who were wounded like her.

LAURA MADELINE WISEMAN

Laura Madeline Wiseman has a doctorate from the University of Nebraska–Lincoln, where she teaches English and creative writing. She is the author of seven collections of poetry, including *Sprung* (San Francisco Bay Press, 2012) and *Unclose the Door* (Gold Quoin Press, 2012). She is also the editor of *Women Write Resistance: Poets Resist Gender Violence* (Hyacinth Girl Press, 2013). Wiseman's writings have appeared in *Prairie Schooner, Margie, Arts & Letters, Poet Lore,* and *Feminist Studies.* She has received awards from the Academy of American Poets and Mari Sandoz / *Prairie Schooner* as well as grants from the Center for Great Plains Studies and the Wurlitzer Foundation.

THE BARRIER

We'd pushed the bed against the door.
Our backs pressed into the box-spring
as we sat on the floor, waiting.

I squeezed his hand grips
with both of my fists. Our sister chewed
the end of her dark hair. Our mother

held the baby and the bottle in her lap.
No one spoke as we listened
to the silence in the apartment.

I could hear her breath, the suckle
from our sister, the creak of the grip's spring.
I'd found it under the bed.

The front door banged open.
After a long time, he climbed the stairs
and ran his shoulder into the door

until the wheels on the bed's metal frame
shifted enough for him to get inside.
She said, *Take your sisters and go.*

SOLO ARTIST

for K.M.

Because, when she practices the cello
in a basement room, the walls muffle

Sonata D, the shut door softens the low moan
of the bow, she urges the strings to whisper,

exerts minute pressure of fingertips, eyes blurry
to not see the punched holes in the walls.

Because once she climbed from the window
flush with ground, left the ripped hinges,

splintered jamb, and wine-stained carpet to serenade
the full moon while he lay passed out upstairs.

Because her new roommate will spot him
a year later in a bar — ripped jeans and unwashed

hair, stumbling with the crooked wound of a smile
— she kicks the music stand over, stands

in the center of the darkening room, the belly
of the cello on the chair. Because the instrument

thunders and bellows, his feet beat an accompaniment
as he descends the stairs, and she pretends for a moment

that this cheap condo is Carnegie Hall and his hands
that rain down on her are applause, his sole word *Encore!*

WISEMAN: My mother married my stepfather in a hurry. They had met at work — she a secretary and he a computer programmer — began dating, and soon found themselves pregnant. Somehow, between bridal bouquet and *I do's*, between buying gold bands and renting their first apartment together, neither he nor his family opted to tell her that he was schizophrenic and required medication but rarely took it. The stories of what that man did to terrorize my mother are epic, the stuff of legend and myth, but because I was only seven, eight, nine, I remember only a few odd moments during the two years we shared the same set of butter knives, which was just before we fled from him to family on the other side of the country. The poem "The Barrier" is based on one of those memories. In anticipation of his return, and because of her fear of his expected violent outburst, my mother had barricaded us in her bedroom by pushing the furniture against the door. We waited. He returned. He forced himself in.

"Solo Artist" grew out of my experience with a roommate who lived with the first boy she'd dated in college, a tall man with mercurial eyes, ruffled hair, and a flirtatious smile that could turn without warning to something dark. It was only after she had left him, after she'd become my roommate, and after she'd seen a therapist for months, that she confessed the emotional violence and threats of physical violence she'd experienced from this boyfriend, a man who was particularly jealous of anything she sought to follow — friends, art, music. She loved to practice her cello but, in fear of what he might to do her in that extra basement bedroom, she played only when she thought he was gone. I wrote this poem for her, for her resistance, for her bravery at getting out, getting help, and getting on with her life.

I believe that poetry is power. Poetry is action, or at the very least has the potential to initiate action. Poets have described the potential of poetry to foster change in the lives of one and of many. From Adrienne Rich to Pablo Neruda, Shelley to Ralph Waldo Emerson, Audre Lorde to Czeslaw Milosz, all of these poets wrote of poetry's power for action. Muriel Rukeyser stated, "If there were no poetry on any day in the world, poetry would be invented that day" (*Lofty Dogmas*, p. 355). I believe that poetry of resistance is a poetry that can break silences about violence against women, as it raises consciousness and enacts a poetry of witness that links the personal, political, and social. Such poetry disrupts hegemonic narratives on gendered violence by employing sassing language and strategic anger. It resists gender violence by earmarking poetry as action, and that's why we need such books as *Women Write Resistance: Poets Resist Gender Violence*, which I edited, and why I'm so honored to be included in *Veils, Halos & Shackles*.

FRANCINE WITTE

Francine Witte lives in New York City. She received her MA from the State Universy of New York at Binghamton and her MFA from Vermont College. Her flash-fiction chapbook *The Wind Twirls Everything* was published by Muscle Head Press. She is the winner of the 2010 Thomas A. Wilhelmus Award in fiction from Ropewalk Press, and her chapbook *Cold June* was published in the same year. Her poetry chapbook *First Rain* was published in 2009 by Pecan Grove Press. Witte is a high school English teacher.

THE GIRL IN THE GARBAGE

11's old and already done.
Raped all the way to old lady.
So many fingers and tongues on her,
it would take lifetimes to undo.

Instead, she moves on, deciding
to leave this girl behind, simply zips
out of the damaged skin. Of course,
she will have to forget the football

huddle of boys who watched, each one
waiting his turn. Forget the underage
beer breath, slop mouth covering hers.
Forget the cold cement floor underneath,

half-dark garage, paint cans on the shelf,
spools of wire — somebody's father
was going to fix something, maybe.
And most of all, she would have to

forget the smallest boy, barely 13, who,
as he lay down on her, whispered *I'm sorry*
in her ear. Some nights, now, the girl
in the garbage wants a drink of water.

Hard, thirsty work pretending not to
exist. She pokes the woman awake,
who, thinking it's a nightmare,
stumbles, shaken, to the bathroom sink.

Quenched now, the woman splashes
her face. At this time of night, anything's
possible — faint smell of cucumber shavings,
sop of coffee grounds, or the stink

of unsaid words that have been rotting
in her throat. And one quick look in the
mirror, where just for a second, she sees
the girl looking back at her through her eyes.

PROM DATE, 1973

6 a.m., and the dark collapsing into the grass,
dew as sudden as the blush on your prom date.
Jimmy Dimples, your mother called him as he pinned you
with a sweet gardenia, careful not to brush your naked
shoulder. You were aswish in tulle and stiff banana curls.
Your mother coaxed his arm around you for a photo.
She winked at Jimmy, who turned scarlet. *Take care
of my girl,* she told him, and he promised, of course,
he would. Only his definition was different. Your mother
would never know how, after the prom, that blue powder
of rented tuxedos and drunken ice cubes swirling in the
punch, Jimmy would drive you out of the parking lot, past
the moon faces of your best friends, past the Denny's
where you were supposed to meet up, and headed, instead,
to McLaren's Field, where he would shut off the motor
and rip off your corsage. Funny part is, you would have
offered your virginity, but he wanted it to hurt, to twist
it from you like a sponge. Afterwards, you checked

your ruined mascara in the rearview and Jimmy
smiled his dimples into the minutes right before dawn.
You waited for him to say something, but he didn't.
The only sounds were the click of the ignition and the flick
of a gardenia petal that had been clinging to his lapel.

WITTE: I am addressing this subject because the aftermath of rape can be another form of oppression. It is less obvious, but the resulting silence a woman is forced into, the sense of shame she always carries with her, and her mistrust of people is part of the damage of rape.

Sholeh Wolpé

Sholeh Wolpé is a poet, playwright and literary translator. Born in Iran, she spent most of her teen years in Trinidad and the UK before settling in the United States. She was awarded the 2014 PEN/Heim, the 2013 Midwest Book Award, and the 2010 Lois Roth Persian Translation prize. Her work, according to Terrain Journal, "transcends the boundaries of language, gender, ethnicity and nationality." Wolpé is the author of three collections of poetry and three books of translations, and is the editor of three anthologies. Her upcoming book *Attar's Conference of the Birds* will be released by W.W. Norton in 2017. She lives in Los Angeles.

Pickles and Donuts

Cold basements remind me of the dead
fruit my mother smothered in sugar, the phallic
pickles souring in tight-lipped jars.

I keep my school uniform stained, my
long hair pulled back tight, my walnut
breasts cloaked with baggy shawls,

tell my friend next door about the red-
jam donut beneath our skirts, teach her
the waist-twisting dance of wrapping childhood's
curtain around her body so soon unfolded
like voodoo air from an uncapped perfume bottle.

I breathe in books that turn my eyelashes
to blue feathers, my eyelid's veins into delicate
wing-bones that flap and lift, travel me
to an island house on stilt legs.

She eats the stone pages of an old Quran,
comes of age at dusk where bombs fall
on paved roads and the sky rains scalding
lava that streams and streams, carries her
to the sharp edge of the world.

THE VILLAGE WELL

You were children, curious. Something splashed
in the belly of the well and she took your hand, descended
into the mouth opened wide,
step by concrete step down its dark spiral throat.

The creature that unhinged the damp stillness
of that well was not a man, not an animal —
just the silhouette of something vast...
You thought it was God, she thought it was a djinn,
and then you with fear did not think at all but ran back up
breathless, the chill of the well at your heels.

That night you didn't wait for his leg to accidently
rub against yours, or his hand to accidentally brush
your thigh as it always did, away from eyes that never
blinked. Instead, you reached for his knee, the flesh and bone
of this gray man who pretended to be daddy's friend. Beneath
the table laden with almond rice your mother had lovingly cooked,
the saffron-stewed lamb, the chicken smothered in herbs...
you squeezed,
squeezed so hard his eyes turned in your direction and melted
into a watery scream like the one still rising in the throat of that well.

WOLPÉ: I have always been keenly aware of the delicacy of fortune, how each of us could have been born elsewhere, been someone else. "Pickles and Donuts" is a poem of movement between two worlds, two possibilities — a girl who was me, and another who could have been me.

When I was a child, my parents took me on many car trips to various parts of Iran, mostly villages and small towns where our relatives and friends lived. These were happy trips, but they were also strange. I often wondered why my father, who was terribly strict with me in Tehran, always let me roam freely with my cousins or other children in the fruit orchards and gardens of the villages we visited. "The Village Well" is a clear memory in liquid fragments. Each droplet is complete in itself, yet it also reflects flashes of other incidents in staccato screams.

ELAINE WOO

Elaine Woo is a poet/librettist and nonfiction writer. She is the membership coordinator of Canadian Women in the Literary Arts (CWILA) and also a creative writing facilitator for *Megaphone Magazine*, Vancouver's award-winning street paper. Woo has written about such issues as breaking racial and gender stereotypes, political philosophy, the environment, and spirituality, in many genres. Her work has appeared in numerous publications, including *V6A*, shortlisted for the City of Vancouver's Book Award 2012, *The Enpipe Line, Arc Poetry Magazine, Ricepaper, Earthwalk,* and the *Poetry Pacific* e.zine. Her first full-length poetry collection, *Cycling with the Dragon,* was published by Nightwood Editions in 2015.

CLOSED IN

I shrink down and cringe
as shooting pain singes
my skin;
my eyelids droop
as though weighted.
The memory of him rolling,
grinding his hips,
arms locking
around my waist,
his slug tongue
thrusting
between my lips,
leaving a trail
of slime
over my tongue.
My synapses explode
and my hands shove him away.
My electrified legs scissor
me into the ladies'.
Fire panic inflames
my throat, burns in my head.

Transformed now, a looming, muscled bull
in rolled shirt-sleeves, he steamrolls
the door open.
I slam my stall door shut and bolt it
tight.

Then silence.
I open the door a sliver.
Bulky bouncers
are scuffling
with the terror.
It takes five of them
to propel him out the door.

They ask if I'm okay.
I want to purify in fire
my polluted clothes,
my sullied skin, my violated mouth.
I want to lock myself in safety,
drop the key down a bottomless well
for eternity, to be invulnerable
to men like him.

Shut eyelids can't seal out the memory.

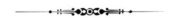

WOO: As a survivor of abuse and an often chaotic world, I wanted to paint a vivid word-picture of the fiery instinct women possess to thrive in the face of oppression.

ANDRENA ZAWINSKI

Andrena Zawinski's book *Something About* received a PEN Oakland Josephine Miles Award in poetry, and her *Traveling in Reflected Light* was a Kenneth Patchen Prize recipient. She has also authored four chapbooks. As founder and organizer of the San Francisco Bay Area Women's Poetry Salon, Zawinski is editor of their anthology, *Turning a Train of Thought Upside Down*. She is also Features Editor at PoetryMagazine.com and a teacher of writing, whose work appears widely online and in print.

THE NARRATIVE THREAD, OR PRACTICE OF KANTHAS

for the Bandit Queen Phoolan Devi, 1963–2001

They stitch as if we need these blankets to crawl under,
these thoughts that toss sweet dreams into fretful nights.
They stitch patches of stories onto a tongue of cloth.

They stitch — girls left to sicken, to die, books torn from them —
stitch in women's fisted faces on a stammer of speech.
They stitch as if we need these blankets to crawl under.

They take to needle and thread in a revolution of stitch,
stitch speaking in streets without asking for permission.
They stitch patches of stories onto a tongue of cloth.

They stitch in women veiled at home, poisoned widows,
stitch mango groves to chemical spills, wheat fields to AIDS.
They stitch as if we need these blankets to crawl under.

They stitch — girls burned by in-laws at husbands' pyres —
stitch palms ripe with fruit to gang rapes in hands of authority.
They stitch patches of stories onto a tongue of cloth.

They stitch quilts for shoppers to slip under with their dreams,
for dreams between borders stitched in a revolution of fingers.
They stitch as if we need these blankets to crawl under.
They stitch patches of stories onto a tongue of cloth.

ZAWINSKI: "The Narrative Thread" villanelle was written in response to the exhibition of quilts, "The Narrative Thread: Contemporary Women's Embroidery in Rural India," at the National Museum of Women in the Arts in Washington, DC. In East India, embroidering quilts (or kanthas) depicting scenes from daily life, which are then given as gifts on festive occasions, dates back to the 18th century. The craft disappeared until the Adithi organization revived and transformed it into grassroots activism in its expression of socio-political concerns, as well as a source of income for housebound women of the lowest caste. Phoolan Devi — to whom the poem is dedicated — was a lower-caste woman from Northern India who came to be known as the Bandit Queen. She suffered multiple rapes, and other brutal attacks, and was finally murdered after her spree of violent vendettas. The unrhymed villanelle, with its lines coming back upon each other, made it possible to add the quality of a stitching movement to drive the poem.

AMANDA ZUNIGA

Amanda Zuniga is a writer from northern New Jersey. She obtained her BA in English, with minors in poetry and women-and-gender studies, from Montclair State University and received her MFA in Poetry & Poetry in Translation from Drew University in 2014.

TO MY UNBORN SON

I will teach you the alphabet
and how to spell your name.
I will read you stories of the wind
and the sun. I will teach you
the numbers you will need for
counting freckles on the back
of the first one you love. I will
teach you why people cry and
I will teach you how to cry. I will
teach you why birds sing and of
extraterrestrial beings. I will teach
you of Lorde, Hooks and Steinem.
I will teach you how to cook fresh
spinach with sea salt and how to
bake your grandfather's favorite
pineapple pound cake. I will teach
you the meanings of "stop" and "don't."
I will teach you how to wash clothes
for when you go to college and how
to sew buttons when you lose one
from your chinos. I will teach you
that "no" means no and to never
blame the victim. I will teach you to
wash behind your ears and how to
keep secrets. I will teach you
to use your voice for those who

cannot. I will teach you magic
and science fiction. I will teach you
how to be an ally and that "yes" means
yes. I will teach you about art and self-worth.
I will teach you about temptation and restraint.

My son, I will not tell you about my drunken
mistakes or the day I lost God.

ZUNIGA: This poem speaks to themes I have struggled with regarding my sexual assault. I feel I must express myself about them because if I do not, who will?

ADDITIONAL BIOGRAPHICAL NOTES
FOR TRANSLATORS

KAMALAKAR BHAT is an associate professor in the postgraduate department of English at Ahmednagar College, in Admednagar, India. He is a bilingual writer and a translator between Kannada and English. His publications include two collections of poems in Kannada and research articles in academic journals. Bhat's translations appear in *Indian Literature, Muse India,* and *Protocol.*

PADDY BUSHE lives in Kerry. He has published nine collections of poetry, seven in English and two in Irish, as well as three books of translations. His most recent collection is *My Lord Buddha of Carraig Éanna* (Dedalus, 2012). He has also edited *Voices at the World's Edge: Irish Poets on Skellig Michael* (Dedalus 2010). *Ó Choill go Barr Ghéaráin* (Coiscéim 2013), a translation into Irish of the collected poems of Sorley MacLean, was recently published. Bushe is a member of Aosdána.

GOPIKA JADEJA edits and publishes a journal and a series of pamphlets for a performance-publishing project called *Five Issues* and has convened a school-specific festival of arts called "Talking Gandhi." A recipient of the Charles Wallace Scholarship for Creative Writing, Gopika has published a chapbook of poems in collaboration with Visthar-Bangalore. She has collaborated on various writing projects for Poets Against War (India), Katha-Xavier's Centre for Translation, *DNA* newspaper, and NID-Ahmedabad and is currently working on English translations of poetry from Gujarat. Her poetry and translations have been published in such journals as *Indian Literature, The Wolf,* and *Four Quarters.* She currently lives and works in Singapore.

PERMISSIONS

THERESA SENATO EDWARDS: "Battered" was first published in print in Chronogram, June 2006, and is reprinted from Edwards' book, *Voices Through Skin* (Sibling Rivalry Press), © 2011. Used by permission of the author.

JANET EIGNER: "Something to Do with Hunted Animals" is reprinted from *What Lasts Is the Breath* (Black Swan Editions), © 2013 by Janet Eigner and used by permission of the author.

SUSAN ELMSLIE: "If There's a Woman on the Street" is reprinted from I, Nadja, and Other Poems (Brick), © 2006. Used by permission of the author.

CARRIE ETTER: "After the Attack" first appeared in *The Beloit Poetry Journal.* © 2016 by Carrie Etter and used by permission of the author.

TRISH FALIN: "The Rape" © 2016 by Trish Falin and used by permission of the author.

CHARLES ADÈS FISHMAN: "A Dance on the Poems of Rilke," "Táhirih: The Seventeenth Disciple" and "Two Girls Leaping" are reprinted from *In the Path of Lightning: Selected Poems* (Time Being Books) © 2012 by Charles Adès Fishman and are used by permission of the author.

CHRIS FRADKIN: "Suzi and the Boob Job" © 2016 by Chris Fradkin and used by permission of the author.

MARISA FRASCA: "Licking Sardines" is reprinted from *Via Incanto: Poems From the Darkroom* (Bordighera Press, 2014) and is used by permission of the author.

BRONWYN FREDERICKS: An earlier version of "Reclaiming" appeared in the *Queensland Women's Health Network Journal* in 2001. The present version is © 2016 by Bronwyn Fredericks, and is used by permission of the author.

SUSAN GARDNER: "Each One" © 2016 by Susan Gardner and used by permission of the author.

CHRISTINE GELINEAU: "Letter to My Rapist" previously appeared in *Remorseless Loyalty* (Ashland Poetry Press), © 2006, and is used by permission of the author.

JUDITH GOEDEKE: "Fiftieth Anniversary" and "Thoughts" first appeared in *Dragonfly Arts Magazine,* © 2013, by Judith Goedeke, and used by permission of the author.

BARBARA GOLDBERG: "After Babel" is reprinted from *The Royal Baker's Daughter* (University of Wisconsin Press), © 2008 by Barbara Goldberg. "Albanian Virgin" is

MICHAEL LEE JOHNSON: "Battered Behind Dark Glasses" © 2016 by Michael Lee Johnson and used by permission of the author.

ELIZABETH D. JOHNSTON: "Dead in Absentia" and "The Stoning" © 2016 by Elizabeth D. Johnston and used by permission of the author.

ADELE JONES: "Severed" © 2016 by Adele Jones and used by permission of the author.

PRIYANKA KALPIT: A slightly different version of the English translation of "Tumor" was included in *The Praktiti Anthology: 2011-2012,* published by The Prakriti Foundation, Chennai. The original Gujarati version first appeared in *Hanshiya Maan Hoon* (My Self in the Margins), published by the Gujarati Dalit Sahitya Academy, Ahmedabad, © 2001 by Priyanka Kalpit and used by permission of the author.

BREINDEL LIEBA KASHER: "The Rabbi Speaks" © 2016 by Breindel Lieba Kasher and used by permission of the author.

J. KATES: "The Woman in My Bed Talks About Her Child" is reprinted from Kates's chapbook, *Mappemonde* (Oyster River Press), © 2001 by J. Kates and used by permission of the author.

DONNA KAZ: "Counting" © 2014 by Donna Kaz. "My Assailant" is reprinted from *Trivia: Voices of Feminism,* issue 13, Fall 2012. Both poems used by permission of the author.

SUSAN KELLY-DEWITT: "Painting Class" is from her book *The Fortunate Islands* (Marick Press), © Susan Kelly-DeWitt 2008. "Sati, 1987" and "My Mother at the Museum of Bound Feet" © 2016 by Susan Kelly-Dewitt. All three poems used by permission of the author.

DIANE KENDIG: "On Three Portraits by María Blanchard" © 2016 by Diane Kendig and used by permission of the author.

ADELE KENNY: "Things Untouched" © 2016 by Adele Kenny and used by permission of the author.

TABISH KHAIR: "Immigration" is reprinted from Khair's collection, *Man of Glass* (HarperCollins, 2010). "Stone" first appeared in *Wasafiri,* London, 2002. Both poems are used by permission of the author.

MOLLY SUTTON KIEFER: "Tripoli" originally appeared in *HEArt: Human Equity Through Art.* "At the start of thunder," "Disposable Woman" and "Tripoli" © 2016 by Molly Sutton Kiefer and used by permission of the author.

DEBORAH KAHAN KOLB: "Eldest Daughter" © 2016 by Deborah Kahan Kolb and used by permission of the author.

ZOE LAMBRINAKOS-RAYMOND: "For Rent" © 2016 by Zoe Lambrinakos-Raymond and used by permission of the author.

GAYLE LAURADUNN: "Telling" is reprinted from *Reaching for Air* (Mercury Heartlink Press). © 2014 by Gayle Lauradunn and used by permission of the author.

GLENNA LUSCHEI: "Men With Their Secret Gardens" is reprinted from *Matriarch* (The Smith), © 1992 by Glenna Luschei and used by permission of the author.

WAYNE LEE: "Camp Fire" © 2016 by Wayne Lee and used by permission of the author.

DANIELLA LEVY: "Stock-Photo Woman" © 2016 by Daniella Levy, , and used by permission of the author.

DIANE LOCKWARD: "The Missing Wife" is reprinted from *Eve's Red Dress* (Wind Publications), © 2003 by Diane Lockward. Used by permission of the author.

KATHARYN HOWD MACHAN: "Les Salles-Du-Gardon" first appeared in *ByLine Magazine.* "Once It's Been Done" first appeared in *The Poets' Touchstone.* Both poems © 2016, and used by permission of the author.

RITA MALHOTRA: "Chrysanthemums" is reprinted from *i remain the ignited woman* (World Poetry Almanac, Ulaanbaatar, Mongolia), © 2012 Dr. Rita Malhotra.

MARIE-ELIZABETH MALI: "Anglerfish" first appeared in *The New Verse News* (2011) and is reprinted from *Women Write Resistance: Poets Resist Gender Violence,* Laura Madeline Wiseman, ed., Hyacinth Girl Press, 2013. Used by permission of the author.

SHAHÉ MANKERIAN: "Picnic at Mt. Sannine" appeared in *Mizna: Prose, Poetry, and Art Exploring Arab America,* Vol. 13, issue 2, 2012, and is used by permission of the author.

MARI MAXWELL: "Recollections at Your Graveside" © 2016 by Mari Maxwell and used by permission of the author.

MARIANA MCDONALD: "Swimming at Lake Cable" © 2016 by mariana mcdonald and used by permission of the author.

GABRIEL ROSENSTOCK: "Billie Holiday" is reprinted from *Rogha Dánta/Selected Poems* (Cló Iar-Chonnacht, 2005) and is used by permission of the author.

SUMANA ROY: "Rape of Sunlight" © 2016 by Sumana Roy and used by permission of the author.

VIMMI SADARANGANI: "Tethered" was first published in her collection *Sonahari rang ji kaaraaN* (Vibha Publications), © 1996 by Vimmi Sadarangani under the title "kahiN gaaiN vaangur man," and is used by permission of the author.

SMITA SAHAY: "The Coronation of Shilavati" and "For Nameless, Faceless Women" © 2016 by Smita Sahay and used by permission of the author.

PERVIN SAKET: "Hands" and "The Left of the Horizon" © 2016 by Pervin Saket and used by permission of the author.

ANU SANGWAN: "I See You, My Daughter" © 2016 by Anu Hada Sangwan and used by permission of the author.

ELLIN SAROT: "Silence" is reprinted from *Women Write Resistance: Poets Resist Gender Violence,* ed. by Laura Madeline Wiseman (Hyacinth Girl Press), © 2013 by Ellin Sarot. "Engraphia" © 2016 by Ellin Sarot. Both poems are used by permission of the author.

K. SATCHIDANANDAN: "That Stone" was originally written in Malayalam and was then translated by K. Satchidanandan into English. The Malayalam version appeared in *Mathrubhumi Weekly,* 6 January, 2013. The English version © 2016 by K. Satchidanandan, and is used by permission of the author.

JANE SATTERFIELD: "Her Familiars" is reprinted from *Her Familiars* (Elixir Press), © 2013 by Jane Satterfield. "Hope" is reprinted from *Assignation at Vanishing Point* (Elixir Press), © 2003 by Jane Satterfield. Both poems used by permission of the author.

ADA JILL SCHNEIDER: "A Ten-Pound Bag" was previously published in *The Why and Later,* edited by Carly Sachs (Deep Cleveland Press, 2007) and in *Behind the Pictures I Hang,* by Ada Jill Schneider (Spinner Publications, Inc., 2007). All rights and permission to re-publish have been granted by both publishers.

LAYLA SCHUBERT: "Nine Volts" © 2014 by Layla Schubert and used by permission of the author.

CATHERINE SERCOMBE: "Special Clearance / Exposed" © 2016 by Catherine Sercombe and used by permission of the author.

RAVI SHANKAR: "Breastfeeding at the Blue Mosque" first appeared in the *Chronicle of Higher Education's* "Arts and Academe Blog," May 8th, 2011, and is reprinted by permission of the author.

MUKTA SHARANGPANI: "Saptapadi" © 2016 by Mukta Sharangpani and used by permission of the author.

K SHARIFA: "Be a Woman, Once, O Lord!" translation © 2016 by Kamalakar Bhat and used by permission of the author and translator.

STEVEN SHER: "My Daughter at Three Asks if God Is a He" originally appeared in *Bridges* Vol. 12, No. 1, Spring 2007, and is used by permission of the author.

ENID SHOMER: "Theater of Dreams" was first published in *Prairie Schooner* and was reprinted in *Black Drum: Poems* (University of Arkansas Press), © 1997 by Enid Shomer. Reprinted by permission of the author.

M. E. SILVERMAN: "Losing My Religion" was published in *Moulin Review* under the title "Sitting Together During Services." "Rain Chaser" © 2016 by M. E. Silverman. Both poems are used by permission of the author.

MYRA SKLAREW: "Violation" © 2016 by Myra Sklarew and used by permission of the author.

AMY SMALL-MCKINNEY: A different version of "Voices" appeared in *The Cortland Review,* 2005. "Voices" © 2016 by Amy Small-McKinney and used by permission of the author.

LUCIE SMOKER: "In a Shard of the Bedroom Mirror" © 2016 by Lucie Smoker and used by permission of the author.

KIRTLAND SNYDER: "Intimacy" © 2016 by Kirtland Snyder and used by permission of the author.

K. SREEKUMAR: "News Review" © 2016 by K. Sreekumar and used by permission of the author.

HANS JORG STAHLSCHMIDT: "Awakening" © 2016 by Hans Jorg Stahlschmidt and used by permission of the author.

JAN STECKEL: "You Could Be a Pretty Girl" © 2016 by Jan Steckel. "Preventive Dentistry" appeared in *Lady Business: A Celebration of Lesbian Poetry* (Sibling Rivalry Press, 2012). Both poems used by permission of the author.

INDEX TO CONTRIBUTORS

AUTHORS

TRANSLATORS

Bhat, Kamalakar – from the Kannada of K Sharifa, "Be a Woman Once, O Lord," p. 434.

Bushe, Paddy – from the Irish (Gaelic) of Gabriel Rosenstock, "Billie Holiday," p. 395.

Jadeja, Gopika – from the Gujarati of Priyanka Kalpit, "Tumor," p. 219, and the Sindhi of Vimmi Sadarangani, "Tethered," p. 399.

Moynihan, Áine – from her own Irish (Gaelic) to English, "Cardinal Sins," p. 288; from the Irish (Gaelic) of Áine Ní Ghlinn to English (with Áine Ní Ghlinn), "The Girl Who Went into the Rain," p. 320.

Ní Ghlinn, Áine – from her own Irish (Gaelic) to English (with Áine Moynihan), "Yourself and Myself," p. 321.

Satchidanandan, K.– from his own Malayalam, "That Stone," p. 411.

INDEX TO POEMS

COVER ART

ABOUT THE FRONT COVER ARTIST:

LUCY LIEW is a Malaysian-American artist whose paintings draw upon her personal experiences and identity as a woman of Chinese-Melanau descent, who grew up in Malaysia. Liew's father, a photojournalist and ethnographer, encouraged her to draw as a child and inspired her penchant for lighting and compositional skills. She also traveled with him, visiting various ethnic groups on the island of Borneo and witnessing their customs and rituals. Those vivid encounters with robust and harmonious cultures helped her develop an artistic language of her own that used indigenous symbolism and botanical motifs as metaphors to express emotions, relationships, and experiences, and made it evident to her that all things in nature are interconnected.

After high school, Liew studied at the Nanyang Academy of Fine Arts, in Singapore, and a Commonwealth Foundation fellowship, in England, allowed her to explore the possibilities of textile design, but it was her travels in Europe, where she was struck by the works of Monet, Klimt and Kandinsky, that she decided to pursue art as a career. Eventually, she immigrated to the United States, where she further developed her artistic style.

Liew's work is now part of the permanent collection of the National Art Gallery in Malaysia and has been featured in numerous solo and group exhibitions in the San Francisco Bay Area and Silicon Valley Open Studios. In addition to receiving several awards and recognitions, Liew has also received a branch-library project grant from the City of San Jose, California, where she currently resides and is part of the vibrant Alameda Art Works community. She is also a member of the Chinese Art Association of San Francisco.

To see more of her work, please visit www.LucyLiewArt.com.

ABOUT THE BACK-COVER PHOTOGRAPHER:

SHERI VANDERMOLEN has served, for fifteen years, as editor in chief of Time Being Books, an independent publishing company based in St. Louis, Missouri. She has an additional decade of experience as managing editor and archivist. Her projects have included overseeing the compilation of The Complete Poems of Louis Daniel Brodsky (a series that comprises verse spanning five decades) and piloting four collected-works editions. She has also facilitated the publication of dozens of individual poetry and short-fiction volumes.

Vandermolen graduated summa cum laude, with Phi Kappa Phi academic honors, in 1990, from the University of Missouri–Columbia, and relocated to Bangalore, India, in 2008. Exploring the subcontinent via camera and pen, for a full six years, she ultimately formed *Jasmine Fractals: Poems of Urban India*, a manuscript of forty-five verse pieces she organically generated from experiences as mundane as her trips to the local city market and as distinct as her visit to the 2013 Maha Kumbh Mela, in Allahabad, which is considered the world's largest single-event gathering of humanity (thirty million people in attendance, on the most auspicious bathing day).

She repatriated in 2014 and now resides in California, with her husband.

Her verse pieces have been published in various international literary journals, including *Ashvamegh, Camel Saloon, Contemporary Literary Review India, Earthen Lamp Journal, Foliate Oak, Muse India, Jersey Devil Press, Papercuts, Shot Glass Journal, Taj Mahal Review*, and *Verse-Virtual*.

COVER ART CREDITS:

Front-cover art "The Core," acrylic on canvas, 30 x 24 in., © 2006 by Lucy Liew, and used by permission of the artist.

Back-cover photo copyrighted by and reprinted with permission of Sheri Vandermolen. The photo was shot by Vandermolen on November 27, 2013, at the Shwedagon temple in Yangon, Myanmar, the city in which human-rights activist Aung San Suu Kyi was under house arrest for fifteen years.

ACKNOWLEDGMENTS

Veils, Halos, & Shackles was born out of our desire to raise collective voices against the oppression of women. It has been a long and extraordinary journey.

We thank each of our contributors for having faith in our vision and for sharing not only their poems but also the stories and life experiences behind them, and we thank the many unknown supporters of this project, who shared our call for submissions and carried it far and wide.

Special thanks to contributors in Australia, India, Ireland, the USA, and elsewhere, who helped organize launch readings for the anthology or, in some other way, assisted us in bringing news of the forthcoming book to the attention of the world.

Our deep appreciation to Sheri Vandermolen and Pushpa Parekh for their invaluable contribution to the proofreading and copyediting of the manuscript.

We are beyond grateful to Lucy Liew for the use of her remarkable painting, "The Core," as our front-cover image, and to Sheri Vandermolen for the use of her luminous photograph, which graces the back-cover of this book.

Our gratitude to Karen Gutfreund, the national exhibitions coordinator for the Women's Caucus for Art, who brought Lucy Liew's powerful work to our attention. Special thanks, too, to our contributor, Donna Kaz, who put us in touch with Karen and who also made two important suggestions about the manuscript, as we neared the conclusion of our editing, and to our contributor, Baisali Chatterjee Dutt, who brought the "Fearless Collective" to our attention.

We also thank Terry Tegnazian, publisher of Aquila Polonica books, for her helpful suggestions regarding distributors and publishers of trade paperback reviews, and Jennifer Perrine, who very kindly sent our media kit to women's and gender studies directors who teach WGS at a wide range of colleges and universities.

We are indebted to Laura Madeline Wiseman for her strong, insightful, and moving introduction to *Veils, Halos, & Shackles*. Her belief in the cause reinforced our belief in the need for this anthology and strengthened our commitment to complete the work.

Don Radlauer and Yael Shahar, our publishers at Kasva Press, have been patient advocates of our work. At every stage of the process of preparing this anthology for publication, they have been our champions and guides. More than that, their tireless efforts to translate their vision for *Veils, Halos & Shackles* into results has been a blessing.

Finally, we thank our families for their timely suggestions and support. Ellen Fishman's wise counsel fortified our conviction and helped us make difficult decisions. Ashish Karan has been a pillar of strength throughout the journey.

Charles Adès Fishman
Smita Sahay
Bellport, Long Island, and Mumbai, India
February, 2016

A PERSONAL NOTE

Veils, Halos, & Shackles will always mean hope for me: hope in the time of barbaric gender violence and hope during a personally difficult time for me.

It all started with a book called *In the Path of Lightning*, which was sent to me by John Amen, editor of *Pedestal Magazine*, who asked me to review the book. Furious, justice demanding, yet celebratory of women and peace-invoking, the book was my pillar and shield, as Jyoti Pandey's death reverberated through India and the world. The book helped me through that period of unbearable pain, uncontrollable tears, and white, blinding, rage.

I reached out to Dr. Charles Adès Fishman who had written the book, and thanked him for his beautiful poetry. He, too, was shocked at the brutality with which Jyoti's innocent life had been snuffed out. And that is when the idea of *Veils, Halos & Shackles* took shape.

Through the long, sometimes arduous, journey, Charles has been an incredible partner: guiding, patient, generous, and trusting. As I have grappled with personal challenges, emotional and medical, Charles' and Ellen's friendship has held Ashish and me up.

As *Veils, Halos & Shackles* gets ready to see the light of day, I feel stronger already. This journey has brought self-discovery, introspection, and healing, and Charles' friendship has reconfirmed my belief in miracles, as I call him my guiding angel.

Thank you, Charles.

Smita Sahay
Mumbai, India
October, 2015

555

About Kasva Press

"Make its bowls, ladles, jars and pitchers
with which to offer libations;
make them of pure gold."
(Exodus 25:29)

וְעָשִׂיתָ קְּעָרֹתָיו וְכַפֹּתָיו וּקְשׂוֹתָיו
וּמְנַקִּיֹּתָיו אֲשֶׁר יֻסַּךְ בָּהֵן
זָהָב טָהוֹר תַּעֲשֶׂה אֹתָם
(שמות פרשת תרומה)

Kasva means "a vessel or jar". The word appears in the Torah exactly once, where it describes the solid gold wine and oil jars used to hold sacrificial liquids in the Sanctuary.

We believe that a book is a vessel for the fluid thoughts of the writer and that, like the wine and oil in the Temple, the words represent the freely-given outpouring of the writer's soul.

It is our aim to provide a worthy vessel for our authors' thoughts.